15.50
AC

Regional and Interregional Social Accounting

Regional and Interregional Social Accounting

Stan Czamanski
Cornell University

Lexington Books
D.C. Heath and Company
Lexington, Massachusetts
Toronto   London

Library of Congress Cataloging in Publication Data

Czamanski, Stan
    Regional and interregional social accounting.

    Bibliography: p. 193
    1. Regional planning. 2. Regional planning—Mathematical models.
3. National income—Accounting.
I.Title. II. Title: Social accounting.
HT391.C93   309.2'5   73-9857
ISBN 0-669-90563-1

Copyright © 1973 by D.C. Heath and Company

Published simultaneously in Canada.

Printed in the United States of America.

International Standard Book Number: 0-669-90563-1

Library of Congress Catalog Card Number: 73-9857

To the memory of
my parents
A. and R.C.

Contents

List of Figures

List of Tables

Preface

The present volume started out as an improved version of my lecture notes, used over a number of years in a graduate course which I taught to planning students at Cornell University. During those years I was also engaged each summer at the Institute of Public Affairs, Dalhousie University, in Halifax, in work dealing with various aspects of the Nova Scotia economy. I thus became deeply involved in the construction, analysis, and interpretation of an extensive set of sophisticated regional studies largely based on regional social accounts consisting of income and product, wealth, and interindustry accounts. My experience made me acutely aware of the inadequacy of the national accounting format for regional purposes and of the weakness of some significant parts of the theoretical foundation upon which social accounts are built. My later, more general research, probing into some of the causes of those shortcomings, was carried out mainly during the longer teaching seasons at Cornell University.

The inherent difficulties met in attempts to construct regional social accounts seem to me to stem from three sources:

1. The weakness of the tools for dealing with, and especially for quantifying and evaluating in money terms, public goods and services, elements of the environment (both physical and social), and the non-pecuniary results of economic activities of public bodies.

2. The low emphasis accorded to stock phenomena. The current preoccupation of economists with flows is not justified at the regional level, where development and locational attractiveness, rather than business cycles and monetary-fiscal policies, are the prime concerns.

3. The relative greater importance than at the national level of disaggregated sectoral accounts for policy planning.

Finally, a striking, not easily remedied weakness arises from the lack of a comprehensive system of regional accounts fusing and summarizing the various types of accounts in a single framework with built-in checks and balances.

I am far from believing that the present work provides solutions to the numerous problems and questions raised. Rather, it simply sums up my long experience in constructing and using these basic tools of regional economic analysis.

My debt to a number of persons and institutions who assisted me in various ways is heavy. My early interest in the subject was aroused by Professor Charles L. Leven, while the incentive for writing this volume was given by Professor Harvey S. Perloff. Two of my former students contributed greatly to the present monograph. Chapter 4, dealing with regional wealth, draws heavily upon the doctoral dissertation of Emil E. Malizia, while Chapter 3, on financial flows, is largely based on an original draft prepared by Andrew A. Dzurik. Both have since assumed independent teaching positions. Professors Andrew A. Dzurik, David Greytak, and Charles L. Leven went carefully over an earlier draft of the present volume and made numerous helpful comments. As in all my previous literary ventures, my linguistic shortcomings were remedied by the excellent editing of Mrs. Margaret Dingley.

The pleasant surroundings conducive to intensive effort at the Institute of Public Affairs, Dalhousie University, are due in large part to its Director, Professor Guy Henson. My thanks go to my Dean, Professor Kermit C. Parsons, for relieving me of part of my teaching duties in order to enable me to finish the present work as well as for his energetic encouragement during the long time my work was maturing. Finally, I am most obliged to my wife Franciszka not only for her last minute help in making the manuscript ready for publication, but for her taking upon herself the normally shared chores, thus enabling me to devote a disproportionate amount of time to my professional interests. In this I have had her constant support.

Financial support for the applied parts of the work was provided by the Department of Trade and Industry of the Government of Nova Scotia and by the Canada Council. The massive effort at Cornell University was financed by a generous grant from Resources for the Future, Inc. I am most obliged for their assistance, although obviously neither they nor the numerous persons who helped me in a variety of ways bear any responsibility for the outcome.

1

Introduction*

Regional Planning Background

Quantitative summaries of regional data, cast in the form of regional social accounts, invariably provide the indispensable factual basis for regional planning and analysis. Yet, their importance extends far beyond the comprehensive approaches to public decision-making as they are widely and frequently used by civil servants, business executives and students of regional problems in an increasing variety of contexts. A separate, somewhat limited, but enormously important class of problems attacked with the help of social accounts is regional development planning. This single issue has exercised a considerable influence upon their early development.

The existence of depressed regions, pockets of unemployment, and poverty in the highly industrialized nations of North America and Western Europe has been attracting increasing attention recently. Awareness that problems associated with the economic stagnation and decline of these regions are very different from those faced by the underdeveloped countries of Africa, Asia, and Latin America and cannot be handled with the models and tools of development economics has been gaining ground. In order to formulate effective policies capable of coming to grips with these complex economic, social, and political issues, policymakers, analysts, and planners need a comprehensive conceptual framework and a sufficient data basis.

The present situation with respect to regional planning bears some similarities to the one prevailing in the early 1930s, when there was neither a valid theory nor sufficient data for pursuit of an effective stabilization policy, or to the one in the years following World War II, when the theoretical basis for a development policy to be followed in the newly independent backward countries was lacking. The vast amount of work in the field of development economics resulted in solid progress in our understanding of the process of growth only in the last decade, although without a dramatic breakthrough similar to the "Keynesian revolution." Thus development of a comprehensive development theory is of fundamental importance for the further evolution of the form of regional social accounts. Whether a single form suitable for regional

*Chapter 1 appeared in a slightly different form in Stan Czamanski, "Regional Policy Planning: Some Possible Implications for Research," *The Annals of Regional Science,* 4, no. 2 (December 1970). Copyright, 1971, by the Annals of Regional Science. Reprinted by special permission.

development planning will prove also useful or usable for the numerous other applications of the accounts is obviously open to doubt.

The problem of regional planning has to be considered against the wider issue of institutional setting, since regional planning with the necessary background studies can only be discussed with reference to a specific organization of the relevant decision-making processes. One of the more interesting phenomena accompanying the rise of the modern welfare state in recent decades has been the penetration of the ranks of civil servants at all levels of government by social scientists, especially by trained economists, often drawn from among practicing scholars. This development stands in marked contrast to the situation prevailing in the liberal state where the political decisionmakers were to a very large extent lawyers by training. Yet the importance of economic problems in a modern welfare state and the fact that many decisionmakers are themselves highly trained economists does not mean that decisions are predominantly, or even often, taken with the help of tools developed in this most advanced of the social sciences. Even decisions affecting purely economic problems or problems having sufficient economic aspects are based primarily on considerations belonging to the political arena in the modern democracy. In matters pertaining to regional development, the situation is complicated by the fact that often several governments participate in the decision processes.

The character of the decision-making bodies provides only a partial explanation of why intuition and hunch are often preferred to the use of highly sophisticated tools and models of modern quantitative economics. Partly at least, this is due to the fact that most of these tools, despite all the impressive recent advances, are not yet developed to the point where the results and forecasts obtained with their help are clearly superior to the simple extrapolation of past trends or to the so-called naive projections. Consequently, few countries rely exclusively or even predominately on quantitative models as guides to governmental economic policy. Actually, Holland and several other countries used econometric models to various degrees for purposes of national economic planning,[1] but mostly as a supplementary source of information or in order to corroborate judgments based on common sense or "enlightened" hunch. As far as regional planning is concerned, there are at least twelve countries in which econometric stochastic models are used for this purpose.[2]

Irrespective of the methods used, there is great variety in the political processes by which decisions affecting regional development are reached. Generally, or perhaps only ideally, one could consider three distinct groups by means of whose participation in the decision process society effects regional development:[3]

1. The elected policymakers and public administrators

2. The experts acting as advisers to the decisionmakers and operating largely within specialized agencies of the central or regional governments of which they are staff, not line, officers

3. The scientists working in research institutes, universities, or private consulting firms

The ultimate decisionmakers at various levels of government do not, as a rule, need or require any regional plans. Regardless of their previous training and experience, their decisions—which ordinarily concern one specific issue at a time—are based mainly on political considerations, although expert opinion may be consulted. At this level, regional plans may play a role only if they are required in order to mobilize public or governmental opinion as a help in marshaling the necessary resources for a specific project.

Those who need and develop regional plans are experts serving as professional advisors to governmental decisionmakers. Their interest in planning is not so much the result of their generally superior training with its orientation towards systematic exploration of all existing alternatives and options, but rather stems from the need for a coordinating document which would enable them to offer consistent advice on a variety of topics. *Planning*, in a general sense, can best be defined as a coordination of future actions so that they may reinforce rather than hinder one another. Regional planning, however, which forms one of the several main types into which planning is divided, is much narrower in scope and is oriented toward coordination from the point of view of harmonious development in geographic space. Regional plans are ordinarily evolved by a combination of common sense, intuition based on the examination of data, and results obtained with the help of quantitative tools.

In their work, planners more often than not use the services of scientists, who almost as a rule rely at least partly upon sophisticated, advanced tools of inquiry and often develop new ones specially suited to the purpose at hand. The role of quantitative models used by regional scientists transcends, however, the limits of background research. Imperfect and unreliable as many of them still are, their use has profoundly influenced regional planning by imposing upon it a more rigorous framework.

Regional Framework

Delineation of meaningful regions for planning of regional policies and designing regional accounts represents the necessary first step and is a major research effort in its own right. There is an extensive and growing literature concerning the problem of regionalization, and the following paragraphs are in no way intended to summarize the recent developments in this field.

The notion of a region obviously has to be distinguished from that of an area or zone. An *area* refers to any part of a two-dimensional space. A *zone* meant, originally, a latitudinal belt cut out from a sphere. But the latter notion has undergone some development, and zone is now used in order to define an area having some characteristic or characteristics in contradiction to the remaining parts of a given space. Of the three, only a *region* represents a wide enough grouping of natural and societal phenomena to function as a more or less distinct part of the whole. It is an area with some causal links, usually to be found only in history; hence, some talk of a region as a four-dimensional area (with a time dimension) while others refer to it as an area with a purpose or with a problem.

The introduction of the concept of a region represents a deliberate departure from the early developments in location theory and space economics.[4] Nonetheless, it undoubtedly represents a step forward because it enables the consideration of feedback effects and a much more extensive application of advanced models and of the theory of spatial equilibrium. Several types of regions are often distinquished: homogeneous regions with a maximum of common characteristics but with little interaction within their boundaries; nodal regions exhibiting great heterogeneity and a maximum of internal contacts, combined with a minimum of interaction with the outside world; problem regions and planning regions which are idealized constructs helpful in dealing with specific situations; or "monocentric" and "polycentric" regions. Various techniques may be used in order to define a region if more than one criterion is applied. They range all the way from simple commonsense tracing of boundaries to very sophisticated mathematical techniques, among which some types of multivariate analyses are often used.

The problem becomes considerable more complicated when dealing with the nation as a whole rather than with a single region. Nodal regions, which are being used for regional planning purposes with increasing frequency, very often fail to exhaust the national territory or, even worse, frequently overlap so that some portions of the territory may belong to more than one region. More important, perhaps, both nodal and homogeneous regions defined at the national level would have to answer a variety of needs, some of which are difficult to foresee at present. If data are to be centrally collected or social accounts disaggregated by region and constructed at the federal level, the fundamental units would have to be relatively permanent over time to ensure the continuity essential for the development of time series. Partly because of this, but more importantly because of institutional constraints, planning regions often correspond to either single administrative units or to their groupings. The importance of following institutional boundaries in defining study areas comes to the fore at the data-collecting stage and in setting up the basic accounting framework preliminary to quantitative analysis.

Models and Accounts

A serious obstacle to the development of regional social accounting is the lack of a comprehensive conceptual framework, as obviously no meaningful methods of analysis can be evolved without corresponding progress in regional theory.

Statistical summaries of economic data not based on theory can hardly prove fruitful or even feasible [5] because, although perhaps not implied, some kind of fundamental theoretical idea underlies any collecting of numbers.

The role which data and quantitative estimates play in the social sciences and in the political decision processes is often overrated. Our basic understanding of socioeconomic phenomena and most political decisions are qualitative and not quantitative in nature. The quantitative aspects which figure so prominently in the recent development of modern economics and of the other social sciences constitute the means toward gaining new insights but are not a purpose in themselves.

Several different types of models are used in regional studies.[6] A crude classification based mainly on their mathematical properties would group them into the following broad categories:

1. Simple multiplier type models, of which the economic base model is by far the most widely used. In its simplest form input-output also belongs in this category.[7]

2. Optimizing programming models, among which linear and dynamic programming are increasingly applied.[8]

3. Econometric stochastic models, of which a great variety exist.

4. Simulation models, used mainly in connection with transportation and land-use planning.

The relative advantages and disadvantages of programming and econometric models as used in regional studies are not easily weighed. The programming models are basically normative and hence fit better into the regional planning context with its obvious emphasis on maximization under constraints. They can be operated at a very disaggregated level, which confers upon them a distinct advantage. On the other hand, they incorporate some rigid assumptions and lack the flexibility of econometric stochastic models. Another great weakness of programming models, which they share with input-output and other simple multipliers, is that there is almost nothing in these models to indicate a basic divergence between the particular hypotheses upon which they are predicated and empirical facts. Input-output, when used as an econometric model, is really an especially simple version of linear programming and shares some of its advantages and all of its rigidities A comparison between input-output, and econometric stochastic models is very difficult. The real choice here is between a highly disaggregated but extremely simple model based on a set of rigid assumptions and a sophisticated analytic tool.[9] Econometric stochastic models are especially adapted for revealing causal or functional relationships and confronting them with data. The statistical estimating techniques and methods of testing the reliability of results have been powerfully developed since the last war. On the other hand, these models so far operate on a level of aggregation which limits their uses in regional studies.

Independent of the form of model, the behavioral relations which describe the assumed reactions of transactors—persons or institutions—to changes in circumstances have to be based on, and supplemented by, a set of economic identities which are given statistical content in social accounts. Taken by themselves, these identities are simply a framework for a consistent description of economic activities of which they cannot provide an explanation.

From the point of view of underlying theories and hypotheses, national growth models may be roughly divided into those dealing primarily with advanced industrialized nations and focusing mainly on effective demand and those addressing themselves largely to underdeveloped nations and focusing mainly on problems of balance of payments and foreign aid. The first group has its roots in the Keynesian model; the second, in the Harrod-Domar type models. In both types, investments are treated as important exogenous variables, but in the first the act of investment and the balance between savings and investments is of prime interest, while in the second the effect of investments upon capacity and their relation to the rate of growth are investigated.

Regional growth models so far developed try to apply some of these concepts to open regions. This approach seems to work reasonably well as long as one is dealing with regions comparable in size and complexity to national economies. It breaks down, however, as soon as one attacks problems of smaller regions, among which are to be found many of the depressed regions which have not had extensive manufacturing development. The fundamental difficulties in applying concepts and models developed at the national level to typical planning regions are largely due to their extreme "openness" combined with the high mobility under modern conditions not only of goods and financial capital but even, to a large extent, of factors of production. More specifically, a region may face a perfectly elastic demand curve for the majority of its products; that is, it can ordinarily sell all its products as long as it is able to produce at competitive prices; hence fluctuations in demand, internal or for exports, should not be treated as the main exogenous variable. Similarly, because of the high interregional mobility of financial capital, local investments do not depend, as a rule, on local savings. Thus in an open region savings and investments may be permanently imbalanced, making models focusing on this particular problem not suitable for handling regional problems.

Types of Accounts

It is doubtful whether the various formats of social accounts evolved at the national level can provide, without considerable changes, a suitable framework for regional studies and the indispensable background for planning. Their form is, after all, a reflection of the theory which they are intended to implement. Besides differences in the theoretical framework, there are also numerous and important differences between national economic planning and regional planning which should find their expression in the form of social accounts.

Social accounts even at the national level are not without their limitations. It is difficult to estimate with their help the externalities which seem to play an ever-increasing role in regional economics. Similarly, they are not a powerful tool for assessing social benefits or costs whenever these diverge from private ones. Furthermore, it is only in the realm of economic interaction and in a market of willing buyers and sellers that the price mechanism can be used to articulate subjective preferences. No similar quantifying mechanism is available in the field of social or political relationships which could provide a means of measuring noneconomic values.[10]

Five main types of social accounts are used, namely: (1) income and product accounts; (2) balance-of-payments accounts; (3) moneyflows or flow-of-funds accounts; (4) interindustry or input-output accounts; and (5) wealth accounts. Four of these accounts deal with flows and one with stock phenomena. They differ widely in the level of aggregation, in the way in which the economy is divided into sectors, in the degree of netting and consolidation, in the amount of imputing, and in coverage. These differences have been abundantly discussed in literature.[11]

Income and product accounts, enormously useful for purposes of business-cycles analysis and for guiding policy at the central level, have been accepted and are quickly becoming an indispensable tool of regional planning and analysis. Their use has paralleled the application of macroeconomic analysis to regional problems. Here, however, a number of important problems are encountered which are a reflection on the differences existing between regional planning and national economic planning, especially in the following areas: (1) scope and objectives; (2) policy instruments; (3) availability of data for specialized research; and (4) methods of analysis.[12]

Some major difficulties in constructing regional income and product accounts or regional social accounts in general, are due not only to the rather obvious data difficulties but also to some conceptual doubts which still persist. First and foremost is the fact that a number of activities do not have any clearcut spatial meaning. Most federal government expenditures and undistributed corporate profits, to quote just two examples, illustrate well the familiar situs problem. Even more important problems are raised by the analytic uses to which income and product accounts can be put at the regional level. Regional planning takes place at a much more disaggregated level than national economic planning and hence the macro approach is not always the most effective one.

Even so, income and product accounts are widely used at the regional level because of the relative ease with which they can be prepared. Their usefulness could probably be greatly enhanced at relatively small additional cost by disaggregating them somewhat, at least to the point which would enable the construction of several production or consumption functions without having to construct a full input-output table.

A far more extensive form is represented by interindustry or input-output accounts, the uses and applications of which at the regional level[13] have been the subject of a long, and at times heated, controversy. The issue has hardly been whether input-output accounts are useful for regional studies (nobody seriously disputed that) but whether the insights gained with their help can justify the very considerable costs involved in their construction. Two features of input-output accounts vastly complicate all discussions.

First, the term *input-output* is used in order to describe both an accounts system and an econometric model. Moreover, as an accounts system, input-output has become so closely associated with a particular econometric model and a specific set of strong assumptions that its other applications are often overlooked.

Secondly, the cost of constructing an even modest regional input-output table is of an order of magnitude altogether different from other types of social accounts and very often not anticipated in advance by regional planners. As a result, the construction of a regional input-output table often replaces, instead of serving as a basis for, regional analysis. Typically, under these circumstances input-output is used simply as a more sophisticated economic base model, which is clearly an inefficient way of applying a very expensive research tool.

The numerous applications of interindustry accounts fall into several categories: (1) prediction of future events, particularly growth forecasts; (2) studies leading to formulation of programs of action; and (3) analysis of regional economic structure.

The first, prediction and forecasting, is an area in which input-output has not been particularly successful even at the national level.[14] When dealing with a regional economy, several additional strong assumptions have to be made which are bound to impair further its forecasting usefulness. The most important is the assumption of the constancy of interregional trading patterns, even in the presence of capacity constraints and despite some evidence that even in large metropolitan areas the amount of cross-hauling is very considerable. Considerable weight is carried by the argument that predictions of future regional growth require inclusion of more elements than the static input-output model encompasses. The very interesting regional applications of dynamic input-output models and uses of input-output as part of programming or econometric models are still in their infancy.

Formulation of programs of action, on the other hand, seems to be the natural domain of input-output. The model was orginally devised, partly at least, in order to explore existing capacity constraints in the presence of shocks to the national economy such as mobilization for war or transition from war to peace. By an extension of this reasoning, interregional input-output models have originally been developed in order to reveal bottlenecks due to separation of plants producing nontransportable services or commodities difficult to transport over long distances.[15] Yet there is little evidence so far that such bottlenecks are numerous or that they affect in an important way a single small region. Modern mobility of goods and services makes it appear rather implausible.

There is no doubt, however, that the model can be very useful when studying "breaks" in the regional structure. It is in this area that a study of historical data pertaining to one particular region may be less relevant than the application of a model broadly based on national phenomena. In some cases, even national input-output tables may be more effective than regional ones in revealing interesting potential relationships.[16]

The following problems, among others, might be investigated with the help of a regional input-output table:

1. Intensity of intraregional interindustry flows

2. Multiplier effects generated in the regional economy by exogenously induced changes in the level of operation of various industries

3. Value added by industry and changes in the employment of factors of production due to direct and indirect effects of changes in the level of demand

4. Impact of investments in various industries upon employment or income

5. The existence of industrial complexes or of industrial complexes in the process of formation

It should be borne in mind, nonetheless, that input-output analysis is primarily a tool for studying interindustry relations, and it does not make sense to apply it to regions which either do not have any manufacturing activities to speak of or possess only a few scattered plants. More generally, this expensive tool should not be applied to regions so "open" as to make the whole notion of bottlenecks irrelevant. If all one needs to know is a production function, even disaggregated by industries, there is no need for an input-output study. Total inputs, use of labor or of capital by industry, can be obtained by other, cheaper methods.

Wealth accounts, which remain today the least developed of the five main types of social accounts, represent the only type of stock accounting. The need for a systematic construction of stock accounts to be incorporated into a comprehensive accounting system stems from three additional considerations:

1. No system of accounts is complete and closed without it

2. Flow-of-funds analysis is based on stock phenomena

3. Dynamic input-output involving a capital assets and a stock matrix is being increasingly studied.

Renewed interest has resulted in a number of recent studies.[17] Despite, however, a relative abundance of data (some of which are of spurious accuracy) the methodological and conceptual issues remain significant. Even the fundamental notions underlying wealth accounting such as capital, wealth, resource, asset, and property are controversial.

In addition, there are numerous practical difficulties in valuation. Not only is knowledge of market transactions fragmentary, but the actual prices at which they are concluded often deviate from those recorded and thus remain unknown. No markets exist for most public goods, some privately owned assets, and human resources. Furthermore, the appropriate interest rates to be used in order to discount future income streams are hard to find.

Nonetheless, the neglect of stock accounts at the regional level is surprising. City planners have always thought that stock variables were important in urban studies but have not brought the social accounting framework to bear in their data collection systems.[18] As has been forcefully pointed out, stock accounts may be more useful than flow accounts for understanding secular trends and structural changes in an open region.[19] They could also relate the concerns and activities of regional economists to those of physical planners.

Wealth accounts are most closely related to flow-of-funds accounts, since both measure a similar set of variables.[20] The former accounts measure stock values, while the latter examine changes in stocks. Their institutional sectoring is another point of similarity. Balance-of-payments accounts are somewhat related to the rest-of-the-world sector of income and product accounts, examining in greater detail the external linkages and emphasizing exports and imports, capital flows, and gold flows over the regional boundaries. Like flow-of-funds accounts, they are more inclusive than income and product accounts by encompassing all transactions involving money or credit, even secondhand goods, and at the same time less inclusive by omitting intrainstitutional flows. Moneyflow accounts and balance-of-payments accounts have also found their way into regional studies. Although data on interregional moneyflows are scarce, these accounts do provide additional descriptive information about the regional economy which might be worthwhile to record. Yet they lack widespread appeal simply because the information provided has considerable more value at the national level in formulating monetary and trade policy.[21]

At the regional level there have been attempts to determine the volume of exports and imports of open regions via an analysis of balance-of-payments accounts, but they do not appear promising because of the intricate structure of the banking system. Moneyflow accounts on the other hand, may hold out some promise. They are, at least theoretically, capable of being integrated into a comprehensive system of regional social accounts and may yet prove quite useful for examining the actual or potential role of various levels of government in promoting regional development.

The main purpose of this survey monograph is to review and assess the various methods and techniques of regional social accounting, to bring to the fore the existing gaps, and to put forward a tentative proposal of a fused, comprehensive accounting system. It is hoped that it will prove useful to planning practitioners, to applied economists, particularly those dealing with regional problems both in the developed and underdeveloped countries and to students of regional science, regional economics, urban and regional planning, and geography. The following six chapters have been organized into two parts, dealing respectively with aggregate accounts treating the economy as a whole or divided into a small number of heterogeneous sectors, and with accounts divided into a substantial number of sectors. The first part covers income and product accounts, balance-of-payments accounts, and moneyflows and wealth accounts. The second part deals with input-output accounts and with interregional intersectional flows. The last chapter presents a tentative model of a generalized accounts system.

**Part One
Aggregate Accounts**

2 Intersectoral Flows of Goods and Services

Origin of Income and Product Accounts

The quantitative approaches to economics and the idea of income accounting can be traced back to the seventeenth century and the work of Petty in England and Boisguillebert in France.[1] These early efforts were directed at measuring the national income in much the same way as the incomes of affluent persons. Petty's major work, *A Treatise on Taxes and Contributions and the Political Anatomy of Ireland,* was the first attempt at applying quantitative methods to what today might be called macroeconomics but which he referred to as "political arithmetic." His objective was to show that in 1665, despite the upheavals of the era of Cromwell and the Restoration, existing taxation did not exhaust the taxable capacity of the country. His work was all the more remarkable since it addressed itself to income and production, or to flow phenomena, at a time when mercantilists placed the stress on wealth. He used in his work the double entry system, but his expenditures and receipts were not balanced by savings. They were limited, moreover, to what corresponds now to disposable income.

The work of Petty was followed in England by that of Gregory King, whose estimates for 1688, like those of his predecessor, were based mainly on taxation statistics. Parallel work was carried out in France by Pierre Boisguillebert and Sebastien Vauban (who was better known as an engineer and a marshal of the French army) whose work was published in 1707. Both were penalized by the French government for attacking the existing inequitable tax system. Further work on national income was carried out by the physiocrats and Antoine Lavoisier, whose estimates were published in 1791 at the behest of the Revolutionary government.

From their beginning, the national income estimates had to face the problem of scope of national production. Of the three concepts which emerged, namely: (1) comprehensive production; (2) restricted production; and (3) restricted market production; the first two survive. The notion of comprehensive production encompasses both goods and services and is widely used today. Restricted production confines production to commodities having physical properties, thus excluding services. Unfortunately, this second concept, following the sterile physiocratic distinction between productive and unproductive labor, was adopted by Adam Smith and later by Marx and became the basis of income and product accounting in the Soviet Union and the Communist

15

countries. The third concept of restricted market production, covers only goods and services which enter the market and thus excludes imputations, but it never had a significant following.

The division between productive and unproductive labor has been firmly rejected by Say, Walras, Rosher, and Marshall, who also underlined the importance of deducting depreciation in order to avoid double counting. With Keynes the concept of comprehensive production finally became firmly established. The depression of the thirties gave impetus to the work on national income, since intelligent decisions on tax rates, borrowing, and government spending required knowledge of the type and magnitude of anticipated effects. Many of the aggregate measures were, moreover, directly required for implementing the Keynesian model. The basic framework of income and product accounting developed during the thirties and forties not only met the requirements of anticyclical policies and of the vastly different needs of a war economy in the early forties, but survived with relatively minor changes till the present. It is only in the areas of long-run, and especially regional, planning that its shortcomings are becoming apparent.

Determination of Income and Output

In our society the organization of basic economic processes such as production, distribution, consumption, and investment is entrusted to, or at least takes place through, the self-regulating market mechanism. It is thus natural to look for indexes of performance of the regional economy in exchange phenomena.

Production, distribution, and consumption can all be estimated by the volume of transactions taking place in a time unit, subject to only two important adjustments. On the one hand, the imputed value of those commodities and services which are both produced and consumed without entering the market mechanism has to be added. This group is comprised of such diverse elements as products of subsistence farming, free food and shelter provided to some classes of employees, and those financial services not explicitly charged to users. On the other hand, transactions which do not correspond to new production, such as sale of nonreproducible and secondhand assets, have to be eliminated. Meaningful aggregates describing the performance of the economy as a whole can thus be derived by consolidating the trading records of primary economic units, be they producers or consumers.

The practical difficulties in constructing income and product accounts, both on the national and subnational levels, are largely due to the fact that many, perhaps most, primary units do not keep records of their transactions. Even in cases where such records exist their format is not uniform, they are ill-adapted for social accounting purposes, and they are often subject to nondisclosure. It is, nonetheless, helpful for developing the conceptual framework of income and product accounting to think of the regional accounts as of an aggregation of profit and loss accounts of basic producing units.[2]

The profit and loss accounts, or income statements, are deficient for purposes of aggregation in several respects. First, they do not list all transactions taking place, since some appear directly in the balance sheet. For example, purchase of materials used for production affects profits, but not necessarily at the time of the purchase, and hence may be recorded at the end of the accounting period in the balance sheet only. Moreover, while as a general rule current transactions appear in the income statement and capital transactions in the balance sheet, some like sale of a used machine may represent a capital transaction for one party (seller) and a current one for the second (scrap-metal dealer). Second, income statements refer to goods sold during the period covered by the report, whereas in deriving income and product accounts for the whole economy the interest is centered on production. Third, business records list purchases of factors of production and of intermediate products indiscriminately as costs. Aggregation over all producing units would result, therefore, in considerable double counting. Two transformations are thus required prior to consolidation of individual income statements: (1) the income statement has to be changed into a production statement, referring to goods and services produced rather than sold during the reporting period, and (2) the production statement has to be changed into an income and product statement limited only to value-added, by eliminating purchases of intermediate products. The hypothetical example in Table 2-1 illustrates the procedure.

Assuming that $480 worth of goods was produced rather than the $470 actually sold would yield the statement presented in Table 2-2. Items marked by an asterisk in Table 2-2 are unchanged, since changes refer only to goods

Table 2-1
Income (Profit and Loss) Statement

Uses		Sources	
Purchases from other firms	207	Sales	470
Depreciation	20	Dividents received	24
Indirect business taxes	9	Interest received	5
Bad debt expenses	1	Subsidies received	1
Charitable contributions	1		
Factor payments:			
wages and salaries	100		
social security contri-			
butions	5		
interest paid	7		
Corporate profit taxes	72		
Dividends paid	40		
Retained earnings	38		
	500		500

Table 2-2
Production Statement

Uses		Sources	
Purchases from other firms	212	Sales*	470
Depreciation*	20	Dividends received*	24
Indirect business taxes*	9	Interest received*	5
Business transfer payments*	2	Net inventory change	10
Factor payments:			
wages and salaries	103		
social security contri-			
butions	6		
interest paid*	7		
Corporate profit taxes	72		
Dividends paid*	40		
Retained earnings	39		
	510		
Less: Subsidies received	1		
	509		509

produced but unsold. Subsidies received have been transferred to the "Uses" side as a negative entry, since they are considered to arise out of the legal environment of the firm and not as payments necessary to elicit services of factors of production.

What remains to be done is the deduction of purchases from other firms and of income from secondary sources, resulting in the income and product statement of Table 2-3.

Table 2-3
Income and Product Statement

Income (Uses)		Product (Sources)	
Depreciation	20	Sales	470
Indirect business taxes	9	Net inventory change	10
Business transfer payments	2		480
Factor payments:			
wages and salaries	103	Less: Purchases from	
social security contri-		other firms	212
butions	6		
net interest paid	2		
Corporate profit taxes	72		
Net dividends paid	16		
Retained earnings	39		
	269		
Less: Subsidies received	1		
Total Gross Income	268	Total Gross Product	268

While total value of transactions may be of interest for some purposes, the objective here is to arrive at costs grouped into: (1) factor payments, and (2) all other costs. The left-hand side, aggregated over all units, adds up to national or regional income at factor cost. Elements of two other aggregates, namely gross regional product, and net regional product, can also be calculated by adding taxes and depreciation. The above example brings to the fore the notion of value-added or payments to ultimate owners of factors of production originating in the firm considered.[3] Before turning to a comprehensive discussion of national or regional aggregates, it is necessary to consider imputations.

Imputed transactions are of particular importance in five types of units: (1) financial intermediaries, (2) unincorporated business enterprises, (3) government units, (4) unincorporated landlords, and (5) households. They arise because of consumption of products which do not enter the market mechanism, barter transactions or other nonmonetary forms of compensation. Transactions in used or secondhand objects are not sufficiently significant in existing records to deserve special handling.

The treatment of financial intermediaries, comprised of commercial banks, insurance companies, investment trusts, savings and loan associations, and other financial institutions, is most controversial. Their main source of income is interest and dividends received. A major source of their funds is checking deposits placed by households and business firms for convenience and not in order to earn interest. The cost of managing the accounts is largely covered by interest earned. Thus the real service performed is not directly paid for and might remain unrecorded in regional income and product accounts. The payment for it appears as difference between interest received and paid. The units paying interest are mainly business firms and since these, like financial intermediaries themselves, are not ultimate owners of factors of production, the amounts involved would be netted out. In order to avoid this, the difference between interest received and paid is often recorded as "imputed service charges" and appears as part of services performed by the local economy. Under this system other business enterprises as well as households have their purchases of services from other firms increased by the imputed service charges for keeping their checking accounts.

The unincorporated business enterprises, comprised of nonfarm, nonfinancial partnerships, farms, sole proprietorships, and producers' cooperatives, present different problems. For one thing the "net income of unincorporated enterprises" covers profits, wages, and interest, and it is ordinarily not possible to separate the contributions of the various factors of production. In fact it is next to impossible to distinguish the activities of owners as forming part of the business and household sectors. Farmers have, moreover, substantial amounts consumed and invested without recourse to the market mechanism, in addition to providing hired hands with free housing and food. All these require extensive imputations the volume of which is, however, relatively easy to establish because of yearly farm censuses.

The ambiguities surrounding the treatment of governments in regional income and product accounts center not on their regulating role but on their active participation in economic processes. To the extent that these are carried out by government-owned enterprises, no difficulties are encountered since their transactions are treated as those of any other business. More complex is the treatment of activities conducted directly by government agencies which fall into three categories: (1) sale of services and products, (2) collecting funds on the basis of regulatory powers, and (3) giving services such as police protection free of charge. Moreover, the amount of depreciation to be applied to their assets is almost impossible to determine, since their expenditures on capital goods form part of the budget and cannot in most cases be cumulated over a number of years for lack of data. Hence, it is customary to consider the contribution of governments to value-added generated in the economy as equivalent to their wage bill.

In deriving the latter figure, the accounts of various levels of government are consolidated, thus eliminating intergovernment transfers and grants; but in constructing regional accounts, an additional problem is raised by the activities of the national, or more generally, higher level governments. These are often treated as part of the rest of the world, even though their installations and agencies may be physically located in the region. Such treatment may be justified only for regions forming a small or insignificant part of the nation, but even there the handling of local employees of agencies of superregional governments becomes rather artificial. They cannot be considered as out-commuters, because the latter category is of importance in other aspects of regional planning.

The treatment in social accounts of unincorporated landlords is, on the other hand, straightforward, their income being equal to rents received, while their expenditures are comprised of maintenance, indirect taxes, interest on mortgage, and depreciation. Conceptual difficulties are encountered only in case of owner-occupied housing, the volume of which is often very substantial. Its omission from income accounting would not only create a significant gap but would violate the principle of accounts being invariant to legal arrangements since purchase of a house by a former tenant would reduce the total amount of services generated in the economy. In order to avoid this difficulty, owners of self-occupied housing are treated in accounts in the dual capacity of business (as owners of property) households. The objection that substantial flows such as depreciation and imputed rents are thus created where none are claimed is hard to avoid.

The treatment of households in social accounts is characterized by a number of arbitrary rules such as the exclusion from major regional aggregates of contributions of wives and other members of the family. These are sometimes substantial but an arbitrary line has obviously to be drawn somewhere since all of these would have to be based on imputations. Only contributions of domestic servants are counted, a significant part of which is also imputed. Households are the suppliers of the overwhelming part of factors of production and consume a major part of the regional product.

It has already been mentioned that regional income and product accounts cannot be derived by combining and consolidating accounts of primary units, since these are usually nonexistent. Except in very small regions, it is even impractical to add up value-added generated in local enterprises, so that indirect methods are the only ones practically available. For this purpose ample use is made of published statistics and other benchmark data. While the techniques used vary according to circumstance, the method of calculating the total product deserves a few passing remarks. It is composed of four main aggregates; consumption by households, investments, exhaustive government expenditures, and exports. Independent estimates, especially for the latter three, are sometimes available but two basic techniques deserve to be mentioned; the commodity flow analysis, and the retail valuation method. The commodity flow analysis, covering some 80 percent of all goods produced, starts with the output of goods (classified into finished durable and perishable, intermediate, and mixed) based ordinarily on a census of manufacturing and traces their flow through the wholesalers, importers and exporters, and retailers, adding at each stage costs and markups. The retail valuation method, on the other hand, limited to some 15 percent of total output, simply multiplies known quantities of commodities produced by their average retail price.

Format and Definition of Sectors

The various approaches to the construction of regional income and product accounts can be classified into (1) those dealing with a particular region in isolation and obtaining the bulk of the required data by field surveys, and (2) those relying on disaggregated national social accounts and data derived mainly from national sources. The differences are not limited to sources of data but affect the format of the accounts, their basic assumptions, and perception of the significant characteristics of the economy studied. Both methods have been fruitfully applied in a number of cases,[4] yet for all its simplicity the first, direct method tends not only to cut artificially the link between the local economy and the larger whole of which it is a part but to be extremely expensive and time-consuming for any but the very small towns. It is doubtful whether the greater accuracy achieved by recourse to direct field surveys is ever justified; even national income and product accounts make use almost exclusively of indirect estimates.

Conceptual differences in approach and practical considerations of data availability have resulted in the emergence of fairly numerous systems and formats of income and product accounts. The differences between the various methods in use relate to:

1. Number and definition of sectors[5]
2. Extent to which legal and decision-making units are preserved
3. Classification of transactions between different accounts
4. Degree of netting and consolidation[6] present
5. Extent and nature of imputations
6. Type of aggregates presented as part of the accounts

Other differences have to do with some key definitions such as investments or consumption, with methods of collecting basic data, and so forth. Whenever indirect methods are followed, the regional accounts have to use to a very large extent the format and general methodology of national income accounting since as a rule they rely heavily upon benchmark data provided by the latter. The various disadvantages and difficulties involved in the indirect approach are due to important differences in scope and objectives of social accounting at the national and subnational level.

The grouping of transactions, or sectoring, is always of critical importance. Of the large number of possible alternatives, one method of organizing sectors is presented in Figure 2-1. It was used in the construction of Nova Scotia income and product accounts.[7] The basic layout was almost identical to the one used in the Canadian accounting system,[8] although seven rather than six sectors were adopted. This resulted from splitting the government revenue and expenditure account into: (1) local governments revenue and expenditure account, and (2) local operations of nonlocal governments account. Thus, the following sectors were used:

1. Personal income and expenditure account
2. Local governments[9] revenue and expenditure account
3. Local operations of nonlocal governments account
4. Business operating account
5. Nonresidents revenue and expenditure account
6. Investment income appropriation account
7. Regional savings account

The first sector, covered by the personal income and expenditure account, groups transactions pertaining to resident households and private and some public nonprofit organizations in their capacity as final consumers and owners of factors of production.[10] The inclusion of nonprofit organizations in the personal income and expenditure account, justifiable to a certain extent on theoretical grounds, is not particularly desirable for purposes of regional analysis. It would be preferable to group private nonprofit organizations with

23

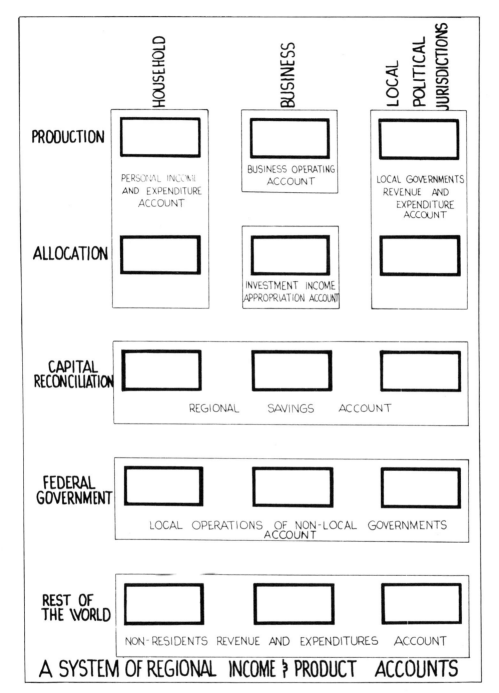

Figure 2-1. A System of Regional Income and Product Accounts.

local governments because their behavior appears to follow more closely that of public administration bodies rather than households.

The income side of the personal income and expenditure account adds up to total personal income and is composed of amounts accruing to owners of factors of production and of transfers such as wages, salaries, and supplementary labor income.[11]

The next group of estimates deals with incomes accruing to other factors of production such as net income received by farm operators from farm production; net income of nonfarm unincorporated business; and interest, dividends, and rental income of persons.

Finally, the account contains an estimate of unilateral transfer payments received by households and private nonprofit organizations, again broken down into those originating from federal and local governments, corporations, and nonresidents.

The expenditure side contains an estimate of personal direct taxes paid by resident households and nonprofit organizations, broken down into income taxes, succession duties and estate taxes, and miscellaneous direct taxes. This item deducted from the total personal income yields personal disposable income. The other entries show how personal disposable income was divided between consumption and personal net savings.[12]

The second sector, covered by the local governments revenue and expenditure account, groups only those transactions which have welfare significance. It thus differs from the total of the budgets of the relative governments and their agencies and affiliated institutions.

The revenue side contains estimates of amounts accruing to local governments. They fall into three major categories: direct and indirect taxes from persons and from corporations, which depend upon the power of local governments to tax; sale of services, including investment income, and employers' and employees' contributions to social insurance and government pension funds;[13] and transfers from nonlocal governments.

The expenditure side contains estimates of exhaustive government expenditures.[14] They are comprised of current expenses in the form of purchases of goods and services from business and payments of wages and salaries, and investments, shown as capital accumulation. The nonexhaustive government expenditures are shown as transfer payments. The balancing item, surplus or deficit on transactions relating to income and product accounts, is derived as a residual and hence contains the total error of estimate.

The third sector, covered by the local operations of nonlocal governments account, is limited in scope to those operations of the federal government and its agencies which influence the regional aggregates forming part of income and product accounts. The approach followed purports to measure the impact of federal government upon the regional economy and not the benefits derived by local residents from the various activities of the federal government. The federal government and its agencies are in effect treated in the context of regional income and product accounts in much the same way as the rest of the world. The structure of both the revenue and expenditure sides of this account differs from the local governments revenue and expenditure accounts only in detail.

The fourth sector, covered by the business operating account, contains transactions without direct welfare significance, because business enterprises are neither final consumers nor ultimate owners of factors of production. The usefulness of the account resides in grouping and balancing various items in a meaningful way.[15]

The revenue side of the account contains estimates of income of local business according to source. Sales are grouped into sales to residents in their capacity as ultimate consumers; investments recorded as sales to business; sales to local and federal governments, both for current consumption and capital formation; and exports of goods and services (with sales to nonresident military personnel and tourist expenditures singled out). Finally, the revenue side contains subsidies from both nonlocal and local governments.

The expenditure side of the account is comprised of costs incurred in production of goods, the sales of which are recorded on the revenue side, such as: wages, salaries, and supplementary labor income; net income received by farm operators from farm production; and net income of nonfarm unincorporated business.[16] Expenditures also include the numerically significant imports and other costs of production such as indirect taxes, payments for services of local government agencies, capital consumption allowances, and miscellaneous valuation adjustments. The balancing item transfers the residual error of estimate to the regional savings account.

The fifth sector, covered by the nonresidents revenue and expenditure account, groups transactions between residents and other economic units domiciled in the region, and the rest of the world. The receipts side is comprised of imports of goods and services; travel expenditures abroad by local residents; and payments to nonresidents in the form of interest and dividends for services of their capital invested in the region. The surplus or deficit representing net disinvestment in the rest of the world resulting from income and product accounts is transferred to the regional savings account.

The payments side of the account contains an estimate of exports and travel expenses of visitors; interest and dividends; and wages, salaries, and supplementary labor income (mainly of out-commuters). The latter refer to factor payments to residents earned abroad.[17]

The sixth sector, covered by the investment income appropriation account, may be viewed as part of the business operating account showing in some detail the allocation of income. On the sources side are grouped investment income (or difference between revenues and costs transferred from business operating accounts) and interest and dividends received from nonresidents and from local and nonlocal governments by both local business and local households. Interest received from governments is not considered part of the gross regional product.[18]

The disposition side shows the division of total investment income between residents and nonresidents. The share of residents is composed of interest, dividends, and rental income of persons; charitable contributions made by corporations; items accruing to local governments such as interest and profits of local government business enterprises; and undistributed profits of local corporations.[19] The share of nonresidents is comprised of interest and dividends paid by business to nonresidents, interest paid to nonlocal governments, profits of nonlocal governments' business enterprises, and corporate income taxes.

The seventh sector, covered by the regional savings account, is analytically the most significant. The sources side indicates the origin of the investment funds available and is comprised of personal net savings; undistributed corporation profits and capital consumption allowances and miscellaneous valuation adjustments, together forming business gross savings; local governments' surplus; and nonlocal governments surplus. In addition, the sources side contains the residual error of estimate.

The disposition side is comprised of fixed capital formation, subdivided into new residential construction, new nonresidential construction, and new machinery and equipment; and surplus on current account with nonresidents. The significance of surplus or deficit on current account with nonresidents resides in the fact that combined with the balance of local operations of nonlocal governments it indicates the volume of investments or disinvestments of residents outside of the region.

Main Aggregates

One of the major objectives of constructing income and product accounts is the derivation of aggregates which form one of the main tools or macroeconomic analysis. Historically, the single figure aggregates preceded the evolution of modern income accounting and were actually largely responsible for their present form.[20]

The five aggregates frequently used in order to monitor the progress of a regional economy closely parallel the main aggregates forming part of the national income and product accounts.

Gross Regional Product at Market Prices (GRP). GRP is the market value of the gross output of goods and services produced during a year by factors of production owned by local residents. Theoretically, gross regional product at market prices can be derived in three ways:

1. By summing incomes accruing to owners of factors of production and adjusting the total to market prices by the addition of indirect taxes less subsidies

2. By summing expenditures, or shares of the product allocated to consumption by households, exhaustive government expenditures, capital formation, and exports

3. By summing value-added created by various industries and accruing to local owners of factors of production.[21]

The fact that GRP is derived in "gross" terms means that the total is calculated without taking into account the value of capital goods which have been consumed in the process. This omission is of little consequence because the relative value of capital consumption does not vary appreciably over time. On the other hand, it greatly facilitates interregional comparisons and, above all, comparisons with other countries whose economies use different technologies and apply different approaches to depreciation.

Net Regional Product at Market Prices (NRP). NRP differs from gross regional product at market prices by the amount of capital consumption allowance and miscellaneous valuation adjustments. Capital consumption allowance is largely composed of, though not identical to, depreciation. It also includes accidental damage to fixed assets and an adjustment for capital outlays charged by business firms to current expenses.

A practical difficulty arises from the fact that depreciation has a different meaning to the owner of the means of production from whose records the total are derived, to the tax collector, and to the economist. The concern of the producer is to keep his capital intact; to society, it is largely the notion of keeping intact the physical productivity of the economy that matters. This distinction comes to the fore, for example, in the case of a new invention which may induce an entrepreneur anticipating obsolescence to apply a quicker rate of depreciation. For society, on the other hand, technical progress could justify allocation of smaller amounts for depreciation because of lower capital-output ratio. Putting it otherwise, the existing machinery would not produce less because of the new invention, but the need to install new equipment would be more remote and more limited. On other scores, too, the problem of keeping capital intact is highly controversial in economic theory. For example, should depreciation be imputed where none is claimed, thus creating a new flow? Depreciation of owner-occupied residential housing is a case in point, with the amounts involved by no means negligible. In this, as in several other instances, a more or less arbitrary solution has to be adopted for purposes of constructing social accounts. Valuation adjustments, which also form part of the difference between GRP and NRP, are numerically unimportant. They result from attempts to derive a uniform valuation of end-of-the-year business stocks despite the fact that several different legitimate methods are used by business firms.

Regional Income, or New Regional Product at Factor Cost (RI). RI differs from net regional product at market prices by the amount of indirect taxes, less subsidies. The difference between the two aggregates represents that part of the market value of goods and services which does not accrue to factors of production. Thus, amounts which may vary unsystematically with changes in the volume of production are eliminated from the index describing the performance of the regional economy.

Sales taxes are a typical example of producers acting as tax collectors. Unfortunately, the treatment of indirect taxes involves the controversial question of incidence of taxation and represents, conceptually and operationally, a complicated problem. The accepted practice is to deduct from net regional product those taxes which are not charges attributable to the use of the factors of production or which do not fall upon any specific factor of production. By a parallel extension of this reasoning, subsidies are treated as amounts accruing to factors of production without which the price of the end product would have to be higher. Whether they are necessary corrections of the market mechanism, bridging the gap between costs and revenues in order to elicit the services of factors of production, or are simply transfer payments deriving from the play of political forces is a relevant but difficult-to-answer question. The first assumption is usually made, and they are deducted from indirect taxes.

Like the other two aggregates, regional income can be measured in two ways. When measured as income accruing to the owners of factors of production, it is called net regional income, or simply regional income. When viewed as a product, net of capital consumption allowance and adjusted for indirect taxes and subsides, it is referred to as net regional product at factor cost. It is unfortunate that the widely used term regional income is particularly confusing in the context of social accounts, dealing as they do with different types of "regional incomes."

The next two aggregates, personal income and personal disposable income, unlike those so far discussed, are not measures of the performance of the local economy but of the means of payment at the disposal of residents of the region.

Personal Income (PI). PI is derived from regional income by the deduction of earnings accruing but not paid out to households such as undistributed corporation profits, employers' and employees' contributions to social insurance, various forms of forced savings, and amounts which accumulate in the hands of the local governments. On the other hand, unearned payments to local households such as government transfers and other unilateral payments, which do not form part of aggregates measuring the level of operation of the economy, are added.

The bulk of unilateral transfers originate from the federal and local governments but in some depressed regions with heavy outmigration an important (but difficult to estimate) part may be due to transfers from former residents.

Personal Disposable Income (PDI). PDI differs from personal income only by the deduction of personal direct taxes. It thus provides an estimate of the amounts available for consumption or saving.

The interrelations between the five major aggregates and their components in terms of flows are illustrated in Figure 2-2 from which some minor flows have been removed for the sake of clarity. The arrows indicate the direction of equivalent money flows rather than movements of goods and services. The four major components of aggregate demand—consumption by households, investments, exports, and exhaustive government expenditures—are indicated at the extreme left. Together they form total resources, not considered to be one of the major aggregates.

The aggregates so far discussed refer to the regional economy viewed as a collection of residents. In regional studies it is customary to look also at economic phenomena taking place within specific geographic boundaries irrespective of the place of residence of owners of factors of production.

A useful measure often applied in this connection is gross domestic product. It differs from gross regional product at market prices by the fact that it measures not so much the total value of goods and services produced by factors of production owned by residents of the region as the total value of production taking place in the region. Hence, it is primarily a geographical concept. Its great advantage is that it avoids some of the ambiguities surrounding measurement of phenomena which do not have any clearcut spatial meaning. The remaining conceptual and operational difficulties are, nonetheless, considerable. In order to derive gross domestic product, the gross regional product at market prices would have to be adjusted for wages of in- and out-commuters, interest and dividends earned from the rest of the world, and interest and dividends paid to nonresidents. This subject has been discussed at length, and all the arguments involved need not be repeated here.[22] Briefly, the transformation of gross regional product into gross domestic product would involve the following adjustments:

Gross regional product

plus: Interest and dividends paid to nonresidents
        Wages earned by in-commuters

less: Wages earned by out-commuters
        Interest and dividends accruing to residents from investments in the
        rest-of-the world

equals: Gross domestic product

In most practical situations, no reliance can be placed on the above aggregate unless the accounts have been computed by summing up value-added created locally. Flows of interest and dividends over intranational boundaries are among the weakest estimates in regional income and product accounts, and it does not seem to make sense to adjust for these very uncertain quantities.

Granting that the use of gross domestic product is conceptually attractive for several reasons, it hardly removes the basic difficulties surrounding the treatment of corporations. The latter do not enter directly into the major aggregates derived from income and product accounts because they are intermediaries and neither final consumers nor ultimate owners of factors of production. Hence, all that is needed for consistent derivation of GRP is the place of residence of stockholders. Income accruing to residents out of dividends of corporations, wherever located, is generally known, although a real difficulty arises in connection with other GRP items pertaining to corporations, namely: (1) undistributed corporate profits, (2) corporate income taxes, and (3) corporate investments.

The difficulty is not due to lack of data but is primarily conceptual since these items form incomes of stockholder whose place of residence is unknown. No satisfactory treatment is currently available, and hence all three items are customarily allocated to the region where the headquarters of the corporation are located. That this is inadequate is glaringly obvious,[23] but numerically these flows are rarely of great importance. The first of the above items, undistributed corporate profits, can hardly be significant in depressed regions since few corporations locate their headquarters outside of the financial centers of the country. As far as corporate income taxes are concerned, reliable published sources of information generally exist, but they are presented according to the place where the headquarters of the corporations are located, which is neither equivalent to where production has actually taken place nor to the place of residence of stockholders. Finally, the third item, corporate investments, is part of usually fairly reliable figures covering business investments, both replacement and new.

Finally, mention should be made of the fairly numerous models employing short-cut methods in order to arrive at crude estimates of the main regional aggregates. Almost without exception such models take as their point of departure published data on personal income. The derivation of estimates of regional income, net regional product and gross regional product is usually predicated on the assumption that the proportions between basic flows and aggregates existing in the national economy apply also to the region under study. For example, the ratio between GNP and NNP is deemed to hold in the region, implying that capital consumption allowance stands in the region in the same proportion to total output of goods and services as in the nation. That such methods can be regarded only as a first approximation is abundantly obvious.

Performance of the Economy

The various flows and major aggregates as well as their changes over time furnish

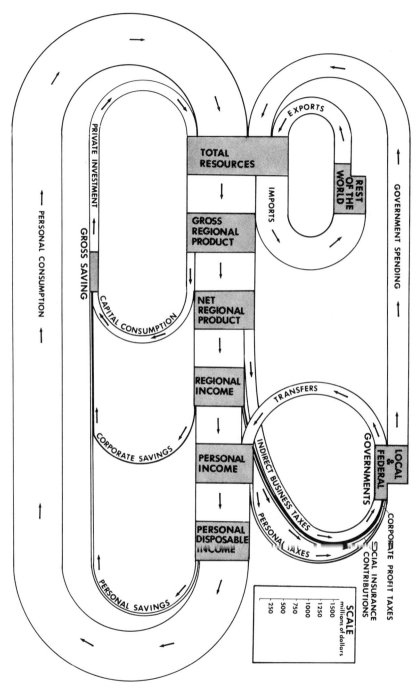

Figure 2-2. Flows in the Nova Scotia Economy, 1965.

the basic numerical material upon which to build or against which to confront hypotheses concerning the regional economy. Yet a vast collection of numbers such as regional income and product accounts can yield meaningful and relevant qualitative insights into the working of the economy only in terms of comparisons with other magnitudes. More specifically, any conclusions have to make use of three types of juxtapositions:

1. Interregional comparisons between similar flows or aggregates in the study area and in other regions
2. Structural comparisons between various flows within the regional economy
3. Temporal comparisons between magnitudes of regional flows and aggregates at various times.

The first problem to which income and product accounts have traditionally been applied is an assessment of the general operation of the economy. Gross regional product at market prices is widely considered to be the best indicator of the overall performance of the economy. Its comparison with the national total shows the region's share in the national economy, while the ratio of GRP or GNP to population yields an easily interpretable measure of productivity. A preliminary assessment of the structure of the regional economy in terms of the relative importance of various sectors also can be derived from a scrutiny of sectoral accounts.

The relation between the three major indicators of the performance of the regional economy gross regional product, net regional product, and regional income is of considerable importance. A relatively small gap between GRP and NRP would point toward a low level of investments, while a substantial difference between NRP and RI may be indicative of low value-added content of local products. Of great significance, in this connection is the level of the local wage bill, since invested capital in many depressed regions is controlled by interests located outside of their boundaries and its share in regional product flows out of the local economy.

An examination of changes over time indicates existing trends. The latter comparisons are often cast in terms of constant dollars, even though there is usually no reason for assuming that fluctuations in the purchasing power of the dollar differ significantly between various parts of the country. The movements over time of the other two major indicators of the performance of the regional economy—net regional product and regional income—usually closely follow those of the GRP. Nevertheless, a widening gap between GRP and NRP is sometimes discernable, indicating an increase in capital consumption allowance following a buildup of invested capital. Comparisons with corresponding national figures reveal the sensitivity of the regional economy to business cycles, the extent to which it is affected by them, and its ability to recover. The depressed regions seem to fall into two distinct categories: the first is confined to regional economies strongly oriented towards the production of a single staple, while the second comprises areas which have lost all vitality and do not have significant industries. The first category is usually hard hit, while the latter often registers relative gains during minor recessions in the national economy. This points toward a greater immunity from cyclical fluctuations due to the importance assumed by transfer payments and other forms of politically motivated federal spending.

Switching attention from indicators of the general performance of the regional economy to those dealing with welfare, the first to be considered is personal income. Its level comes close to being an index of the well-being of local residents, but its comparison with the national average may fail to portray fully the plight of a depressed region in countries comprised of heterogeneous parts. In such cases, juxtaposition with other regions, even forming part of different systems, may shed more light and prove more revealing. More conclusions remain unaffected when per capita personal disposable income is considered instead of personal income, although interregional differences are somewhat scaled down in the latter case due to progressive taxation.

Even more illuminating are structural comparisons between various aggregates describing the local economy. Typically, in depressed regions personal income is persistently greater than regional income and may even exceed GRP. In extreme cases personal spending may exceed earnings accruing to factors of production owned by local residents.[24]

A scrutiny of components of personal income sometimes bring to light interesting facts concerning the relative share of income accruing to households in their capacity as owners of factors of production. Not only may the overall share lag behind the corresponding national figure, but a depressed region may show lower relative wage income and a higher share of nonfarm unincorporated business than the more economically mature parts of the nation. In this connection wages and salaries are of particular interest, for they may be viewed as a crude index of industrialization and of social change. A particularly dangerous sign is a downward trend in the relative share of wages and salaries in personal income compared to the rest of the country.

Per capita wages and salaries provide no information about wage rates or wages and salaries paid per employee or per man-hour. The two ordinarily tend to move together but their interpretation may be different. While socially and politically low wage rates are a negative phenomenon, the economic significance of cheap labor is more difficult to assess. Low wage rates may induce or stimulate outmigration, with its detrimental effects. On the other hand, they may act as a force attracting new industries. The desirability of attracting industries dependent on cheap labor presents a complex problem from the long-run point of view. Moreover, the analytically relevant relationship is not the ratio of total wages and salaries to total number of employees but comparison of the wage rate with the marginal productivity of labor. This comparison can hardly be made on the basis of data derived from income and product accounts alone.

A preliminary step for such an analysis would be to disaggregate the accounts by sectors. Very often, however, some important industries such as mining have to be eliminated because their levels of employment may depend upon sociopolitical considerations and not be correlated with levels of output. Consequently, earnings accruing to their employees are partly at least in the nature of transfer payments. This circumstance makes the derivation of production functions and the calculation of marginal productivities of labor in those sectors extremely difficult.

Turning next to an examination of the distribution of personal income in terms of its allocation to various uses, direct personal taxes have to be deducted first, leaving personal disposable income to be apportioned between consumption of goods and services and savings. Analytically significant is the relation between consumption and regional income or income accruing to resident owners of factors of production. Excess of consumption over regional income is again typical of depressed regions, which are often supported to some extent by transfer payments.

Among the most analytically significant components of GRP are investments. Their importance derives from their impact upon (1) the short-run equilibrium of the economy, and (2) the productive capacity and long-run growth. The first finds its simplest analytic expression in the relation between savings and investments on the one hand, and foreign investments and balance of foreign trade on the other. The second is found in the relations between the rates of capital accumulation, and growth of the labor force and output.

In regional studies, with their emphasis on long-run growth, the various analyses of investments can be classified into those probing into the forces responsible for the level of investments and those examining the effects of either total regional investments or their components upon employment and production. In both types of studies ample use is made of comparisons with corresponding national magnitudes.

For purposes of analysis either net or gross investments may be used. Net investments provide a measure of the increase in the stock of real capital assets and thus represent additions to the productive capacity of the economy. Gross investments, on the other hand, include both new and replacement capital. While replacement investments would see to do no more than maintain intact a given stock of capital with respect to size, quality, and value, financed automatically from depreciation allowances, the distinction between new and replacement investments is, in reality, not a clearcut one. Because of constant shifts in such factors as technology, prices, and costs, investment expenditures even when financed from depreciation reserves rarely represent a simple replacement of capital assets that have become worn out or obsolete. Hence, the usual analytic treatment of investments concentrates on gross rather than net investments.

Another important distinction is between autonomous and induced investments. Induced investments are those which can be determined and explained statistically from within the economy, being usually linked in some way to current output or demand, while autonomous investments are considered to be exogenous, or independent of current operation of the economy. Attempts to pinpoint and explain statistically the factors influencing investments, even at the national level, are fraught with great difficulties. Precisely what these factors are is by no means as clear as for the consumption or production function. Nor is the relationship of an investment function to a production function obvious. In some macroeconomic models, an investment function seems to be a substitute for a production function, while in others both an investment and a production function are included as complementary to one another.

The factors which are thought to influence investments fall into three categories. First, there are the relationships between the price or cost of assets and the expected future flow of net yields. Irrespective of the specific form of this relation, under appropriate market conditions the rate of return should be equal on the margin to the rate of interest. The main difficulty in practical applications of this relationship is a technical one and pertains to the difficulty of estimating the rate of return on assets.

The second group of variables is related to the demand for the product. In one-factor, macroeconomic models demand is often represented by aggregate income. In those models net investments depend upon the aggregate level of income, upon its rate of change, or sometimes on both.

The third group of variables trying to measure factors affecting investments relates them functionally to profitability of production. In macroeconomic terms, these factors may be represented either by the rate of profit on invested capital (rather than by the level of profits) or by the rate of change of profits.

Finally, the three sets of factors may be treated as interrelated. Application of these concepts to the study of a regional economy may have to contend with several complicating circumstances which are in some respects due to the role and importance of government investments. The efforts of governments to stimulate the local economy may assume a variety of forms and either be directed toward economic overhead capital and infrastructure or take the form of overt or covert government subsidies, in which case the volume of investments is not necessarily a function of economic considerations alone.

Investments can be disaggregated according to their character into machinery and equipment, nonresidential construction, residential construction, and government investments. The first two refer largely to productive capacity, whereas the latter form components of the physical infrastructure. Disaggregation helps to pinpoint which investments were reponsible for the peaks and troughs in the level of total investments.

Relating a complex phenomenon such as investments in a highly aggregate form to one or two causal factors at a time involves a severe simplification of reality. The following remarks are in the nature of a preliminary exploration. A deeper analysis using broader data would have to be based on a more rigorous econometric formulation. Simple regression techniques are likely to yield spurious results due to the presence of time trends in several of the series examined.

Of the several factors which may possibly cause fluctuations in the level of investments, usually the first to be attacked are anticipated yields of assets and profitability of production; but they cannot be examined on the basis of data available from income and product accounts alone. Some of these factors are not directly obtainable from the accounts in their aggregate format, while the accuracy of quantities derived as differences between estimates of much larger magnitudes is open to doubt.

The second set of factors which might explain fluctuations in gross business capital formation is demand for commodities and services produced with their help. In the absence of better and more detailed data, GRP is often taken as an index of aggregate demand. It is usual to conduct such analysis in terms of constant dollars, thus eliminating the effects of fluctuations in purchasing power of the money. Frequently the analysis is carried out in terms of first differences.

A relationship between business gross fixed capital formation and private savings is considered fundamental to the internal equilibrium of the national economy. The conceptual basis of this approach in the case of a small regional economy is questionable. It is not at all certain that regional industries have to depend upon local private savings for their sources of financing. It may well be that under modern conditions of high mobility of investment capital, productive investments in a region forming a small part of the national economy simply follow the general investment trends modified by factors related to local attractiveness. Hence, a relevant study would perhaps consider locational factors affecting various industries, but this is clearly beyond the scope of a simple analysis of data derived from income and product accounts.

Another problem to be examined is the effects of investments upon the productive capacity and its rate of growth (particularly as compared to the expansion of the labor force). They are not amenable to simple analysis without considering simultaneously such important and closely related phenomena as formation of urban-industrial complexes or growth poles, and creation of economic overhead capital and infrastructure. Both are capable, in time, of becoming an attractive force for new investments, thus changing the whole economic structure of the region.

An essential characteristic of Keynesian economics, from the simple multiplier to the complete model of short-run equilibrium, is that income determination is based firmly on aggregate demand defined by the flow conditions of the product market. Extensions of this model to long-run equilibrium and its applications to the theory of growth of industrialized nations all stress the central role of effective demand.

There are four main components of aggregate demand: consumption by households, investments, foreign trade, and government spending. Thus aggregate demand can be described by the basic accounting identity distributing the gross regional product;

$$Y \equiv C + I + G + (E - M) ;$$

where

$Y = GRP$ (gross regional product) ;

C = consumption of goods and services by households;
I = total private and government investments;
G = exhaustive current government expenditures;
E = exports of goods and services;
M = imports of goods and services.

Foreign trade has traditionally formed the basis of many regional models. Of particular importance are exports, the low volume of which may be due to lack of demand for regional products or to a generally low level of production. Foreign trade deficits often experienced in depressed regions may or may not be accompanied by an unfavorable balance of payments. The divergence between the balance of foreign trade and balance of payments may be substantial, due mainly to the following four factors, or a combination of them: (1) investments made in the area by nonresidents; (2) growth of indebtedness of the region toward nonresidents; (3) selling out of fixed assets by residents; (4) government and other transfer payments.

Consumption of goods and services by households forms easily the largest component of aggregate demand and is widely used as the main endogenous variable in simple multipliers.

Personal consumption is of considerable welfare significance. It is customary to relate it to income, using for this purpose the notion of average propensity to consume, (c).

$$c = \frac{C}{Y} ;$$

With the help of this ratio the basic product identity can now be transformed into:

$$Y = cY + I + G + (E - M) ; \text{ or}$$

$$Y = \frac{1}{1-c} \ [I + G + (E - M)] ;$$

where $\frac{1}{1-c}$ is the average demand multiplier. It indicates the impact upon total output or income of exogenous changes in the remaining components of aggregate demand. The analytic uses and their validity depend upon the stability of the multiplier and may be also slightly misleading, since it fails to account for important "leakages" due to the extreme "openness" of a small economy. Hence, a second multiplier taking into account the effects of imports has to be derived.[25] For this purpose the average propensity to import (m) is defined as

$$m = \frac{M}{Y} \; ;$$

Inserting this into the basic identity yields

$$Y = cY - mY + I + G + E \; ;$$

or

$$Y = \frac{1}{1-c+m} \; (I + G + E) \; ;$$

where

$\dfrac{1}{1-c+m}$ is the modified multiplier.

The size of the multiplier indicates the effects of a unit change in the remaining elements of aggregate demand (investment, exhaustive current government spending, and exports) upon the level of operation or GRP. A low value may signify that a considerable part of the anticipated multiplier effects of new investment or heavy government spending may be felt in other parts of the country or even abroad. This finding has obvious implications for efforts to boost the local economy with the help of government spending or induced business investments. Another possible refinement would consist of splitting government expenditures into those which can be manipulated in order to induce regional development and into those more or less rigidly tied to various given factors. Should it prove possible to estimate this second part as a constant function of GRP an improved multiplier could be introduced, perhaps of the form

$$Y = \frac{1}{1-c+m-g_c} \; (I + G_d + E) \; ;$$

$$g_c = \frac{G_c}{Y} \; ;$$

where

G_d = government expenditures aimed at regional development;

G_c = ordinary government expenditures;

g_c = average propensity of ordinary government expenditures.

Because of the size of government expenditures, this would by itself greatly improve estimates of the impact of the remaining exogenously determined elements of aggregate demands.

The validity of analytic uses of the multiplier depends upon the stability over time of both average propensities to consume and to import, even in the face of major structural breaks in the regional economy following important investments, introduction of new industries, or formation of an industrial complex. Moreover, the value of the multiplier might also fluctuate among the various components of aggregate demand, namely investments, government spending, and exports. It is difficult to imagine that the average propensity to import is the same in case of investments involving purchase of plant and machinery, current government spending, and production for export.[26]

The existing data basis and format of the income and product accounts do not allow implementation of such an improved multiplier. An expanded and improved accounting framework would involve consideration of the sectoral structure of the economy. Its discussion is best deferred to Chapter 7.

3 Financial Flows*

Foreign Trade and Balance of Payments

Commodity flows and to a lesser extent financial transactions between regional economies are important elements for understanding processes of growth and development. A rigorous analysis of these interrelations is usually carried out with the help of balance-of-payments and moneyflows accounts.

At the national level, the balance-of-payments account shows the relations between a national economy and the rest of the world, reflecting a country's international trading posture. The flow of goods and services between regions is often taken as an indication of their relative resource endowment, resulting in comparative advantage. For a system of regions, interregional trade frequently results in an increase in real income for all through increased specialization in each region in the production of goods in which it enjoys a comparative advantage. Human resources may be viewed in this context in a way similar to natural resources, explaining interregional division of labor. Specialization in each region is the outcome of a unique combination of resources, capital, and labor improving its relative advantage on the international market.[1] Accompanying specialization in certain goods and services is the demand for goods and services produced by others, leading to an import demand. A nation exporting more than it imports has a favorable balance of trade and, since it is producing more than it is consuming, it is likely to develop what was once thought to be a favorable economic position relative to other nations.[2]

The transactions taking place in international trade are recorded in some detail in the balance-of-payments account. In scope and coverage the account is wider than the rest-of-the-world sector in the income and product accounts,[3] since it covers also movements of goods not currently produced, all unilateral transfers, grants of loans, and movements unrelated to the performance of the economy.

Study of elements of interregional trade reveals the role and significance of the following factors influencing growth processes:

1. Distribution and utilization of natural resources
2. Interregional division of labor (specialization) related to both differences in natural endowment and technology
3. Distribution of population and the level and structure of consumption in various regions
4. Regional differences in the rate of economic growth[4]

---

*This chapter was originally drafted by Andrew A. Dzurik.

41

While it is believed that specialization, reflected in interregional trade, leads to more rapid progress, the concept is not equivalent to the economic base theory of regional growth. According to the latter, a region's economic growth depends upon the level of its export or basic industries relative to the service industries since exports bring in new money while services only recirculate money already in.[5]

But whatever its effects, interregional trade is largely caused by differences in the supply of factors of production, relative scarcities, and differences in demand for goods and services among regions. Ohlin who introduced the "mutual interdependence" theory to explain the causes of interregional and international trade, maintained that international trade is a special case of interregional trade in which differences in factor endowments provide the basis for cost variations. The mutual interdependence of factor and commodity prices, trade, and factor movements lead to an equilibrium both at regional and national levels.[6]

The counterpart of the movement of goods and services are moneyflows complemented by, and often undistinguishable from, capital movement and government and private transfers of funds. In the United States, these transactions are consummated primarily through checks drawn on commercial banks and, in turn, by Federal Reserve Banks acting on behalf of banks in their districts. Unlike nations, however, subnational regions do not have their own monetary systems. This makes the construction of a regional balance of payments even more difficult because regional boundaries (if defined at all) are relatively open and no accurate records are kept of the interregional flows of money.

The balance-of-payments account can best be described as a systematic summary record of all economic transactions between residents of a nation, or of a region, with the rest of the world in a given time period. Its primary purpose is to inform the government about the international economic standing of the nation in quantitative terms for use in formulating monetary and trade policies.

The components of the balance-of-payments account, presented in the form of a double entry system, can be divided into three major parts. The current account measures the flow of goods and services, or is a record of exports and imports. The capital account keeps track of lending and investing, while the cash account records the flow of gold, foreign exchange, and credit in response to current and capital transactions.

The setting up of a balance-of-payments accounting system must overcome deficiencies of the data available in terms of their accuracy, thoroughness, and currentness. Some of the required data cannot be obtained, and thus estimates and assumptions must be made.

In addition to data problems, arriving at a set of agreed definitions is difficult. The fundamental notion on which much of the work in balance-of-payments accounting hinges is that of a resident, including both persons and corporations, since transactions measured in the balance-of-payments account are those between residents of different countries. *Residence* is defined as the place where one ordinarily lives, but there are numerous exceptions. As an example, citizens working for their government abroad are residents of their home country, while a corporation "resides" where it is incorporated, regardless of who owns the stock. Similarly, foreign branches of firms are considered residents of the home countries, while subsidiaries in a foreign country are considered residents of that country. A true measure of whether a transaction is international (or interregional) is not necessarily the actual movement of goods or services, but the residence of the parties to the transaction.

A detailed examination of the credit and debit entries appearing in the balance-of-payments account provides more insight into its construction and use. Because of the double-entry system used, every movement of goods or services is recorded twice, as both a debit and credit. The current account shows debits and credits related to exports, imports, and unilateral transfers which do not give rise to claims, the capital account records transactions whose net result is a change in total investments abroad or foreign investments in the country, and the cash account shows changes in monetary and gold balances and collects the balancing items for transactions recorded in the other two parts.

A simplified hypothetical regional balance-of-payments account is shown in Table 3-1. Every transaction appears twice in the accounts, because it involves goods, services, or securities and simultaneously a corresponding transfer of cash, bank loan, or some other debt instrument. Debits (negative sign) increase the supply of goods and services in the region, add to claims on "foreigners," or reduce the region's debts. Credits (positive sign) reduce the supply of goods and services, reduce claims on "foreigners," or increase the region's debts. Every increase in assets is accompanied by a decrease in some other assets or an increase in liability. In the account, increases in assets and decreases in liabilities are considered debits whereas decreases in assets and increases in liabilities are credits. Thus, if a commodity is imported, assets increase but a debt is incurred to cover the value of the import. A credit may be viewed as decreasing a nation's assets, increasing its liabilities, constituting a claim upon residents of foreign countries, or giving rise to a receipt of funds. Some examples of credits are exports of goods, interest and rent paid by foreigners to residents, and expenditures by foreign travelers in the country. A debit works in the opposite direction, increasing assets, decreasing liabilities, and giving rise to a payment of funds.

In actual practice, a fourth category is often included: errors and omissions. This is the inevitable result of the many data limitations and conceptual problems encountered in estimating flows. The errors-and-omissions entry is used to reconcile the accounts in such a way that debits equal credits in the overall account.

The balance-of-payments account clearly focuses on the interregional trade in

Table 3-1
Hypothetical Balance of Payments

Item	Credit (Exports)	Debit (Imports)	Net	
A. Current Account				
Commodities				
Automobiles	800	1200	−400	
Medicine	400	0	+400	
Ore	0	500	−500	
Other	1100	800	+300	
Services				
Transportation	0	100	−100	
Education	400	100	+300	
Recreation	900	200	+700	
Other	0	400	−400	
Gifts & Unilateral Transfers	20	0	+20	
Balance on Current Account				+320
B. Capital Account				
Direct Investment				
Factory in region B		600	−600	
Federal loan	500		+500	
Balance on Capital Account				−100
Balance on Current and Capital Accounts				+220
C. Cash Account				
Currency Movement				
Commodities	2500	2300	+200	
Services	800	1300	−500	
Transfers		−20	−20	
Investment	600		+600	
Loan		500	−500	
Balance on Cash Account				−220

goods and services. By systematically recording summary data on flows resulting from trade, it provides quantitative information useful for rigorous analysis.

Intersectoral Moneyflows

Flow-of-funds or moneyflow accounts are a fairly recent development[7] and, as a form of social accounting carried out by a government agency, were until recently limited to the United States. Their objective is to provide a complete record of flows of money and credit between sectors. The transactions covered are comprised of payments for goods and services (both new and used), transfers of ownership, unilateral and government transfers, and borrowing and lending. In fact all transactions, irrespective of their character, which take place in the economy between two or more distinct legal units and which involve transfer of money and credit are covered by the accounts. Thus defined, moneyflow accounts differ sharply from other types of social accounting primarily in their wider scope or coverage, preservation to a very considerable extent of decision-making and legal units, and almost total absence of imputations.[8] There is little netting, and no major aggregates form part or are indirectly derived from the accounts—a circumstance which has been the subject of considerable criticism.

In form moneyflow accounts resemble a set of interlocking balance-of-payments statements in which the regional economy and the rest of the world are replaced by a number of sectors, only one of which is external. The sectoring emphasizes financial institutions which in the most succinct form of the accounts comprise four of the eleven sectors into which the more than sixty million economic units are grouped. A theoretical guide for sectoring is provided by the principle of homogeneity, which implies combining units which are similar with respect to the structure of their assets and liabilities and in their behavior and reactions to changes in capital markets.[9] Table 3-2 shows the eleven sectors typically used in flow of funds accounting.

Although the accounts show the sources and uses of funds for each of the sectors, they do not indicate the intersectoral flows in any detail. Such information would be useful in regional analysis to determine the sources and uses of funds among sectors, but the flow-of-funds accounting system deals not with commodities but with the means by which economic sectors finance their transactions and allocate the financial resources available to them. Aggregating economic units into sectors eliminates information which may be useful

Table 3-2
Sectors in Flow-of-Funds Accounting

1. Consumer and nonprofit organizations	
2. Corporate Business	Business
3. Noncorporate Business	
4. Farm	
5. Federal government	Government
6. State and local government	
7. Commercial banking	
8. Savings institutions	Financial
9. Insurance companies	
10. Other financial institutions	
11. Rest-of-world	Foreign

regarding flows within that sector. Among the factors which are considered in defining sectors are the following:

1. The type of transactions and the nature of economic characteristics to be explained

2. The strategic role of the financial sectors in a flow-of-funds system, and the characteristics of the financial structure of the economy under investigation

3. The quality of the available statistical data

4. The possibility of integrating the flow-of-funds system with other national accounting systems.[10]

Because of the focus on money flows, sectors and transactions dealing primarily with finances are treated in detail. The financial sectors are especially important because of the fact that a large proportion of flows from surplus sectors to those with a deficit pass through the financial intermediaries. They are not merely passive agents, but assume a major role in determining the size and destination of financial flow.

Breaking down sectors and transactions into sources and uses, a summary of flow-of-funds account is derived as shown in Table 3-3.[11]

A summary table of this type is constructed from separate balance sheets and flow of funds statements developed for each of the sectors. In the summary account, each sector balances with respect to total nonfinancial sources and uses of funds, and each type of transaction balances with respect to sources and uses of funds over the total of all sectors. The reason for this is that every economic transaction involves simultaneously both a source and a use of funds, and at the end of any period the flow-of-funds account must be in balance. The summary table provides a useful display of net changes in assets and liabilities for the various sectors in the time period under consideration and is an important element of comparative analysis over time and among regions, especially with regard to investigating the reasons for the results. The account can be used to measure (1) the effects of monetary policy on the general functioning of the economy, (2) the effects of legal and institutional policies, and (3) the effects of business cycles on the economy.

The intersectoral money and credit flows can be cast in matrix form, with funds supplied by sectors appearing in rows and funds received appearing in columns. The table records financial flows among major sectors of the economy by showing the sector providing funds and the sector using them, as indicated in Table 3-4. The row and the column totals in this table should correspond to the column totals for sources and uses in each sector shown in the region's flow-of-funds account. In this case, however, the entries are broken down by interacting sectors rather than by type of transaction.

Extending the input-output analogy further, the interregional-intersectoral accounting system can be established as shown in Table 3-5. Note that the elements of the matrix are denoted by X_{ij}^{gh}, where g and h represent the

Table 3-3
Format for Flow-of-Funds Account

	SECTORS											
	Consumer and nonprofit	Business			Government		Financial Institutions				Rest of World	Total
		Corporate	Non-corp.	Farms	Federal	State & Local	Banks	Savings	Insurance	Others		
Transactions	S U	S U	S U	S U	S U	S U	S U	S U	S U	S U	S U	S U
Nonfinancial												
A. Payroll												
B. Investment receipts & payments												
C. Insurance & grants												
D. Taxes & tax refunds												
E. Capital acquisitions												
F. Purchases & sales of other goods & services												
Subtotal												
Financial												
G. Currency & Deposits												
H. Federal Obligations												
I. Mortgages												
J. Corporate Securities & state & local obligations												
K. Other												
Subtotal												
Total												

Note: S = Sources of funds, U = Uses of funds

Table 3-4
Intersectoral Flow-of-Funds Format

Supplier \ User	1. Consumer; Nonprofit	2. Corporate Business	3. Noncorporate Business	4. Farm	5. Federal Govt.	6. State-Local Govt.	7. Bank	8. Savings	9. Insurance	10. Other Financial	11. Rest of World	Total Sources of Funds
1. Consumer; Nonprofit	x_{11}	x_{12}	.	.	.	.	.	.	.	.	$x_{1,11}$	
2. Corp. Business	x_{21}	x_{22}	.	.	.	.	.	.	.	.	.	
3. Noncorp. Business	.	.	.	.	.	.	.	.	.	.	.	
4. Farm	.	.	.	.	.	.	.	.	.	.	.	
5. Federal Govt.	.	.	.	.	.	.	.	.	.	.	.	
6. State-Local Govt.	.	.	.	.	x_{ij}	.	.	.	.	.	.	$\sum_{j=1}^{11} x_{ij}$
7. Bank	.	.	.	.	.	.	.	.	.	.	.	
8. Savings	.	.	.	.	.	.	.	.	.	.	.	
9. Insurance	.	.	.	.	.	.	.	.	.	.	.	
10. Other Financial	.	.	.	.	.	.	.	.	.	.	.	
11. Rest of World	$x_{11,1}$	.	.	.	.	.	.	.	.	.	$x_{11,11}$	
Total Uses of Funds						$\sum_{i=1}^{11} x_{ij}$						$\sum_{i=1}^{11}\sum_{j=1}^{11} x_{ij}$

supplying and using regions respectively, while i and j represent the supplying and using sectors. The matrix consists of $n \times n$ submatrices representing n different regions. Whereas a matrix for a single region contains 11 rows and columns—one for each sector—any submatrix of the combined interregional format contains 10 rows and columns, because the rest-of-the-world sector is eliminated and replaced by submatrices for all of the other regions. In addition, there is no vector for final demand as in the usual input-output case. Thus the structure presented is a closed system showing flows among sectors and regions, with values entered in the table representing actual dollar flows.

An alternative approach to measuring intersectoral flows is to determine

Table 3-5
Intersectoral-Interregional Flows-of-Funds Framework

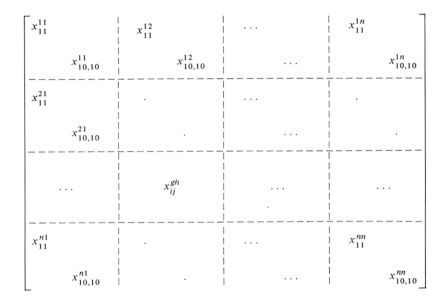

$$\begin{bmatrix} x_{11}^{11} & x_{11}^{12} & \cdots & x_{11}^{1n} \\ x_{10,10}^{11} & x_{10,10}^{12} & \cdots & x_{10,10}^{1n} \\ x_{11}^{21} & . & \cdots & . \\ x_{10,10}^{21} & . & \cdots & . \\ \cdots & x_{ij}^{gh} & \cdots & \cdots \\ x_{11}^{n1} & . & \cdots & x_{11}^{nn} \\ x_{10,10}^{n1} & . & \cdots & x_{10,10}^{nn} \end{bmatrix}$$

intersectoral credit flows.[12] Rather than determining sources and uses of funds, the same sectors are used in terms of lending and borrowing sectors. Considering the usual data limitations, this approach is perhaps the most practical means of measuring intersectoral flow when based on changes in credit balances between the beginning and the end of the period.

A table of flows, then, would be set up with total credit given by each sector appearing in rows and credit received by each sector in columns. The table developed by Heth (see Table 3-6) shows credit relationships between sectors in both gross and net terms.[13] "The net credit flows are derived by offsetting the gross flow against one another, and they show whether a sector gave more credit to another than it received from it or vice versa."[14] For example, if gross credit flows from banks to corporations is 100 units, and gross flow from corporations to banks is 25 units, the net flow from banks to corporations is 75 units, and no net flow is recorded from corporations to banks. The net change in financial claims of one sector upon another during the period is represented by this amount.

An intersectoral accounting system of this type is particularly useful in identifying surplus and deficit economic units. In a modern economy with a complex system of financial institutions, some sectors spend less on goods and services than they earn in a given time period while others spend more. Those that earn more than they spend are able to finance the difference between

Table 3-6
Intersectoral Credit-Flows Format

Lending Sector	Borrowing Sector 1.	2.	...	m	Total Credit Granted
1. Gross	C_{11}^{G}	C_{12}^{G}	...	.	$\sum\limits_{j=1}^{m} C_{1j}^{G}$
Net	C_{11}^{N}	C_{12}^{N}	...	.	$\sum\limits_{j=1}^{m} C_{1j}^{N}$
2. Gross	C_{21}^{G}	C_{22}^{G}	...	.	.
Net	C_{21}^{N}	C_{22}^{N}	...	.	.
$\vdots$	$\vdots$	$\vdots$	$\vdots$	$\vdots$	$\vdots$
m	.	.	.	C_{mm}^{N}	.
Total Credit Received					
Gross	$\sum\limits_{i=1}^{m} C_{i1}^{G}$				$\sum\limits_{i=1}^{m} \sum\limits_{j=1}^{m} C_{ij}^{G}$
Net	$\sum\limits_{i=1}^{m} C_{i1}^{N}$				$\sum\limits_{i=1}^{m} \sum\limits_{j=1}^{m} C_{ij}^{N}$

Source: Meir Heth, *The flow of funds in Israel,* Praeger 1970, p. 263.

payments and receipts of the other sectors. The importance of the size and direction of these flows is in itself enough to justify flow of funds accounting. It should be remembered, however, that it is difficult to determine the regional flow of funds within a nation in such detail that types of funds and investments can be separated.[15]

Interregional Financial Flows

Study of interregional flows of funds is gaining in importance as the volume of transactions among regions continues to increase. A substantial part of the growing financial interdependence between various parts of the nation is due to the mounting pressure upon state and local governments to provide ever more sophisticated and expensive public services and facilities, thereby expanding their financial needs. These needs are typically met through transactions with agencies of the federal governments, or through the sale of state and local government securities on the national market. Interregional financial flows, likewise, are increasing rapidly in various private sectors, including the housing market and capital investments in industry.

Interregional moneyflows can be studied within the framework of flow-of-funds accounts and may include analysis of (1) financial self-sufficiency of regions, (2) "foreign" investments in regions, and (3) the regional banking system. Such studies were carried out in the United States, using states,[16] Federal Reserve Districts,[17] and in some cases, smaller administrative units.[18] Some studies were limited in scope. The Lees study, for example, measured the capital flows into and out of each state stemming from sale of state and local government securities for the period 1957-62, while the study by Leven concentrates on a single small region in order to determine its financial transactions with the rest of the world, particularly the sources and uses of investment and savings funds. Others, like the studies of Grebler[19] and Romans[20] were more comprehensive.

The main difficulty in developing any set of reliable interregional moneyflows accounts is the availability of data, with greatest difficulties encountered with respect to financial transactions. Hence, the most successful attempts used the Federal Reserve Districts as regions. In essence, the twelve Federal Reserve Districts are autonomous regions, each having its own central bank. Cash flows between two regions are the result of financial transactions undertaken by persons located in each of the regions. "Every transaction which results in a payment between two different regions will cause an interdistrict movement of funds. The net amount of all interregional transactions of any single district for one year is shown in the net credit or debit of that reserve bank in the Interdistrict Settlement Funds for that year."[21]

The individual reserve banks may redistribute their holdings of financial assets to regions which need capital. In addition, the U.S. Treasury may shift its deposits to capital-short areas as a supplement to the redistribution of federal tax money. It is thus evident that knowledge of the flow of funds among regions may be useful in formulating monetary and fiscal policy. The usefulness of flow-of-funds analysis with respect to regional development is more limited except in cases in which implementation of a credit policy is feasible.

The Federal Reserve System data on interregional moneyflows make possible studies of flows between a Federal Reserve region and the rest of the world without regard to specific interregional relationships.[22] Of much greater significance to the regional analyst is going one step further to determine transactions among specific regions. The flow of funds between a single region and the rest of the world is well illustrated in Hartland's study of New England's balance of payments.[23] The study estimated gold and currency movements from transactions of the Federal Reserve Bank of Boston through the Interdistrict Settlement Fund. The financial movements affect the banking reserves of the districts concerned, and thus the region's reserves increase or decrease. The extent and nature of the flow of funds in a given region is analyzed with respect to each of the other regions,[24] by using gross rather than net data. A somewhat more comprehensive study was carried out by Bowsher, Daane, and Einzig who presented a matrix showing net flows among the 36 Federal Reserve head and branch offices developed from weekly Interdistrict Settlement Fund data on district clearings.[25] Such a matrix reveals patterns of financial flows useful in temporal comparisons. The study shows the relationships among all regions rather than between a single region and the rest of the world.

Table 3-7 presents a possible format for studying flows between a region under study (i) and other regions, listing separately sources and uses of funds. The subtotal column gives the overall transactions with the rest of the world (sum of all other regions), and the total column gives the total sources and uses of funds for transactions in the study region.

The policy implications of interregional flows of funds are far from obvious. Such evidence as exists[26] seems to indicate that national banking systems often collect savings in the depressed parts of the nation in order to invest them in the more prosperous regions. The phenomenon, to the extent that the mechanism behind it is known, seems to have its roots in the goods, not in the monetary sphere, and whatever remedies may be available will hardly be found in monetary and credit policies. Equally unexplored are differential regional impacts of federal monetary and fiscal policies, and few theories and models deal with them explicitly. In the absence of further progress in our theoretical understanding of the complex interrelations between flows of money and credit and of goods and investments in the spatial context, regional and interregional flow-of-funds accounts can make a contribution to our factual knowledge but will hardly be of much help in solving policy problems.

Table 3-7
Format for Interregional Financial Transactions

		Region															
		Rest of World															
Transactions	i		a		b		c		d		...		n		Subtotal		Total
	S	U	S	U	S	U	S	U	S	U	S	U	S	U	S	U	S	U
Nonfinancial																		
A. Payroll																		
B. Investment receipts and payments																		
.																		
.																		
Subtotal																		
Financial																		
G. Currency and deposits																		
H. Federal obligations																		
.																		
.																		
Subtotal																		
Total																		

4

Regional Wealth*

Place of Stock Accounting and Notion of Wealth

Wealth was the first economic aggregate to be measured. The concern of early economists with accumulation as a measure of economic progress, and of differences in factor endowment responsible for specialization, division of labor, and trade, took a number of forms. Whereas the mercantilists emphasized the value of precious metals and money, others, notably Adam Smith, broadened the concept of wealth, although the lack of a clear distinction prior to the twentieth century between wealth and income left an element of confusion.

The early work of Petty[1] and King[2] aimed at assessing the wealth of England, followed in the eighteenth and nineteenth centuries by a long series of studies in various countries, brought important progress in the methodology of stock accounting but simultaneously underscored the tenuous assumptions and concepts underlying wealth estimation. Ever since the invention of marginal analysis and the development of economic statics by Marshall, the emphasis of economics has been shifting toward a study of flow phenomena, a tendency further reinforced by the application of Keynesian macroeconomic theory to the study of business cycles. During a period of severe business recessions of the interwar years, which loomed larger than problems of growth and development, interest in wealth estimates faded, while advances in the theories of value and capital have further eroded the conceptual bases of this form of social accounting. With its theoretical foundations in dispute, its methodologies relatively crude and few in number, its optimum formats and alternative uses unexplored, wealth accounting remains the least developed form of social accounts.

Parallel to the renewed interest in economic growth, a significant amount of work has been devoted to the study of stock phenomena in the past twenty five years. Actually, no system of social accounting can be considered closed or complete without wealth accounts. There is a basic symmetry between stock and flow phenomena since the latter can properly be viewed as changes in stock variables occurring over time.

Kuznets[3] was responsible for historical studies of United States wealth, and his work has been extensively used by Goldsmith,[4] whose significant theoretical and practical contributions laid the foundation of modern national wealth

---

*This chapter draws upon the doctoral dissertation of my former student Emil E. Malizia, *Regional Wealth Accounting as a Means of Quantitative Evaluation of Regional Resources,* Cornell University dissertation, 1969.

accounting. After reviewing many different approaches to making wealth estimates, he suggested the perpetual inventory method, based on cumulating capital expenditures adjusted for capital retirements, while Scott[5] presented a case for the inclusion of natural resources in wealth estimates.

With the scope of wealth accounting no longer limited to reproducible assets but encompassing also nonreproducible assets, financial capital or claims, natural resources, and human resources, the question of format and of possible cross-classifications gained in importance. Ideally, all elements of wealth could be grouped along three different dimensions, corresponding to different criteria: (1) type of asset, or its physical properties and uses, (2) ownership, according to both legal form and economic sector of the unit exercising control, and (3) location within the region. For subnational regions, however, the paucity of data ordinarily precludes a full cross-classification, and a double- or triple-entry balance sheet is the closest approximation so far achieved.

The introduction of financial assets and the netting of claims and counter-claims within the system permits the determination of the net worth of each sector and of the economy as a whole. In its most aggregate form, the net regional worth represents the difference between tangible assets, intangible assets, human resources, and foreign assets on the one hand, and foreign liabilities on the other. The relative importance of various components in a fairly typical depressed region is illustrated in Table 4-1.

In regional studies the long neglect of stock variables is particularly unfortunate, since most flow phenomena dealt with are simply symptoms of deeper causes to be found in the structure of existing assets. Flows may show strong fluctuations over time in response to changing, transitory causes, whereas

Table 4-1
Regional Wealth by Type and Control: Nova Scotia, 1961

	(In Millions of Dollars)			
Control over Wealth	*Natural Resources*	*Man-Made Captial*	*Human Resources*	*Total*
Nonfarm households	302.2	1,001.0	16,198.0	17,501.2
Unincorporated farms and farm households	78.1	111.8	557.8	747.7
Business corporations	105.5	581.9		687.4
Unincorporated businesses	29.5	128.7		158.2
Nonprofit organizations	4.0	125.2		129.2
Local and provincial governments	749.1	154.1		903.2
Federal government	19.6	195.0		214.6
Non-Canadian foreign units	69.8	142.0		211.8
Total	1,357.8	2,439.7	16,755.8	20,553.3

the relative longevity of some stocks and virtual permanence of others makes them important factors in studies dealing with the long run. Wealth represents in many ways a summary of the area's economic history, the result of past economic, social, and political decisions, while the interregional distribution and relative size of existing assets and resources critically influences the location of new private and public investments which in the long run are the prime factors determining economic progress of open regions. Wealth accounts are a conceptually necessary complement to, and bridge between, successive flow statements.

Unfortunately, regional models dealing explicitly with stock variables are still few. The lack of data, as a direct consequence of the state of regional wealth accounting, is probably as much responsible for this as the peculiar bias introduced into regional studies by the strong influence of regional economists trained in the use of flow variables. Yet planners typically start regional studies with an inventory of regional resources, and the lack of formal models dealing with stocks creates an uncomfortable gap between model builders and planning practitioners. It tends also to increase the distance between industrial location theory, with its preoccupation with existing factors and facilities, and regional growth theory.

A rigorous definition of the related notions of wealth, capital, and natural resources encounters a number of difficulties. The widest definition of the three, that of wealth, has evolved continuously with developments in economic theory and is still the subject of considerable disagreement among economists. In general terms the concept of wealth includes all stocks possessing the four attributes of usefulness, scarcity, appropriability, and transferability.

The attribute of utility is the most fundamental one. It refers to the potential of an item to satisfy human needs, either through direct consumption or, more frequently, by its use in the production of other commodities or services that are capable of satisfying human needs. Attempts to measure utility on a cardinal scale have met with limited success. While ordinal utility has been sufficient for a solution of the general equilibrium system, it does not offer a one-to-one correspondence between preferences and values. The cardinal utility of an object may be considered as being comprised of seven distinct components, of which only the first is a free gift of nature:

1. Elementary utility—referring to the desirable characteristics of the good while in its natural state

2. Form utility—conferred when the good is changed or transformed by the production process

3. Place utility—added when the good is moved to a more desirable location

4. Time utility—often resulting from storage or scheduling of production to provide the good at an appropriate time

5. Intangible utility—deriving from information on the quality and relevant characteristics of the good

6. Quantity utility—resulting from the bridging of quantitative differences between supply and demand

7. Assortment utility—referring to the presence of a range of goods in proximate locations, enabling comparison or simultaneous satisfaction of a whole range of needs.

The development of these notions in some ways parallels the evolution of concepts of productivity in economic thought. While the physiocrats would have recognized elementary, quantity, and assortment utility as conferring value to a good, classical economists would include form utility as well. Time, place, and intangible utility are recognized only when services are viewed as productive. Any attempt to define, let alone quantify natural resources must come to grips with the problem of separating the contribution of elementary utility.

The attribute of scarcity is somewhat ambiguous. In the context of regional analysis, items that are not scarce in absolute or relative terms and thus should not be classified as components of wealth may well have to be considered. Such free goods as sunshine may go a long way toward explaining price differentials of agricultural land in Alaska and Florida. Despite the fact that the presence of free goods is ordinarily reflected in the value of various items forming part of total regional wealth, their explicit consideration in regional studies may be warranted. The argument applies equally to public goods which are not scarce from the point of view of an individual.

Scarcity may be even more fundamental to price formation and the operation of the market mechanism than utility. While the subjective perception of marginal utility orders individual preferences, the price, which relates the pooled preferences of all individuals to quantity, becomes the objective or collective value of the good. Prices, however, are not determined by demand alone but by the intersection of demand and supply. They are established by the marginal buyers and sellers and act as a signal for action establishing equilibrium.[6] This underscores the importance of the attribute of scarcity, for without it buyers would not be willing to pay a positive price and sellers would not go through the trouble of providing the commodity. The more extreme form of the scarcity theory of value deems market price, determined by supply-demand relations alone, as an appropriate measure of value, without reference to production costs. This theory applies not only to marketplace but to any type of valuation. For example, we seem to enjoy the sunset in proportion to its rarity.

A related issue is raised by the question of whether the wealth of a region viewed as a whole is different from total wealth derived by summing up individual components. In social accounting this notion has been called the "indeterminancy principle."[7]

The attribute of scarcity can impair the use of value in regional studies in another more subtle but hardly less drastic way. The total value of a resource is sensitive to shifts in demand as well as in supply. Consequently, relative or local scarcity may (by affecting the unit price) increase the total value of a resource. For example, a comparison of two cities possessed of an equal number of housing units may reveal that the total value of the housing stock in one is substantially higher than in the other. The difference, however, may be due to either of two very different causes: higher average quality of the housing units, or higher demand resulting from population pressure. Hence, interregional or intertemporal comparisons based on value cannot be made independent of fluctuations in demand. To the extent that they reflect social needs, these are obviously legitimate influences to be reckoned with, but should not be confounded with differences in absolute or potential abundance. Total value of several resources as an index of relative attractiveness of a region may thus be deceptive.

The attribute of appropriability refers to the ability of an asset to be owned by physical or legal persons. Both the physical ability to deny the use of an item to others and the existing legal system are involved here. Whether an item possesses this attribute may often depend upon the point of view—upon whether we are considering an individual acting within the social matrix or society as a whole. Each particular social system establishes a set of rules, embodied in codes and legal precedents or in informal norm values and mores, that define which objects are appropriable.

While appropriability, under the existing legal and social system, tends to restrict the notion of regional wealth, it also extends it by including elements beyond the purely physical objects. Given the openness of regions, the interaction among economic units generates claims on wealth that include claims on wealth located beyond the regional boundaries as well as offsetting foreign claims on wealth located within the region. Thus the notion of regional wealth also encompasses financial assets and liabilities.[8] Furthermore, since a region contains mutually exclusive but interacting economic sectors or entities, the organizational structure influencing the efficiency of the system is itself part of regional wealth. The intangible values thus created are of importance from both individual and social points of view.

The fourth attribute, transferability, is more restrictive, referring to the ability of an item to be exchanged in the market. It is rarely rigorously applied in defining wealth.

The notion of capital is narrower than that of wealth but almost equally ambiguous. The definition of capital is a controversial issue, but it is generally accepted practice to classify as capital those elements of wealth which were themselves produced, and as resources, those which were not. This distinction is, however, too general to bring into sharp focus the fact that the same asset may be capital from one point of view and resource from another. For example, a locally available trained labor force is, for the entrepreneur who considers locating his plant in a particular city, a resource, while the very same labor force may be viewed by the local community, which has expended considerable amounts of money on training, as human capital.

The notion of a natural resource restricts the concept to those physical assets which are gifts of nature. The only outlays necessary to make them available would be those connected with exploration and accessibility. Because of the considerable number of stock variables, with at least several possible ways of measuring each one, the use of physical measures in order to quantify them is hardly feasible. An obvious alternative would be to place money values on them, thus providing a common measuring rod with additive properties, but progress in this direction has so far been slow. The main stumbling block seems to be the fact that thy concept of value applies to commodities and services defined within a specific societal context. At variance with the older theories, which tried to explain the determinants of value by considering the amounts of labor, satisfaction, utility, or welfare involved, the modern view is that the formation of value depends upon exchange or mutual interaction. Goods involved in economic exchange owe their value to three elements: the object being valued, the person placing the value on it, and the sociopolitical environment.

The three approaches to valuation of assets or wealth are: market value, depreciated past outlays or replacement costs, and capitalized future income stream. The three approaches evolve from a slightly different time perspective. While the first explores market prices at the present point in time, the second looks backward in time, cumulating investments or past costs in previous time periods. With the third approach, the existing stocks are measured by discounting the expected returns. Each approach has its advantages and disadvantages, which are more or less pronounced depending upon circumstances. Ideally, all three should be applied as a check on one another.

It has already been mentioned that many resources cannot be considered as commodities; but even for those which can, persistent difficulties typical of attempts to evaluate wealth are aggravated by several circumstances. Market price, which is fundamental to valuation, is established by the equilibrating mechanism that balances supply and demand during some time period. Price itself is a ratio of two flows, and as such it cannot be entirely removed from the temporal context. The very concept of market price applied to a stock is therefore conditional. What would the market price of the stock be if it were sold in the marketplace? This involves at least three critical considerations.

First, a fairly active market with numerous transactions must exist—a condition not often encountered with respect to natural resources.

Second, in order to be able to apply the market price of a good, based on current transactions, to the entire stock, the flow of goods would have to be representative of the entire stock or form a fair or random sample of it. In addition, a complementary condition would require that the market price be invariant to changes in sample size. In other words, the market price would have to be constant regardless of whether the entire stock or only a few items are offered for sale. This implies a perfectly elastic demand curve, again a condition not often met in the case of natural resources, which are often subject to important legal limitations and government controls.

Third, the very concept of market price cannot be of much help with respect to resources that are lacking some of the basic attributes of commodities. Valuation of resources that are not transferable or appropriable can be based only on imputed values or opportunity costs. Hence, either the cost of a marketable substitute or, less frequently, the value of the resource in some alternative use has to be applied. This often raises serious practical difficulties, because the highest marginal contribution of a resource can be hard to estimate empirically.

Natural Resources

Among characteristics which distinguish the physical and socioeconomic environment of one region from another and significantly affect regional growth, a prominent place is held by natural resources. Their impact upon regional development is twofold: on the one hand, their relative abundance or scarcity crucially affects the productivity of capital and labor; on the other, they may go a long way toward explaining the attractiveness of the region for both entrepreneurs contemplating new investments and for households. Yet attempts to incorporate them explicitly into regional growth models have so far been few, the preoccupation of development economics with capital, labor, and technical progress only partly explaining this rather surprising omission. The obvious difficulties of quantifying the important but elusive elements of the environment in a meaningful way provide another reason for the relative neglect.

There are important differences between commodities and even those natural resources which have tangible physical properties. With respect to resources which lack two or three of the essential attributes of a commodity (some even have to be classified as free goods), recourse has to be taken to roundabout methods. Typical of a class of natural resources devoid of marketable physical properties is sunshine or scenic beauty, which may nonetheless go a long way toward explaining local development trends.

Lack of marketable properties makes the conceptual basis of valuation controversial. Ordinarily, any good supplied in excessive quantities and thus superabundant has no value, because its marginal utility is zero. In other words, the demand curve for this good intersects with that of supply at the zero price point or no intersection takes place at all. This abnormal situation rarely arises with respect to produced goods, at least under competitive market conditions, but in the case of goods supplied by nature in locally unlimited quantities, the mechanism to stop production of superabundant resources does not exist. Hence, the market price of those natural resources is demand determined.

The above discussion indicates that the very heterogeneity of natural resources may require, for purposes of their valuation, a classification into four broad categories: (1) mineral resources produced for national or world markets for which an infinitely elastic demand and an exogeneously determined price level exist; (2) land, both agricultural and urban; (3) living populations such as forest, game or aquatic resources; and (4) free goods, devoid of value within the social matrix.

The first category to which the term "gifts of nature" may be applied is comprised of resources that are tangible and at some stage of processing have the attributes of a transferable commodity. All are available in finite quantities; that is, they do not multiply or increase in total volume, although additions can occur through new discoveries. Another important characteristic of subsoil resources setting them apart from land or free goods is that when brought to the surface and manufactured into goods capable of satisfying needs, they are transformed or destroyed in the process. Because of it their unit value can be derived as economic rent or as a residual after deducting from the obtainable price the cost of extraction, bringing the resource to the pithead, and transportation. There would obviously be no rent on marginal deposits. If the total physical quantity of existing deposits can be estimated, no major conceptual difficulties remain, although consideration of subsoil resources cannot be entirely divorced from actual operation of the industries involved. The mineral or subsoil resources can be classified into four subgroups, namely: (1) base metals, (2) nonmetallics, (3) structural materials, and (4) fuels.

The economic rent of a resource corresponds to its contribution to the value of final product and reflects the productivity of the deposit. Average or unit rent can be derived as the difference between revenue at site of production (representing international price less transportation costs) and production costs (composed of cost of raw materials, fuel, supplies, labor, and capital). This approach recognizes, for example, that the price of coal at the market is not the unit value of coal reserves underground; these are two different commodities, located at opposite extremes of the production process. Also, it assumes that local deposits can supply only a small part of world demand. Unfortunately, the result is bound to overestimate the value of subsoil resources because in most cases it is virtually impossible to deduct the cost of land and the opportunity costs of entrepreneurship. Further difficulties may be experienced with subsoil resources whose potential supply is almost unlimited. In deriving total value, the estimated physical quantity of such resources has to be replaced by expected long-run market demand.

Another method of valuing subsoil resources would view them as capital goods supplying productive services over time.[9] Cost value might be assigned by keeping a physical inventory of each type of resource, noting new discoveries and depletion. The value of the inventory would be increased with new discoveries and decreased by the value of extracted resources. This approach is similar to the valuation of business inventories.

A slightly different approach would derive present worth by capitalizing future returns at a given discount rate, casting the analysis in the profit maximizing framework where the goal is to maximize future net returns. This brings to the fore two problems worth mentioning. First, if natural resource utilization is viewed from a social rather than a private point of view, the rate of discounting will be lower since societal time preferences are lower than the time preferences of individuals. Second, monopolistic elements on the supply side might work for the benefit of society since the rate of resource utilization would be slower.[10]

Valuation of land encounters several complicating circumstances, not only because it is indestructible (whether used for agricultural purposes or serving as support for manifold human activities and artifacts), but because value due to differential fertility often has to be combined with locational rent. In the latter case all the ambiguities and uncertainties surrounding the valuation of urban real estate have to faced. Moreover, location rent is a function of city-wide land-use patterns, which are subject to shifts over time.

Of all natural resources, land has longest occupied the attention of economists and been discussed most extensively. Historically this was due to the importance which classical economists ascribed to it, defining it as one of the elementary factors of production; more recently it is due to the renewed interest in location theory. The quantity and quality of available land has long been viewed as a prime consideration in regional development, its importance being obviously related to the role which agriculture has historically played in many presently depressed areas.

An attempt to assess the available land resources must be preceded by classification or grouping of all parcels of land into several broad categories. The criteria for classification vary depending on objectives of the study, and include: (1) present, or sometimes potential use; (2) chemical qualities and inherent physical characteristics such as topography and drainage; and (3) location with respect to climatic conditions, proximate man-made improvements, or accessibility. The first criterion is ordinarily preferred although it requires, in order to be relevant, rather detailed subdivision of the major classifications such as agriculture, forestry, recreation, or wildlife. The second criterion has the great advantage that the characteristics used are unchanging over time even though their relative importance responds, albeit slowly, to socioeconomic developments. The difficulty of this approach resides in the very considerable number of characteristics which have to be considered and in the uncertainties involved in weighing them. The third criterion, rarely applied, would include socioeconomic or agro-climatic classifications.

For a variety of analytical purposes, a single index of the regional land resources would be most useful. A straightforward approach toward such a unidimensional index would be the value of land measured in dollar terms. Unfortunately, valuation of land is beset by many ambiguities.[11] It depends to a high degree upon societal phenomena. Not only emergence of alternative uses, accessibility, and relative scarcity, but such rapidly fluctuating factors as business cycles or changing expectations affect land values. Not all land is saleable, but even for those areas which do at one time or another enter the market mechanism, for which sales data are reported and assumed to be representative of the entire land market, the problem still presents numerous difficulties. The market price will vary with the conditions surrounding the transaction, as, for example, when the sale is the result of foreclosure, or due to eminent domain proceedings.[12] The existing and potential use of the land may be affected by scale factors and indivisibilities, adding another distortion. For example, a parcel of land of less than minimum size may yield a lower than average price because it cannot reach its full productivity.

Market price as an index of availability of land resources raises questions when used for interregional comparisons. Physically, the total supply of land in a region is fixed, making market price primarily demand determined. Since changes in demand following variations in population size and urbanization would force up the price of land by making it more scarce relative to other factors of production, it is intuitively obvious whether a region with highly priced urban land is better off than one with less valuable urban land.[13] The higher total land value might reflect the presence of a positive factor in the form of external economies or of diseconomies due to excessive crowding. On the other hand, however, the quantity of land is fixed only physically and not economically, because land uses can change. Thus the supply of specific types of land fluctuates, making market price of land at least partly determined by both supply and demand.

Another approach to land valuation is to estimate its worth as the capitalized flow of future returns for services. Rent, forming the basis of this approach, would depend primarily upon fertility in the case of agricultural land and upon accessibility for urban land. In theory, location rent would be a function of transportation cost savings to either consumers or producers, thereby reflecting scarcity value.[14] A hypothetical rent cone reflecting mainly accessibility in urban areas and productivity in rural areas offers a crude approach to land valuation.

A third method often applied to urban land consists in treating land as residual, or as the difference between capitalized returns and depreciated replacement cost of improvements. The obvious difficulties involved in this method derive from the fact that land value is obtained as a difference between much large quantities, thus compounding any valuation errors.

Assessed values are one of the most readily available sources of information on the value of land and are often used in land studies, but this method must be treated with care. Assessed values are often placed on real estate, which includes land and improvements.[15] They are subjective, since assessors put values on land, for tax purposes, that are not identical to future worth of land.[16] Furthermore, much land is tax exempt, and the assessed values for this land are usually considerably lower than potential market price.

The third broad category would comprise living populations such as forest, game, or ocean resources. Their common characteristic is that they grow and multiply, thus conserving their value as long as they are not overexploited (or in some cases underexploited). The evaluation of the actual or potential contribution of such resources to production or consumption has therefore to be predicated on the preservation of an ecological balance. Hence, the discounted future income stream approach may be more appropriate than imputed cost calculations, but the practical difficulties attending its application are considerable. Forested areas, for example, are a source of timber, but they also provide recreational facilities, serve as an abode for wildlife—a resource in its own right—and supply modest amounts of forest fruits. The various commodities and services originating in the forest are to a very large extent complementary to one another rather than mutually exclusive, so that the inherent ambiguity in assigning values to the various benefits derived makes valuation of the resource uncertain. Moreover, with respect to wildlife and recreation the forested area is rarely used to capacity and is thus devoid of the attribute of scarcity. In addition, intensity of use for recreational purposes is a function not only of the resource itself but also of investments existing in the region as a whole, of availability of access roads, and of on-the-spot facilities. Valuation of living populations has thus to reflect both the ecological balance and developments in the regional economy. The interdependence between equilibrium in the ecosystem and in the socioeconomic system has been fused into a general framework by Isard and others,[17] who analysed the reactions between the various natural and economic processes with the help of an extended input-output model. In order to assess the value of the regional forests, it is perhaps best to deal first with the contribution of the living population of trees only, disregarding other benefits derived from forested areas. The valuation of forests as a source of timber can either proceed by considering the allowable annual cut or the total standing stock. The first approach recognizes that the forest should be harvested in such a manner that the growing stock will maintain itself and defines the allowable annual cut as the harvest of wood that may be taken from the forest without reducing its ability to produce a sustained yield. By following the alternative approach, the value of forest reserves is obtained as the product of the estimated quantities of standing timber by average market values. The total figure has to be corrected in order to account for the fact that not all forest reserves are marketable at any time. Some of the growth is too young and will only become marketable with maturity, depending upon the age distribution of standing timber.

The value of standing timber is to be distinquished from the value of land in forest use. The separate treatment of the population of trees and of land on which they are growing seems the more justified as some forested land could potentially be put to other "higher" uses. The latter is usually estimated in the most likely alternative use.

Measurement and valuation of game and wildlife is based on the assumption that their economic value can be viewed mainly as an attractive force for sportsmen and campers, both residents and visitors. Several approaches to measuring the contribution of game and wildlife to the local economy are theoretically possible. Market prices for meat and skins could be applied to yield total value. Another approach, feasible in principle, would call for household surveys as a means of estimating total outlays related to wildlife. Such studies can only rarely be carried out due to paucity of data and to the prohibitive cost (beyond the importance of the subject) of research based on a field survey. A crude estimate is sometimes made on the heroic assumption that the value of game and wildlife equals direct payments made for hunting and angling privileges. This approach, followed of necessity, almost certainly results in a gross underestimate, because the fees imposed on hunters and anglers are institutionally determined and quite inelastic. It can hardly be considered as representing the user's valuation of satisfaction derived or the value of the resource to the region seeking to develop its tourist industry. Moreover, while hunters and anglers actually deplete the resource, other individuals such as campers, naturalists, and photographers consume wildlife services free of charge. The recreational value of forest resources or the closely related issue of their potential contribution to the development of a tourist industry is fraught with very great conceptual and measurement difficulties.

With respect to marine or, more generally, aquatic resources, the importance of which varies from region to region with fish species usually forming the most valuable component, the problem is not in finding an appropriate price but in estimating quantity and determining ownership. The fishing grounds are usually in international waters, accessible to fleets of many nations, all of which are often competing for the same natural resource. The physical supply is limited, with the total catch of many species close to the maximum permitting survival. Thus, with respect to offshore fishing, one can often only discern a locational advantage, the importance of high declines with increasing size of fishing vessels and the appearance of large and more sophisticated fish-processing units.

The problem is different with respect to territorial waters, in which only national, although not necessarily local, fishing vessels are allowed. While the legal basis for measuring the extent of waters denied to foreign vessels is not ordinarily disputed, local as opposed to national ownership has to be determined by legal and political processes. Yet almost all individuals harvesting within national waters are ordinarily residents of adjacent shores.

As a basis for assessing the value of accessible marine life, a number of assumptions have to made, including: (1) balance for each species between death and birth rates, (2) fixed proportion between yearly catch and total population, and (3) constant share of regional fishermen in total landings.

The fourth category of regional resources, ordinarily referred to as free goods, often defy attempts to quantify them, and the very concept of value is in their case inapplicable despite the considerable significance in explaining interregional disparities and differences in growth rates. Their contribution to the value of capital assets or other natural resources or to the regional productivity can at best only be established indirectly by considering differences and shifts in regional production functions. Since in some cases their usefulness is potential only and contingent upon the emergence of new industries or new needs, consideration of their actual contribution would assign them zero value but would hardly provide a measure of regional attractiveness. The dominant feature of many free goods encountered in regional studies is that while capital and labor combined in their presence yield higher returns, their unlimited or currently unconstrained supply precludes a straightforward application of imputed or shadow prices.

In this category, water has to be singled out because of its importance. The difficulties attendant on attempts to evaluate its contribution to regional development stem from the manifold uses which are to a large extent complementary to one another rather than mutually exclusive. Not only do water transportation, generation of hydropower, and recreation frequently represent noncompeting results of a single investment, but the subsequent use of water for residential and industrial purposes falls largely into the same category. The major applications of water can be grouped for purposes of analysis into the following broad categories:

1. Residential, including consumption by households and for municipal purposes

2. Industrial, comprising numerous applications: as raw material (for example, in beer production), conducting processes in liquid state (for example, dyeing, many food-processing operations, and, in fact, most chemical processes), washing of raw materials and products, cooling, transport of heat, humidifying, steam and power generation, and transportation of solids in water streams

3. Irrigation

4. Generation of electricity, both in thermal and hydropower stations

5. Transportation, on both fresh and salt water

6. Fishing or, more generally, as a source of aquatic life

7. Recreation.

Almost every one of these manifold applications imposes different constraints on quality, acceptable cost, and regularity of supply.[18] Because of its heterogeneous uses, differences in quality, price, and temporal availability, water cannot be treated as a homogeneous commodity. The fact that water may cause damage (flooding) or adversely affect the environment (standing water or flows of polluted water) and thus require heavy investments in preventive measures has also to be reckoned with.

The supply and demand for water have to be balanced within relatively small areas because, though there are few technical restrictions on transporting water over long distances, the costs involved are forbidding and preclude the utilization of water hauled from remote sources for most purposes.[19] Hence, the very notion of region-wide abundance or scarcity is meaningless, except in cases in which the study area corresponds to a water supply region. The estimates of total requirements for water covering its various uses remain elusive; in addition, the demand often turns out to be price inelastic, while multiple reuses further compound the difficulties.

The evaluation of total supply is just as uncertain as that of total demand. The first problem is whether to measure supply as a stock or as a flow. The total stock of water could be defined as the sum of surface water contained in lakes and estuaries plus groundwater reserves. Alternatively, total water supply could be defined as the annual flow of surface and groundwater available under normal climatic conditions. The first definition would be more suitable as a measure of the stock of water available for recreational use and as a potential source of power; however, the total stock of fresh water usually forms only a fraction of yearly circulation, or even of residential and industrial consumption. Hence, the availability of fresh water is often measured as a flow phenomenon.[20]

Total supply of fresh water does not determine the quantity available unambigously. Water used for residential and industrial purposes is often recycled and reused—in some areas up to twelve to fifteen times—before being finally discharged into the sea or used for irrigation. It is not obvious whether the processing of water should be treated as part of making the supply available. In other words, should supply be defined as supply of untreated and hence ordinarily not usable fresh water or as supply of water ready for use? In the latter case, because of recycling, quantity will often exceed that supplied by nature.

The fact that untreated water is seldom usable supports the view that, at least with respect to residential and industrial consumption, water should be considered as the product of a highly capital-intensive water purification industry, the relative abundance or scarcity of untreated water being reflected in differences in returns of the water purification plants operating in different regions. In principle these differences could perhaps be capitalized to yield an index of the regional availability of water. Such an approach would run, however, not only into practical but into far more serious theoretical objections. To begin with, the quantitative demand for water is a function of, among other factors, the existence of closed looped systems in the local water-using industries. The considerable investment outlays required for their installation are ordinarily forced upon these industries by local authorities, but it is not obvious whether they should or should not be considered as part of the cost of supplying water. Furthermore, water has many properties of a public good, with its price being as a rule unequal to either cost or marginal utility and demand being price inelastic. More generally, neither the supply nor the demand curve are well behaved; both have kinks and do not respond to price changes which are not market determined.

Moreover, the low value of local water resources may be the result of lack of demand as much as of abundant supply. In depressed regions especially, water is sometimes potentially superabundant and hence commands zero value. This, however, may be taken as a positive characteristic, making the region attractive for water-consuming industries. Of interest would be an index indicating the distance from the threshold beyond which water would have a positive value or, still better, a supply curve.

Human Resources

The treatment of human skills in economics has been the subject of a long controversy. It has been argued that the ultimate goal of resource allocation is satisfaction of human wants, and thus it is inconsistent to consider humans as means to that end. Furthermore, human resources in a nonslave economy lack one of the essential attributes of a good—namely, transferability—and hence were usually excluded from consideration of wealth. The very idea of assigning money value to a human being based on amounts invested in his education or his anticipated or potential contributions to the product of goods and services appears unattractive, because the manifold activities of a member of the human community are not limited to being, and perhaps are not even primarily, economic in character. Hence, an approach based on his cost to society or on his future contributions to production seems desperately too narrow, underestimating his value to society.

Yet the productive capacity of the labor force is a resource capable of affecting future development of a region to the same extent as the presence or absence of natural resources or man-made investments. The difficulty of assigning a cardinal measure of value to human resources, combined with the ambiguities familiar from attempts to measure some natural resources, might have contributed to the marked lack of interest on the part of many economists.

Nonetheless, even among the early economists there were many notable exceptions,[21] beginning with Petty[22] in the seventeenth century, and Adam Smith in the eighteenth century, who insisted that "the acquired and useful abilities of all inhabitants" are part of the nation's fixed capital.[23]

With Fisher[24] and Marshall,[25] the debate over the treatment of human beings in economics came to a head. The prevailing Marshallian view of labor as a homogeneous commodity is predicated on the implicit assumption that labor is largely unspecialized or at least unskilled. Whatever the merits of this position might have been in the past, it is certainly more in keeping with present conditions to consider each man as possessed of a stock of skills and knowledge acquired at some cost and capable of yielding measurable returns.[26]

The renewed interest in human resources or human capital after last World War II originated largely in studies of national economic growth. It was found that changes in the level of national production could not be adquately explained by changes in quantities of inputs without explicitly including human resources. According to Schultz,[27] moreover, the greater diversification of skill and knowledge employed in modern production processes requires the introduction as an independent variable not only of labor but also of changes in the quality of the labor force. More recently, the view has been gaining ground that human capital is the most important factor in explaining the phenomenon of economic growth. Interest in human resources has been further stimulated by concern for education and training, and their social and economic implications. This aspect has become the subject of considerable research.[28]

The present concern for interregional disparities and regional development has strongly underlined the necessity of quantifying human resources, not only in order to make simple interregional comparisons or to compare human, natural, and other locally available resources, but increasingly for use in sophisticated growth models. In some regional models, labor—sometimes disaggregated by level of skills—has been included along with natural resources in local production functions, while in others the impact of government policies and public expenditures on human resources became the major focus of attention.

The practical difficulties of valuation of human resources are considerable and obvious. In the total absence of market prices for humans, value estimates can be based either on: (1) the income approach or (2) the cost approach. Either of these two approaches can be applied on a net or gross basis. On a net value basis, consumption expenditures are not added to past outlays on education and training but are deducted from the discounted future income streams, thus applying to human beings an approach similar to the one used for valuation of livestock. On a gross or total value basis, consumption outlays during the period of training (cost approach) are added but are not deducted from future incomes flowing from productive activities. Net measure reflects, perhaps, the value from the society's point of view, while gross or total measure, which transcends the purely economic aspects, is more relevant to the individual or social group. Total value has been used more often as a measure of human capital, but the choice between these approaches depends ultimately upon the purpose of the study.

The data requirements are always considerable and are not easily met. The cost approach requires estimates of all past expenditures made for education and training of the existing population and, if on gross basis, of past consumption, expenditures for food, shelter, and clothing as well. If the estimates are made on a net basis, the often elusive division between investment and consumption expenditures has to be made, with health expenditures particularly difficult to categorize.[29] Income forgone during education and training is sometimes added to explicit costs,[30] but whether the opportunity cost of childrearing might be equated to the amount forgone by a mother who could have joined the labor force is an open and difficult-to-answer question.[31]

Past expenditures often differ considerably from what their present cost would be. In order to correct for this and establish a uniform basis for outlays incurred at different times, price deflators have to be applied expressing past costs in terms of their present value.

Measurement of human capital based on discounted future income is the more often used approach.[32] For this purpose, the population is divided into relatively homogeneous groups by age, sex, education, and/or occupation, depending on the detail of available data. Assuming constancy of the relevant parameters such as death rates, labor-force participation rates, existing occupational structure, and incomes, the population is aged and reduced by the repeated application of a survivorship matrix. Applying to the results the labor-force participation rates and average earnings, a declining future income stream is obtained. Refinements may be introduced by making allowances for changes in average incomes, occupation, and education and for additional outlays for retraining and improving education standards of the existing population.

A sensitive conceptual problem for which no generally accepted operational solution exists is posed by the fact that human capital appreciates over time even without specific outlays. These changes in value due to increases in skill and proficiency are most difficult to measure[33] and have so far hardly been practically estimated. Furthermore, part of the present population may emigrate from the region in the future. Under these circumstances, it is not obvious whether their discounted future earnings should be added to the value of regional resources.

The two methods of valuation—the income approach and the cost approach—are unlikely to yield, even in principle, identical results when applied to labor resources. Human beings have innate abilities that would allow them to earn some income even in the absence of specific and identiable expenditures to develop their skills; thus valuation using the total outlays or cost approach would always tend to be slightly lower than valuation based on discounted value of future contributions to production. Moreover, to be commensurable with other components of wealth accounts the unit value of human resources should be established by the intersection of the supply and demand schedules. Unfortunately, both concepts are surrounded by major ambiguities when applied to labor. The supply schedule—or as applied to labor, the relationship between the size of the labor force and the average wage rate—may be very complex. It is generally considered that the supply of labor depends primarily upon the following three factors: (1) the age-sex structure of the population, (2) the labor-force participation rate, and (3) migrations.

The relative importance of the various factors is unknown and their dependence upon absolute or relative wage rates uncertain. The age-sex structure is unrelated in the short run to economic considerations, although labor-force participation rates probably are. Higher wage rates might, on the one hand, induce women, older people, and youngsters to enter or reenter the labor force, but on the other hand, by increasing the earnings of the head of the households, may also have the opposite effect. Empirical evidence is lacking as to which of the two effects is stronger. Moreover, labor-force participation rates depend also upon such factors as the type or sectoral structure of the local industries.

The causes of interregional migrations are difficult to establish in a form enabling rigorous testing. Wage-rate differentials and employment opportunities, the two most often quoted factors, are not independent of one another. According to A.W. Phillips[34] and Bowen and Berry,[35] the rate of change of money wages responds negatively to both the level and the change in unemployment rate. This need not be true at the regional labor-market level because of the possibility of substantial migrations. Bell[36] has tested the Phillips hypothesis for the state of Massachusetts, but the results of the tests were clearly negative.[37] Studies by Bell[38] in Detroit and Ross[39] in eighty-four SMSAs confirm that unemployment has no impact on wages.

In a study carried out in Nova Scotia, outmigration was found to be significantly negatively correlated with unsatisfied demand for labor lagged one year (at the 1 percent level of significance).[40]

$$M_t = -3.007 - 0.3718 D^L_{(t-1)}; \quad R^2 = 0.3687 \qquad (4\text{-}1)$$

where

M = outmigration

D = surplus labor or unsatisfied demand for labor, measured as the difference between total employment and potential labor force. This latter was defined as the product of a population vector and age-sex specific Canadian labor-force participation rates, taking into consideration structural unemployment of 4 percent.

Further tests carried out with such explanatory variables as relative wage levels, per capita income, and the "image" of the province created by relatively rapid industrial growth were all negative.

The economic effects of migration upon both regions involved are manifold and easy to point out but difficult to quantify. Depopulation is bound to bring about a drop in investment activity or even negative net investment and thus ordinarily further reduces the possibilities for productive employment. Migrations due to economic motives are a highly selective process involving not only a high proportion of persons in prime productive age but the most highly skilled, educated, and energetic. The loss of these people, who are lured away first when local opportunities falter, is particularly undesirable because of their potential contributions to regional output and income. The depletion of the labor force caused by their departure imposes a heavier burden on those left behind and has important socioeconomic effects beyond those measured by the ratio of dependents economically active. This often-advanced proposition stems from the recognition that labor is not a homogeneous stock but is composed of persons of different ages, strengths, family state, skills, training, and energies. Research on labor mobility generally shows that in areas of declining job opportunities there is a potential core of workers who are unable or unwilling to move, even though the existence of this core of immobility may be obscured by a high rate of total outmigration.

In spite of the numerous negative effects of outmigration, the positive side should be mentioned too. Whenever a basic change in industrial structure causes high chronic unemployment in an area over a long period of time, outmigration may be the only factor preventing poverty and social disintegration. There is a strong presumption that when the marginal productivity of labor is zero or very low, emigration is likely to increase the region's per capita income.[41] Even in such extreme situations however, the waste of social capital involved may be such as to justify attempts to attract new industries and employment to a declining region.

In the receiving region, the inflow of migrants from a depressed area may by itself be a mixed blessing. A substantial sudden inflow of low quality labor may lower average output per worker, canceling the positive influence of the rise in the proportion of population in the labor force. The new investments required, both for new productive facilities and for infrastructure, may severely tax the existing resources. In addition, besides the most highly qualified members of the parent population, migrants include substantial numbers of people ill-prepared for the metropolitan labor market, often found at the very bottom of the social scale.

It is not immediately clear whether human or labor resources can even in principle be considered as a whole without disaggregating them according to skills. The pertinent question is whether labor is homogeneous enough to be treated as a single factor of production, but efforts to disaggregate it by skills and quality is a complicated task. Among the factors influencing the aptitudes of labor, one would have to distinguish the psychomotor area and the intellectual area. The first is influenced by nutrition, mortality and morbidity, each of which may be to a certain but unknown extent a function of income. In the intellectual area, one has to consider to a greater extent age and heredity besides the socioeconomic factors. Skills are largely influenced by education, but the link between motivation and demand for education, on the one hand, and incentives provided by the labor market, on the other, is hard to establish. Since education, and especially college-type education, is hardly priced according to costs or demand, and because of the several years lag between effective demand for a particular type of labor and the entry of students into labor force, the relations are most difficult to study empirically.

On the demand side for labor, the relationship between quantity and price or, in other words, between employment and wage rate, is no less ambiguous. Not only is the paradox of zero marginal productivity of labor encountered in many underdeveloped countries, but the problem of the contribution to output of labor with various skills has hardly been explored rigorously. A far more disaggregated production function treating various types of labor as separate, identifiable factors would have to be implemented. Finally, the relation between the demand for labor, the capital labor ratio, and the current interest rates is not clear. Nor has the relationship between the intellectual characteristics and the education of the labor force, and its contribution to production been fully explored.

Man-Made Capital

With modern technological progress, an overwhelming role in regional growth is assumed by the part of wealth consisting of man-made capital. There are several criteria according to which the various items of invested or man-made capital can be classified. The first, and often used, division groups assets according to type or some inherent characteristics, yielding the following major categories: (1) reproducible assets, (2) nonreproducible assets, (3) intangible assets, and (4) financial capital.

The first category is self-explanatory and encompasses objects forming the bulk of national or regional wealth.

The nonreproducible assets category includes historic buildings, galleries, museums, book collections, works of art, precious gems, antiques, monuments, and the like. Although economically less significant than reproducible capital, nonreproducible assets often enhance the quality of living in a region, while some elements like historic buildings and museums are often directly productive as tourists attractions.

Intangible assets consist of numerous and heterogeneous items such as the existing legal system or the presence and quality of certain social institutions. It is generally considered that this form of accumulated capital has an important though indirect impact upon economic processes taking place in a region, but the conceptual difficulties in rigorously defining its role in regional growth are far from being solved. Mainly because of the conceptual and operational problems encountered, there have been hardly any attempts so far at measuring it.

Financial capital, on the other hand, referring to claims between economic units, is well defined and its contribution to regional progress is clear and, in principle, measurable. Yet lack of sufficient regional data ordinarily foils attempts to evaluate the financial assets owned by regional residents.

A second criterion for classifying assets is their main use, sometimes combined with some secondary characteristics inherent in the assets themselves. This classification, very often used for a variety of analytic purposes, is comprised of the following categories:

1. Producer capital
   a) Machinery and equipment
   b) Nonresidential construction
   c) Livestock and inventories

2. Consumer capital
   a) Housing and residential structures
   b) Consumer durables

3. Defense installations

4. Infrastructure
   a) Transportation and communications
   b) Water supply, sewerage, engineering constructions
   c) Urban facilities meeting cultural, communal, sports, or entertainment requirements
   d) Educational facilities
   e) Health and welfare installations
   f) Investments related to administration and protection (police, fire, etc.)
   g) Recreational facilities

Producer capital represents those regional investments whose prime object is production of goods and services to be sold or supplied to other units for consumption or further processing. The bulk of producer capital is owned and operated by business enterprises, although a substantial part is held by nonprofit organizations and various governments. The major subdivisions of producer capital are self-explanatory. The inclusion of business inventories is justified by the fact that they are largely composed of produced but as yet unsold items and of goods in processing, which form part of the circulating capital of business enterprises.

The first and by far the more significant component of consumer capital is residential structures, which for purposes of analysis can be classified in a number of ways. Taking location as the relevant criterion, one could distinguish urban and rural housing, while according to tenure one might divide residential housing into owner-occupied and renter-occupied. From the point of view of structural type, one could list separately: single detached houses, duplexes, attached houses, walk-up apartment houses, and high-rise apartments. Still other relevant classifications are based on characteristics of construction (such as concrete, brick, or wooden frame), on size of housing units, on the extent to which structures are equipped with utilities, or on average value and age.

Consumer durables, despite the fact that their total value is usually smaller, comprise an even wider group of assets, of which the most important are automobiles, electric stoves, refrigerators, home freezers, automatic dishwashers, washing machines, clothes dryers, sewing machines, vacuum cleaners, television sets, radios, phonographs, and record players. Other items such as furniture, carpets, pictures, antiques, jewelry, or clothing may occasionally reach considerable value but are rarely recorded in published statistics. The common characteristic of all consumer durables is that they are already owned by their ultimate users. In fact, consumer durables are often defined as those consumption expenditures which release their utility over a period of time, the generally accepted, although arbitrary, cutoff point being one year.

These characteristics would be sufficient to describe the wider notion of consumer capital, except that the expected lifetime of the other component of consumer capital—housing—is of a different order of magnitude. Moreover, a significant part of the total value of housing is represented by rental housing, which is not owned by ultimate users but cannot, for a variety of reasons both analytical and statistical, be treated separately. For regional studies the main, important difference between consumer durables and residential structures is the fact that while the former are mobile, the latter are not.

The interest of regional scientists in consumer capital in general, and in housing in particular, is centered on three distinct though related aspects:

1. Welfare implications of endowment in consumer capital

2. Economic implications of housing, representing a huge, spatially immobile investment

3. Sociopolitical consequences of the distribution of various types of housing within metropolitan areas

Only in the crudest sense are the welfare aspects of housing easily measurable. Such indices as number of rooms per capita or average age of structures, while lending themselves to interregional and intertemporal comparisons, bring to the fore only one aspect of an essentially multidimensional phenomenon. Nor is total, average, or per capita value of the housing stock a suitable measuring rod, since it is strongly influenced by local demand conditions, precluding its use for comparative studies. The development of suitable indicators encompassing the manifold characteristics of housing is badly needed. The huge value, immobility and longevity of the housing stock make it an important locational factor, while the changing spatial pattern of industrial developments engenders obsolescence of the housing stock, often outpacing its physical wear and tear. Since the range of commuting is severely circumscribed, the existence of a large housing stock often leads to efforts to induce new industries to locate in labor market areas no longer attractive under changed conditions. Housing may thus contribute to perpetuating inefficient spatial patterns of production. The locational obsolescence of housing is mainly evident at the regional, not at the urban level of inquiry, and this partly explains the fact that it has attracted rather scant attention. Despite its imperfections, the measurement of capital invested in social services, utilities, and housing is all the more important since the market prices of inputs and of the stream of services produced do not reflect their capital content.

The assessment of the economic implications of existing consumer capital, on the other hand, presents few conceptual issues, but is beset with difficult measurement problems, some of which have already been alluded to. In economically developed countries, the housing stock represents an accumulation of investments exceeding social overhead capital in value. The capital outlays on housing per urban household do not lag far behind investments required to provide a place of work for its head. This statement obviously has to be qualified somewhat, since investments per place of work depend upon industry, with capital-labor ratios varying over a tremendous range.

The existence of a defense establishment is an important aspect of development in many regions, for while its assets do not form part of either producer or consumer capital, their presence generates important multiplier effects in the regional economy. The fixed assets, once they reach a certain size, tend to perpetuate themselves through constant additions. Whether only immobile assets should be counted or some part of the mobile military hardware as well depends upon the objectives of the study. An even narrower approach sometimes taken would only consider assets with alternative or subsidiary civilian uses or capable of being converted to such uses.

The size and value of the physical infrastructure have long been recognized as significant elements influencing regional development. Yet the preparation of an inventory of assets classified as forming part of infrastructure has to be preceded by the resolution of a definitional difficulty. The division of assets into "productive" and belonging to infrastructure has to be qualified in view of the meaning attached to those terms in classical economics. During the whole classical period of economics from Smith to Veblen, the notion of productivity of capital was dominated by the view of the physical nature of capital. The idea actually has antecedents stretching back to Aristotle, and has survived as part of Marxian economics in the contemporary social accounting practices followed in the socialist countries. Since capital was deemed to be composed of physical objects, only activities generating as their output physical objects were considered productive. According to this view, services, in our time rapidly growing in relative importance, are considered as necessary but not productive, and hence are explicitly not counted as part of the total output of the economy.

The dichotomy sometimes introduced in regional studies is based on an entirely different criterion, namely the way in which the objects or services produced are made available to consumers. Sectors selling their products or services for prices determined by the market mechanism are considered as "productive" and thus guided in their production or investment decisions by existing or anticipated supply and demand conditions. Sectors classified as infrastructure, on the other hand, are those either producing public goods or goods and services subject to such important externalities that they are either given away or charged at prices that stand in no relation to either costs or characteristics of demand. The levels of output and investments in such sectors usually follow the general growth trend of the regional economy, but may depend largely upon population size, desired level of welfare, or degree of urbanization. More usually, they are to a very large extent subject to sociopolitical considerations and cannot be treated as endogenous variables in models confined to economic factors. Moreover, the marginal contribution of investments in these sectors to the production of goods and services cannot ordinarily provide the basis for valuation since they are often indirect and difficult to trace.

Several other, albeit less frequently used criteria for classifying elements of wealth ought to be mentioned briefly. The third criterion is the sectoral structure of industries using assets as capital goods, while the fourth, related criterion is the sectoral structure of industries producing them. The two approaches are obviously different, but both are of practical importance and often applied in regional studies.

The fifth classification uses control as the main criterion. In view of the progressive scattering in modern law of the bundle of rights to assets forming property, control seems to be a more significant characteristic. Ownership increasingly becomes limited to the right to income produced and to inheritance, while real control of regionally important assets is often exercised by individuals or bodies without any property rights in them. The conceptual difficulty inherent in this classification derives from the implied abandonment of the profit maximizing principle on which much of economic theory is based.

Two other criteria—degree of mobility and location within the region—are self-explanatory. They are sometimes used in conjunction with some of the other systems of classification.

The assessment of the volume of man-made capital invested in a region and placing of money values on its components is beset with a number of statistical difficulties in addition to some more fundamental conceptual problems. Because of their significance for a variety of economic analyses, the intricacies of estimation have been explored to a much greater extent than in the case of natural and human resources. The method of valuation ultimately adopted depends in each instance to a large extent upon the purpose of the study. Wealth, according to Parsons and Smelser, "is not so much an inventory of commodities as an instrumentality for achieving goals and inducing the cooperation of actors in that achievement."[42] The most common use of estimates of invested capital is in studies of production functions and in various direct and indirect methods of assessing the technology of the regional economy. Among the significant potential applications are estimates of the extent to which economies of agglomeration are generated, and the closely related studies of absolute and relative attractiveness of the region for new investments.

For purposes of implementing production functions, capital must be measured in a way correlative with production, since at bottom the measurement of product and of capital are identical problems. Yet the technical difficulties involved in the measuring of income flows and of stocks are very different in nature. Since they have already been discussed elsewhere, it is sufficient to recall here that while items composing income flows are for the most part goods and services currently valued upon the market, the volume of capital goods changing hands is small compared to the total existing, and few are traded at dates near to measurement. Hence, market prices as basis for valuation are the exception rather than the rule.

In a perfect market, prices are proportional to marginal utilities and reflect marginal costs. Any deviations between the two are signals to stop or to step up production, thus ensuring an efficient allocation of goods and resources. If the market for a good is not perfect, its marginal utility may be unequal to its marginal cost, although both may exist, with the price diverging from either or from both; but in the complete absence of a market there is no price. In the face of imperfect markets or in their absence, valuation in terms of utility or in terms of costs may still be possible, but there is no reason why the two should be equal.

Since markets are imperfect and transactions few, for most capital items actual prices are at best poor indicators of value. Two possible principles of valuation for capital assets are often involved—a utility principle and a cost principle—answering two basically different questions. The utility principle corresponds to a comparison of two bundles of consumption goods from the point of view of their capacity to satisfy wants. The cost principle, on the other hand, corresponds to a comparison of two bundles of consumption (or production) goods generating identical utility in terms of resources and factors of production used in their manufacture. The former approach has received more attention, but for measuring capital goods the cost aspect may well be more important.[43]

Practically, seven different methods of valuation of capital assets are possible:

1. Book value, used mainly for corporate assets

2. Original cost to owner

3. National original cost, or cost to the first owner in the nation or in the region

4. Face value, used in case of financial assets

5. Replacement value

6. Market value

7. Capitalized net income.

The selection of methodology, or of the combination of methods to be used, depends upon the objectives of the study and data available, but the basic choice to be made is between uniformity of valuation of the assets covered and adherence to the motives of authors of the original data. The difficulties arising are due to differences between the principles upon which are based business accounts, forming the main source of data, and social accounts. The methods used in reported attempts at constructing wealth accounts can be classified into the following four categories:[44]

1. Sample survey of statistical data, which involves discovering economically meaningful questions that can be answered by data obtained from business records of a sample of firms. This approach has been developed and used by Barna at the National Institute of Economic and Social Research in London.

2. Sample survey of engineering data, obtained from plans or projects of new establishments submitted in support of applications for government or other financial assistance. This method has been extensively used by the Harvard Research Project and by the Rand Corporation.

3. Estimates derived from book values of business firms, adjusted for changing levels of prices and for revaluations, although without attempting to correct unrealistic depreciation policies. This approach has been followed by Creamer and Bernstein at the National Bureau of Economic Research in New York.

4. Perpetual inventory method,[45] based on adjusted income and product accounts. This was originally developed by Goldsmith in the United States, by Redfern in England, and by Krengel in Germany and in many ways seems to be the most promising approach.

The perpetual inventory method is based on, and provides a welcome link to, income and product accounts. Capital stock invested in an industry or sector of the economy at any particular time is derived by adding up purchases of capital goods, as recorded in income and product accounts, over a period of years. In order to determine net additions capital consumption, encompassing depreciation due to physical wear and tear, obsolescence, and accidental damage to fixed assets, has to be deducted. Two methods can be used for estimating yearly capital consumption: (1) historical time-series data on capital consumption allowances, which form part of income and product accounts, or (2) independent estimates on capital withdrawals, based on average economic life of capital goods; that is, the length of time that, on average, similar capital goods remain in useful economic production before discarding or scrapping occurs.

The first method has the advantage of consistency, since both investments and capital withdrawals form part of the same set of balanced income and product accounts. Its main drawback, besides the difficulties involved in adjustments, is that the use of two time series does not permit the estimation of the value of the initial stock. In order to minimize the size of the error, it is necessary to go very far back in time, when the total reproducible capital of the economy was small. Some estimates, in fact, reach back for over 100 years, which considerably reduces the discrepancy without completely eliminating it.[46] The use of such long time series, partly reconstructed from imperfect records, involves, however, a number of other difficulties that are mainly statistical.

The second method (followed for estimating Canadian capital in manufacturing[47] and in Nova Scotia[48]) is conceptually simpler and provides a consistent estimate but rests on a number of rather strong assumptions concerning the average economic life of various assets. In following this last method, three sources of data are needed for deriving the estimates: (1) historical time series of gross fixed capital formation by every industry, in current dollars; (2) price indexes pertaining to the types of capital goods being estimated, to be used as deflators; and (3) data on average economic life by broad categories of assets.

The derivation of the estimates can be succinctly explained as follows:

$$GK_{hT} = \sum_{t=1}^{T} (GI_{ht} - R_{ht}) \; ; \qquad (4\text{-}2)$$

where

GK = constant dollars gross stock of capital in terminal year T;

GI = gross fixed capital formation or gross capital formation in constant dollars;

R = withdrawals from capital stock in constant dollars;

and where the subscripts

t = time in yearly intervals: $1, 2, \ldots, T$;

h = industrial sector: $1, 2, \ldots, H$;

L = average expected economic life of capital goods in years;

$$R_{ht} = GI_{h(T-L_h)} \; ; \qquad (4\text{-}3)$$

Substituting and simplifying

$$GK_{hT} = \sum_{t=1}^{T} GI_{ht} - \sum_{t=1}^{T-L_h} GI_{ht} \; ; \; \text{or} \qquad (4\text{-}4)$$

$$GK_{hT} = \sum_{t=T-(L_h-1)}^{T} GI_{ht} \; ; \qquad (4\text{-}5)$$

In order to arrive at net capital formation, the estimated depreciation is deducted by applying the straight line method.

$$NI_{ht} = GI_{ht} - D_{ht} \; ; \tag{4-6}$$

where

NI = net fixed capital formation in constant dollars;
D = estimated capital consumption allowance in constant dollars;

$$D_{ht} = \frac{1}{2L_h} \left[GK_{ht} + GK_{h(t-1)} \right] \; ; \tag{4-7}$$

Net capital formation and net capital stock are simply found by substituting

$$NI_{ht} = GI_{ht} - \frac{1}{2L_h} \left[GI_{ht} + GI_{h(t-1)} \right] \; ; \tag{4-8}$$

$$NK_{ht} = \sum_{T=t-(L_h-1)}^{T} NI_{ht} = \sum_{t=1}^{T} GI_{ht} - \sum_{h=1}^{T} D_{ht} \tag{4-9}$$

$$= \sum_{t=1}^{T-L_h} GI_{ht} + \sum_{t=T-(L_h-1)}^{T} GI_{ht} - \sum_{t=1}^{T} D_{ht}$$

$$= GK_{hT} - \frac{1}{2L_h} \sum_{t=t-(L_h-1)}^{T} \left[GI_{ht} + GI_{h(t-1)} \right] \; ;$$

where

NK = constant dollar end-year net stock of capital.

For all industries

$$NK_T = \sum_{h=1}^{H} NK_{hT} \; ;$$

The last step to be carried out is the conversion of gross-fixed capital formation data from current to constant dollars with the help of price indexes of capital goods.

The various types of wealth can be summarized in a double-entry system showing on the left hand side the various types of assets and on the right the amounts controlled by various sectors. An alternative system is a complete cross-classification illustrated for a fairly typical depressed region in Table 4-2.

The advantages of combining and contrasting the various elements of regional wealth are obvious, but their detailed analysis and evaluation is possible only within the context of regional models in which stock phenomena are combined with changes and developments taking place in the economy.

Table 4-2
Net Capital Stock Estimates by Sector: Nova Scotia, 1961 (In Millions of 1961 Dollars)

Sector	Machinery and Equipment	Nonresidential Structures and Engineering Constructions	Business Inventories and Agricultural Livestock	Total
Agriculture	22.3	22.1	26.1	70.5
Fishing	22.8	4.2		27.0
Forestry	3.2	6.4		9.8
Mining	27.7	16.4		44.1
Construction industry	22.2	1.7		23.9
Manufacturing	103.0	77.6	72.3	252.9
Trade and finance	54.7	80.4		135.1
Commercial services	13.3	8.3		21.6
Subtotal	269.2	217.1	98.4	584.7
Utilities	177.4	147.5		324.9
Schools, hospitals, and other institutions	14.4	110.8		125.2
Provincial and local governments	7.1	120.3		127.4
Federal government in Nova Scotia	22.7	117.0		139.7
Total	490.8	712.7	98.4	1,301.9

**Part Two
Sectoral Accounts**

5

Interindustry Flows

Regional Industrial Structure

The various types of accounts so far considered failed to attack the important problem of sectoral structure and existing interrelations in a consistent, systematic way. For while income-and-product, balance-of-payments, and moneyflow accounts provide some illuminating insights into numerous aspects of the working of the regional economy, they are as a rule incapable of generating guidelines for regional development policies, which almost invariably have to address themselves to specific sectors or industries. Moreover, an examination of individual industries does not probe deeply into multiplier effects comprised of indirect and induced repercussion which accompany large investments and which are often considered to be the main elements of major economic advances.

The study of interindustry effects has to be based upon an examination of intersectoral flows and leakages, the strength and diversity of which is directly related to the structure of the regional economy. One of the most useful indicators measuring the degree of industrialization of regional economies is the index of industrial specialization[1] derived by adding up positive and negative differences between the percentage shares of various industries in total regional and national employment. More specifically,

$$I_s = \sum_{i=1}^{n} \left| \frac{E_i^R}{E^R} - \frac{E_i^N}{E^N} \right| \bigg/ 2 \, ;$$

where

I_s = index of industrial specialization;

E_i^R = employment in the i-th industry in the region;

E^R = total employment in the region;

E_i^N = employment in the i-th industry in the nation;

E^N = total employment in the nation.

The use of this crude yet convenient device raises some serious doubts when applied outside of the United States. In many countries the national economy is highly specialized and far from self-sufficient; hence, the implied comparison of the sectoral distribution of productive activities of the region with its consumption patterns is spurious.

For purposes of interregional comparisons, a useful complement of the index of regional specialization is the localization curve. The curve is constructed by marking on the abscissa, at equal intervals from the origin, industries ranked in order of decreasing employment. The elevation plotted on the ordinate corresponds to the cumulative percentage share of total employment. The more employment is concentrated in one or a few industries, the more the curve deviates from the 45° line. For purposes of interregional comparisons, a diagram may contain several curves, although in such a case the sequence of industries marked on the abscissa will be different for each curve.

When dealing with many regions, it is often convenient to use instead of a multitude of curves summary coefficients derived by taking the ratio of the area bounded by each localization curve and the main diagonal, to the maximum area which could be bounded if employment were concentrated in one industry only. The derivation of this coefficient (C_e) is straightforward and is illustrated for a hypothetical case of three industries in Figure 5-1.

The area $OABCD$ (α) is equal to

$$\alpha = \sum_{i=1}^{n} \frac{(Y_i + Y_{i-1})}{2} (X_i - X_{i-1}) = \sum_{i=1}^{n} \frac{(Y_i + Y_{i-1})}{2} \frac{1}{n}$$

$$= \frac{1}{n} \left[\sum_{i=1}^{n-1} Y_i + \tfrac{1}{2} Y_n \right] = \frac{1}{n} \sum_{i=1}^{n-1} Y_i + \frac{1}{2n} \; ;$$

The area of OCD (β) is equal to

$$\beta = \frac{X_n Y_n}{2} = \frac{1}{2} \; ;$$

The area of OEF (γ) is equal to

$$\gamma = \frac{X_1 Y_n}{2} = \frac{1}{2n} \; ;$$

Hence, the value of the coefficient (C_e) is

$$C_e = \frac{\alpha - \beta}{\beta - \gamma} = \frac{\dfrac{1}{n} \displaystyle\sum_{i=1}^{n-1} Y_i + \dfrac{1}{2n} - \dfrac{1}{2}}{\dfrac{1}{2} - \dfrac{1}{2n}} = \frac{2 \displaystyle\sum_{i=1}^{n-1} Y_i - (n-1)}{(n-1)} \; ;$$

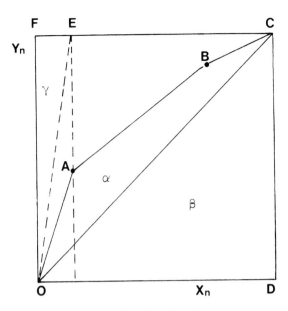

Figure 5-1. Localization Curve.

These and several other similar measures can at best provide a useful starting point for a study viewing the regional economy as a system. Such an analysis has to start by considering the interindustry flows taking place per unit of time. Intersectoral models of this type to which the name input-output has been applied can be traced to the celebrated *Tableau Economique* of Quesnay (1758) and to the theories of Walras (1877) and Marx (1848),[2] but its modern form is almost entirely the creation of Leontief.[3] Walras, in laying the foundation of general equilibrium analysis, stressed the interdependence among productive sectors in terms of their competing demands for factors of production, production costs, possible substitutions among outputs, and effects of changes in consumers' incomes. Yet, the theory was cast in highly abstract terms, yielding few interesting conclusions and precluding empirical verification. Leontief simplified the Walrasian system to the point where implementation became possible. He rejected the Austrian division into primary and secondary processes by assuming that all are equal with each trading, in principle at least, with all others, thus describing the economy as a whirlpool of interrelations. In the early versions of the model, households were also treated as an industry, consuming products of other sectors and supplying in turn labor services.

In this form input-output is purely an accounting device, but its important contribution resides in the rigor which it introduces, in the cross-checks which it provides, and in the possibility of filling in the gaps in basic data. In order to transform it into a forecasting tool, some strong assumptions are required, among which three are of particular importance:

1. Sectors are defined in such a way that a single production function can be assumed for each. Hence, each commodity is supplied by a single industry or sector, and each sector produces a single commodity or at most a group of commodities with closely related characteristics. It also implies that one method is used in producing each commodity (no factor substitution).

2. Inputs purchased by each sector are a fixed proportion of the level of output of that sector. The extremely simple and rigid production function thus postulated precludes any substitutions. It takes the form:

$$X_j = \min\left[\frac{x_{ij}}{a_{ij}}\right]; \quad (i = 1, \ldots, n);$$

The isoquants are right angles with the expansion path becoming a straight line. (The elasticity of substitution is zero.)

3. The total effects of carrying out several activities are the sum of their separate effects (constant returns to scale). The assumption bars from consideration the effects of economies of scale which traditionally have played an important role in economic theory, as well as external economies and diseconomies of agglomeration and urbanization which are of special interest to regional scientists and planners.

While these strong assumptions yield a strange picture of the economy, it is helpful to distinguish the input-output table from the analytical system to which it is related. The table is a statistical description of the inputs and outputs of different branches of an economic system during a particular period of time. The distinction commonly made in economic analysis between the production of goods and services and their final disposition is reflected in the division of the sectors of the input-output table into two groups: the producing or intermediate sectors on the one hand, and the final sectors on the other. Schematically the system of accounts may be represented by the diagram on the following page.

The first quadrant shows the intermediate or interindustry transactions, that is, the flow of goods and services which are both manufactured and consumed in the process of current production without reaching the ultimate users. Since it is precisely upon these relations between the intermediate sectors that input-output analysis focuses attention, they are shown in greater detail, so that the first quadrant usually occupies the largest part of any table. The transactions table may be regarded as a disaggregation of the production account of an income and product accounting system. In the latter, all intermediate flows are netted out on the grounds that they represent double accounting, but this double-counted production is the main concern of the input-output system.

Corresponding to the expenditure side of the production account, are the transactions recorded in the second quadrant of the input-output table, while the third quadrant corresponds to the primary inputs side of the account. Total primary inputs are equal by definition to all factor payments, plus depreciation, net indirect taxes, and imports.

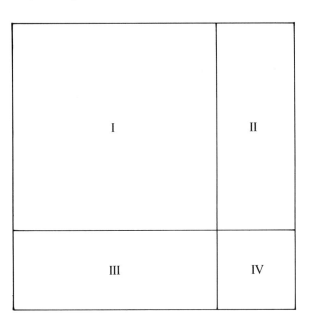

Given an economy divided into sectors, the total disposition of the output can be described by the following set of equations:

$$X_1 = x_{11} + x_{12} + x_{13} + \ldots + Y_1;$$
$$X_2 = x_{21} + x_{22} + x_{23} + \ldots + Y_2;$$
$$\vdots$$
$$X_n = x_{n1} + x_{n2} + x_{n3} + \ldots + Y_n;$$

where: X = total output
x = intermediate flow
Y = final demand

The equations are known as balance equations. The assumption characteristic of input-output economics is that the flow from production sector i to production sector j is always directly proportional to the output of sector j. This assumption can be formally expressed in the following equation, often referred to as a structural equation:

$$x_{ij} = a_{ij}X_j;$$

where a_{ij} is treated as a constant.

The solution of the input-output system, or the derivation of levels of operation of all sectors, necessary in order to satisfy any given or assumed vector of final demands, is possible by substituting for each x_{ij} in the n balance equations the corresponding structural equations, thus yielding a new set of n equations:

$$(1 - a_{11})X_1 \qquad - a_{12}X_2 - a_{13}X_3 - \ldots \qquad - a_{1n}X_n = Y_1;$$
$$- a_{21}X_1 + (1 - a_{22})X_2 - a_{23}X_3 - \ldots \qquad - a_{2n}X_n = Y_2;$$
$$\vdots$$
$$- a_{n1}X_1 \qquad - a_{n2}X_2 - a_{n3}X_3 - \ldots + (1 - a_{nn})X_n = Y_n;$$

In the usual matrix notation in which capital letters denote matrices, lower case letters with subscripts are numbers or elements of a matrix, lower case letters without subscripts are column vectors, capped letters denote diagonal matrices the nonzero elements of which are those of the corresponding column vector, and superscripts $'$ and $^{-1}$ denote transpose and inverse respectively. Using this notation, the basic relations of an input-output system are few and derived directly from the three assumptions mentioned.

Let: $\mathbf{X}$ = matrix of intersectoral flows, the elements of which are x_{ij}, or

$$\mathbf{X} = \begin{bmatrix} x_{11} & x_{12} & \cdots & x_{1n} \\ x_{21} & x_{22} & \cdots & x_{2n} \\ \cdot & \cdot & \cdots & \cdot \\ x_{n1} & x_{n2} & \cdots & x_{nn} \end{bmatrix}$$

i = unit vector, all elements of which are unity;
$I = \hat{i}$ or identity matrix;
y = vector of final demand;
v = vector of value added;
x = vector of total outputs, or

$$x = y + Xi; \tag{5-1}$$

or alternatively

$$x = v + X'i; \tag{5-2}$$

Together equations (5-1) and (5-2) imply the equivalence of total inputs and outputs of the economy.

$$i'v = i'y; \tag{5-3}$$

since

$$i'v + i'X'i = i'y + i'Xi;$$

and $(i'X'i)$ and $(i'Xi)$ both represent simply the sum of entries of matrix $\mathbf{X}$.

Let: $\mathbf{A}$ = matrix of technical coefficients a_{ij}, or

$$\mathbf{A} = \begin{bmatrix} a_{11} & a_{12} & \cdots & a_{1n} \\ a_{21} & a_{22} & \cdots & a_{2n} \\ \cdot & \cdot & \cdots & \cdot \\ a_{n1} & a_{n2} & \cdots & a_{nn} \end{bmatrix}$$

where

$$a_{ij} = \frac{x_{ij}}{X_j}; \text{ or}$$

$$A = X\hat{x}^{-1}; \tag{5-4}$$

Thus by definition

$$X = A\hat{x}; \tag{5-5}$$

and since the matrix $\mathbf{A}$ is independent of the level of output, it enables the determination of intersectoral flows X for any postulated level of total outputs x.

Substituting equation (5-5) into (5-1) leads to

$$y = x - Xi = x - A\hat{x}i = x - Ax; \text{ or}$$
$$y = (I - A)x; \tag{5-6}$$

Similarly, by substituting into (5-2) yields

$$v = x - X'i = x - \hat{x}A'i;$$

Defining $a = A'i$;

$$v = x - \hat{x}a = (I - \hat{a})x; \tag{5-7}$$

Equations (5-6) and (5-7) lead to

$$x = (I - A)^{-1}y; \tag{5-8}$$

$$x = (I - \hat{a})^{-1}v; \tag{5-9}$$

and substituting the latter into (5-6) results in

$$y = (I - A)(I - \hat{a})^{-1}v; \quad \text{and} \tag{5-10}$$

$$v = (I - \hat{a})(I - A)^{-1}y; \tag{5-11}$$

which connects the bill of goods with the level of demand for services of factors of production. The elements of the inverse matrix $(I - A)^{-1}$ can be interpreted as quantities of good i required to satisfy directly and indirectly unit final demand for j. Matrix **D** of coefficients of value added can be defined as:

$$D = (I - \hat{a})(I - A)^{-1}; \tag{5-12}$$

Elements d_{ij} of D are interpreted as amounts of value added v_i of sector i needed to satisfy unit final demand of sector j. Elements of vector $(i - a)$ give the share of value added in total inputs of each sector. By using (5-12) in (5-11) it is possible to write

$$v = Dy; \tag{5-13}$$

The inverse of the **D** matrix is

$$D^{-1} = (I - A)(I - \hat{a})^{-1}; \tag{5-14}$$

Clearly $D > 0$, while $D^{-1} \geqq 0$; Notice also that

$$i'D^{-1} = i'; \tag{5-15}$$

since by substituting

$$i'D^{-1} = i'(I - A)(I - \hat{a})^{-1} = (i' - a')(I - \hat{a})^{-1} = i'(I - \hat{a})(I - \hat{a})^{-1} = i';$$

Moreover $i'D^{-1}D = i'D$; or

$$i' = i'D; \tag{5-16}$$

The conditions imposed upon the elements of D^{-1} by (5-15) are insufficient in order to identify A given D^{-1}. From (5-14) one can derive

$$A = I - D^{-1}(I - \hat{a}); \tag{5-17}$$

since $D^{-1}(I - \hat{a}) = I - A$;

To derive A under these circumstances some additional constraints have to be imposed. An assumption that is frequently used deals with elements on the main diagonal of A. If $a_{ii} = 0$ for all i's $(I - \hat{a})$ defines value added per unit of output. This is sufficient to derive A from D.

Sectoring and Aggregation

The feasibility of a solution and the stability of parameters of the structural equations (a_{ij}) loom large in constructing an input-output table. The first and perhaps the most important and difficult problem in this connection is that of aggregation. The data upon which the system is based originate usually in firms and have to be aggregated into large groupings.

Before discussing the problems involved in defining industries, it might be worthwhile to consider briefly the basic units of which they are comprised. Four such units, often merely representing different ways of viewing the same entity, may be distinguished: firm, enterprise, department, and establishment or plant.

A *firm* is essentially a legal notion and, despite its decision-making powers (of considerable importance in behavioral studies), has few characteristics of interest in the present context. While extensively used in some types of economic studies, it has yet to find its way into regional analysis.

An *enterprise* represents a related concept, referring to a firm or an aggregation of firms under common ownership and financial control. Most enterprises correspond to individual firms, sometimes very large and engaged in economically heterogeneous activities, although occasionally an enterprise might be comprised of separate legal entities bound by common ownership or by financial and managerial control. The concept often proves useful, though mainly for data-collecting purposes.

A *department* refers to a part of an operating organization concerned with one aspect of its operation, usually associated with a particular activity.

Finally, the notion of an *establishment* or *plant* plays a fundamental role in defining sectors. For statistical purposes, an establishment or plant is defined as the smallest unit that is a separate operating entity capable of reporting all elements of basic industrial statistics. Its importance in regional studies derives from its homogeneity and ability to report on the main inputs and outputs. Typically, an establishment is a factory, mine, or store having, in most cases, the legal form of a firm, although an individual working on his own account may form an establishment. While the majority of plants are firms, many firms have more than one establishment. Originally the notion referred to a unit producing similar goods and services under one roof, but nowadays a plant may be located in several buildings on a single plot of land.

Among the aggregate notions the simplest is that of an occupation which refers to a job or a set of tasks requiring a body of skills, knowledge, experience, or aptitudes, or to a group of individuals performing these tasks.

Commodities refer to raw materials, processed materials, or end products viewed either as outputs of industries or as materials and supplies used by industries or final consumers. The importance of the concept rests on the fact that some commodities tend to be associated with particular industries, so that industries are often defined in terms of their principal products.

For purposes of economic analysis, the most important notion of industry or sector refers in broad terms to a grouping of plants having some characteristics in common. The criterion on which the definition is based may be similarity of products, usually made from related materials, or similarity of technical processes and equipment. The two criteria have a slightly different origin but basically represent merely different ways of describing the same phenomenon, because a change of technology is usually (and according to some, always) followed by a change in input structure. Hence, a description of inputs and outputs is considered to define the technology adequately. The definition stressing similarities in technology and equipment is sometimes viewed as being more applicable to industries, while the one stressing similarity in input-output structure is more applicable to sectors, although the two notions are so close that they are used interchangeably.

In combining the basic units (establishments or plants) into sectors, two problems have to be faced: (1) the technical one of grouping, and (2) the criterion according to which the basic units are to be aggregated.

The technical question of grouping or reducing the size of vectors and matrices is solved with the help of grouping and weighting matrices. Grouping matrices, derived from identity matrices, form a special case of permutation matrices. The way they are applied depends on whether they are used for reducing the size of vectors, of matrices of interindustry flows, or of matrices of technical coefficients. In the first case, that is, in order to aggregate a column vector, the vector is premultiplied by the appropriate matrix. For example, in order to reduce a 5 x 1 column vector of final demand into a 3 x 1 vector by combining sectors three, four and five, the following operation has to be performed:

$$
\begin{bmatrix}
1 & 0 & 0 & 0 & 0 \\
0 & 1 & 0 & 0 & 0 \\
0 & 0 & 1 & 1 & 1
\end{bmatrix}
\begin{bmatrix}
Y_1 \\
Y_2 \\
Y_3 \\
Y_4 \\
Y_5
\end{bmatrix}
=
\begin{bmatrix}
Y_1 \\
Y_2 \\
Y_3 + Y_4 + Y_5
\end{bmatrix} ;
$$

In symbols: $Y^* = GY$;

where $Y^* =$ the reduced vector;
 G = grouping matrix;
 Y = the original vector

In order to reduce the size of an input-output flow matrix, the matrix has to be premultiplied by a grouping matrix and postmultiplied by a transpose of the grouping matrix. The case of a 3 x 3 matrix reduced to size 2 x 2 by combining sectors two and three is illustrated below.

$$X^* = G \times G'$$

where X = original flow matrix;
  $X^* =$ reduced flow matrix;

G = grouping matrix;
G' = transpose of grouping matrix;

$$\begin{bmatrix} 1 & 0 & 0 \\ 0 & 1 & 1 \end{bmatrix} \begin{bmatrix} x_{11} & x_{12} & x_{13} \\ x_{21} & x_{22} & x_{23} \\ x_{31} & x_{32} & x_{33} \end{bmatrix} \begin{bmatrix} 1 & 0 \\ 0 & 1 \\ 0 & 1 \end{bmatrix}$$

$$= \begin{bmatrix} x_{11} & x_{12} & x_{13} \\ (x_{21}+x_{31}) & (x_{22}+x_{32}) & (x_{23}+x_{33}) \end{bmatrix} \begin{bmatrix} 1 & 0 \\ 0 & 1 \\ 0 & 1 \end{bmatrix}$$

$$= \begin{bmatrix} x_{11} & (x_{12}+x_{13}) \\ (x_{21}+x_{31}) & (x_{22}+x_{32}+x_{23}+x_{33}) \end{bmatrix} \; ;$$

which is what one would expect to obtain.

Notice that the first entry is unchanged because the flows from the first sector to itself are unaffected. The second entry $(x_{12}+x_{13})$ combines the flows from the first sector to the former sectors 2 and 3, which now form a unique new industry. The third entry $(x_{21}+x_{31})$ combines the flows from sectors 2 and 3 to sector one which remains unaltered. Finally, the entry $(x_{22}+x_{32} +x_{23}+x_{33})$ combines the flows from sector 2 to itself and to sector 3, with flows from sector 3 to sector 2 and 3.

In order to reduce the size of a matrix of input-output coefficients, the matrix has to be premultiplied by a grouping matrix and postmultiplied by the transpose of a weight matrix in which the nonzero entries are formed by appropriate weights. The case of a 3 x 3 matrix of coefficients, reduced to size 2 x 2 is illustrated below.

$$A^* = GAG'_w \; ;$$

where A = original matrix of coefficients;
A^* = reduced matrix of coefficients;
G'_w = transpose of weight matrix;

$$A^* = \begin{bmatrix} 1 & 0 & 0 \\ 0 & 1 & 1 \end{bmatrix} \begin{bmatrix} a_{11} & a_{12} & a_{13} \\ a_{21} & a_{22} & a_{23} \\ a_{31} & a_{32} & a_{33} \end{bmatrix} \begin{bmatrix} 1 & 0 \\ 0 & \beta \\ 0 & (1-\beta) \end{bmatrix} \; ;$$

where $\beta = \dfrac{x_2}{x_2+x_3}$; and $(1-\beta) = \dfrac{x_3}{x_2+x_3}$;

Notice that the weights are proportions of output of each sector to total output of the combined sector.

$$A^* = \begin{bmatrix} a_{11} & a_{12} & a_{13} \\ (a_{21}+a_{31}) & (a_{22}+a_{32}) & (a_{23}+a_{33}) \end{bmatrix} \begin{bmatrix} 1 & 0 \\ 0 & \beta \\ 0 & (1-\beta) \end{bmatrix}$$

$$= \begin{bmatrix} a_{11} & [\beta a_{12}+(1-\beta)a_{13}] \\ (a_{21}+a_{31}) & [\beta(a_{22}+a_{32})+(1-\beta)(a_{23}+a_{33})] \end{bmatrix} ;$$

Substituting for β and $(1-\beta)$ and recalling that $a = \dfrac{x_{ij}}{X_j}$,

yields,

$$A^* = \begin{bmatrix} \dfrac{x_{11}}{X_1} & \left\{ \dfrac{X_2}{X_2+X_3}\dfrac{x_{12}}{X_2} + \dfrac{X_3}{X_2+X_3}\dfrac{x_{13}}{X_3} \right\} \\ \dfrac{x_{21}+x_{31}}{X_1} & \left\{ \dfrac{X_2}{X_2+X_3}\dfrac{x_{22}+x_{32}}{X_2} + \dfrac{X_3}{X_2+X_3}\dfrac{x_{23}+x_{33}}{X_3} \right\} \end{bmatrix}$$

$$= \begin{bmatrix} \dfrac{x_{11}}{X_1} & \dfrac{x_{12}+x_{13}}{X_2+X_3} \\ \dfrac{x_{21}+x_{31}}{X_1} & \dfrac{x_{22}+x_{32}+x_{23}+x_{33}}{X_2+X_3} \end{bmatrix} ;$$

The first entry

$$a_{11} = \frac{x_{11}}{X_1} ;$$

is unchanged and simply indicates the flow of products of sector 1 to itself per unit of output. The second entry

$$\beta a_{12} + (1-\beta)a_{13} = \frac{x_{12}+x_{13}}{X_2+X_3} ;$$

indicates the flow from sector 1 to the combined new sector composed of former industries 2 and 3, per unit output of the new sector. The third entry

$$(a_{21} + a_{31}) = \frac{x_{21} + x_{31}}{X_1} ;$$

indicates the flows from former sectors 2 and 3 to 1 per unit output of the latter. Finally, the last entry

$$\beta(a_{22} + a_{32}) + (1-\beta)(a_{23} + a_{33}) = \frac{x_{22} + x_{32} + x_{23} + x_{33}}{X_2 + X_3} ;$$

indicates the flow from the new combined sector 2 and 3 to itself per unit output of the new sector.

Notice, incidentally, that the grouping matrix postmultiplied by the transpose of a weight matrix yields an identity matrix, as can be seen from

$$GG'_w = I ;$$

$$\begin{bmatrix} 1 & 0 & 0 \\ 0 & 1 & 1 \end{bmatrix} \begin{bmatrix} 1 & 0 \\ 0 & \beta \\ 0 & (1-\beta) \end{bmatrix} = \begin{bmatrix} 1 & 0 \\ 0 & 1 \end{bmatrix} ;$$

The same result holds true whatever the number of sectors aggregated, although the notation becomes slightly more complicated. When n sectors are aggregated into one, the entries in the weight matrix become

$$g_{w.ij} = 0, 1, w_{ij} ;$$

subject to

$$0 \leqslant g_{w.ij} \leqslant 1$$

and

$$\sum_{i=1}^{n} g_{w.ij} = 1 ;$$

In other words, the weights have to be nonnegative and to add up to unity.

The second problem involved in aggregation, that of an appropriate criterion, raises far greater difficulties since there are no ideal criteria for classification of activities or for aggregation of establishments into sectors. In the oversimplified example discussed above, the input coefficients of the aggregated input-output sector were weighted sums of the coefficients of the constituent original sectors, the weights being the relative size of each sector's output in the base period. This is very often the case in practical situations, but the shortcomings of this approach should not be overlooked.

To be acceptable, aggregation should not affect the basic characteristics of the system, especially the requirement that for all possible variations in final demand the output of the aggregated sector should be equal to the sum of outputs of the individual ones. More rigorously, this requires that $a_{i(m+n)}$ should be unchanging when the two sectors m and n are combined or $X_m + X_n = X_{(m+n)}$;

Now

$$a_{i(m+n)} = \frac{x_{i(m+n)}}{X_{(m+n)}} = \frac{x_{im} + x_{in}}{X_m + X_n} = \frac{a_{im}X_m + a_{in}X_n}{X_m + X_n}$$

$$= a_{im}\left[\frac{X_m}{X_m + X_n}\right] + a_{in}\left[\frac{X_n}{X_m + X_n}\right] = a_{im}w_m + a_{in}w_n;$$

It is clear that even if the original coefficients are all stable, the aggregate coefficients may change in response to a. shift in the relative value of outputs of the sectors of which the aggregate sector is comprised, since these will affect the weights w_m and w_n. There are only two cases in which the values of the coefficients of the aggregate sector will not be affected by nonproportional change in the level of output of the composing sectors:

1. If the technical coefficients of the two sectors are equal, or $(a_{im} = a_{in})$. Here no change in the weights (w's) resulting from changes in demand (Y) for the products of the two industries will affect the aggregate coefficients. Aggregation will result in a loss of information since demand for each good will no longer be known, but this is of minor importance.

2. If products of the two industries m and n are demanded always in fixed proportions, the weighted average of the input coefficients will be always the same. In this case, there is no loss of information because demand for X_m is always a fixed proportion of total demand for $X_{(m+n)}$.

The first condition refers rather to aggregating productive activities and the second to commodities. Under any of these two conditions aggregation would be perfect, and no error would be introduced by it but such circumstances are rarely encountered in practice and hence compromises are necessary.

Attempts to define an industry as a grouping of plants to which a single production function might be applied hurt themselves against the fact that few plants are limited to a single product.[4] Moreover, overlap is not the only problem besetting attempts to define an industry. In multiproduct plants the criterion used to assess their relative importance is of considerable significance but is often ambiguous. Physical measures of quantity could be, and sometimes are, used, but this may be an awkward unit if aggregation is required or if the products are very dissimilar. Other obvious units are value-added, value of shipments, and employment. Each represents some advantages and difficulties of its own but they generally lead to slightly different classifications. Employment, frequently used because it is readily available, has the serious disadvantage of being sensitive to differences in productivity.

Industries defined as aggregates of plants using similar technology (as opposed to sectors having similar input and output structure) respond to slightly different analytic needs. Any economic theory or hypothesis has to be predicated on the assumption of uniformity of characteristics and behavior of basic units such as households, firms, or organizations, but it is by no means clear that the groupings are the same for purposes of various studies. Depending upon the problem studied, sectors or industries based for example on similarity of behavior in business cycles, or on identical income elasticities, may be more relevant than those defined by the criterion of similarity in the use of factors of production or of inputs. In regional studies, aggregates based on similarity in the main locational factors would assume great significance, and their omission in official statistics presents a major difficulty in the quantitative testing of hypotheses dealing with space. Clearly, no definition could satisfy all requirements.

In defining sectors, one has to contend not only with main products but with subsidiary products, by-products, and joint products as well.

Subsidiary products are those which form the main product of another industry.[5] They may or may not be technologically linked to that of the main product, the latter case being simply the result of integration or of growth in scope of activities rather than size. The output data of subsidiary products are usually easily obtainable but not the associated inputs which are hard to identify, especially since few units keep records appropriate for this purpose. In order to implement input-output accounts, one might use input coefficients of the industry in which the subsidiary product is the main line of activity, but this implies that the same technology is used in both cases which is frequently not the case, since the subsidiary product may be produced in a highly mechanized modern industry while at the same time forming the main product of a more primitive traditional activity. In terms of input-output accounts, the subsidiary products are best removed from the industry in which they are actually produced and the total output ascribed to the industry where they form the main line of activity. This turns out several products as well. Hence, both sales and inputs have to be allocated and all have to be balanced.

The easiest way to proceed is to seek engineering-type data, from which to calculate input coefficients, directly from the industry concerned, but such information is frequently not available. An alternative is to introduce a simplifying assumption. Two assumptions are most often used: (1) each industry produces a fixed proportion of product, and (2) output of each industry is comprised of several products manufactured in fixed proportions.

For example, assuming two industries A and B and two products X and Y, one could postulate one of the following two cases:

Example 1

		Products	
		X	Y
Industries	A	.8	.1
	B	.2	.9
		1.0	1.0

Example 2

		Products		
		X	Y	
Industries	A	.8	.2	1.0
	B	.3	.7	1.0

The two assumptions are far from equivalent and lead to very different results except in the trivial case when there are no subsidiary products.

By-products are second products related technically to the main products usually forming a fixed proportion of output. For example, the quantity of cotton seeds turned out in a cotton gin depends strictly upon the level of operation of the mill. The treatment of by-products in input-output studies presents various difficulties.[6] It is perhaps best not to attempt to separate out the costs of the by-products—since this is statistically next to impossible and conceptually often unsatisfactory—but to remove their output from the industry concerned. The following example illustrates the handling of by-products in an input-output table. Let us assume that industry one produces eight units of its main product and one unit of a by-product which is the main product of industry two. The relevant facts are illustrated in the following example, in which the by-product is market by an asterisk:

Example 3

	X_1	X_2	Y	Σ
X_1	0	2	6+1*	8+1*
X_2	0	0	10*	10*
V	9	8		

Since in a large input-output table products cannot be differentiated by asterisks the following two alternative ways of recording the situation are available.

Example 4						Example 5			
(1)	X_1	X_2	Y	Σ		(2)	X_1	X_2	Y	Σ

(1)	X_1	X_2	Y	Σ
X_1	0	2+1	6	8+1
X_2	0	0	11	11
V	9	8	0	

(2)	X_1	X_2	Y	Σ
X_1	0	2	6	8
X_2	−1	0	11	10
V	9	8	0	

The disadvantage of the first method is that it does not preserve the homogeneity of rows, because different products are recorded in each row. Moreover, more output is shown (20 units) than actually took place. The second method is generally preferred, even though the negative entries cause some difficulties in computations.

A hypothetical increase in final demand for the by-product by 4 units (from 11 to 15 units) would be recorded as:

Example 6

	X_1	X_2	Y	Σ
X_1	0	2.78	6	8.78
X_2	−1.10	0	15	13.90
V	9.88	11.12	0	

Notice that the second industry in which the by-product is the main line of activity had to step up its output by only 3.90 units rather than 4, because in order to enable the second industry to increase its output the first industry had in turn to step up production in order to supply the second industry with its product. This increased the supply of the by-product by 0.10 units since it is technologically linked to the first product. In a larger table, the inverse of the matrix of coefficients would have to be used in order to derive the necessary quantities.

Let us now assume that consumers increased their demand for the first product rather than for the second. The result is illustrated in the following:

Example 7

	X_1	X_2	Y	Σ
X_1	0	1.90	10	11.90
X_2	−1.49	0	11	9.51
V	13.39	7.61	0	

Notice that the net result has been a curtailment of the activity of the second industry because a greater volume of the second product has now been supplied to the consumers as by-product of the first industry.

The treatment of joint products requires the introduction of dummy industries which play an important role in input-output studies. Joint products refer to several outputs of a plant which are of roughly equal importance and are not produced elsewhere; for example, meat and hides in a slaughterhouse. They may or may not have to be produced in fixed proportions, and may not even be technically related. Whenever the proportions of the several products in total output are fixed by technology, as for example in the production of meat and hides or of cotton and cotton seeds, the allocation of inputs can be determined with the help of statistical data although considerable difficulties are encountered whenever there are several joint products sold to different users. The second case of joint products manufactured in variable proportions is even more complex, and more often than not engineering-type coefficients have to be resorted to, since there is usually no industry specializing in a single process.

The following example illustrates a way of introducing a dummy industry.

Example 8

	X_1	X_2	X_3	Y	Σ
X_1	0	5	0	15	20
X_2	5	0	0	5	10
X_3	−2	−1	0	3	0
V	17	6	0	0	

The first two industries contribute two and one units respectively to the third industry—a dummy industry. The contributions are shown by negative entries. Notice that total output of the dummy industry is absorbed by final demand even though it may represent merely an increase in stocks. In the technical coefficients table, the coefficients relating to the dummy industry are all of the indeterminate 0/0 form, but they are actually not needed. The final demand vector is applied only to real industries.

Supposing that the demand for the main products is increased by one unit each (16 instead of 15 and 6 instead of 5). The situation is shown in example 9.

A rather obvious conclusion of the preceding discussion is that product groups should be set up in such a way that:

1. Each product should appear as output of only one group

Example 9

	X_1	X_2	X_3	Y	Σ
X_1	0	5.71	0	16	21.71
X_2	5.43	0	0	6	11.43
X_3	−2.17	−1.14	0	3.31	0
V	18.45	6.86	0	0	25.31

2. Within each group, products should be homogeneous in the sense of their input structure.

Practically, the first step in setting up an input-output table is an examination of the joint-product industries. Outputs produced in fixed proportions are dealt with first and their individual input structures determined. Next, artificial joint-product or dummy industries are created by combining processes forming part of plants classified as belonging to different sectors. The difficulty resides not only in the determination of input structures but often even of total output, since sometimes all that is known is joint demand.

One type of dummy industry deserves special attention. In the early input-output tables, it was customary to set up dummy industries for the unallocated inputs and outputs. The logic of input-output analysis requires, however, that the total value of all unallocated outputs be equal to the total value of all unallocated inputs in all industries. As a consequence, the dummy industry with a column collecting the unallocated outputs and with a row collecting unallocated inputs generated demand for outputs of industries with large unallocated outputs. For some industries, this caused considerable and unrealistic deviations from actual facts. It is now considered much better to allocate inputs and outputs in the face of lack of statistical information on the basis of judgment rather than to use for this purpose a dummy industry.

The important problem of aggregation deserves one more comment. Aggregation arises either involuntarily because of data deficiencies or by design if it is deemed not useful to keep industries separate or in the face of difficulties with inverting large matrices. For purposes of constructing interindustry tables, it is assumed that every industry stands in input-output relations with every other industry in the system, but in reality many flows do not exist and the corresponding technical coefficients are zero or very nearly so. This property offers two possibilities for an important simplification of the work involved: (1) by assuming a hierarchical structure of industries, a triangular matrix could be obtained, or (2) by assuming the existence of groups of industries with little trade between them, a partitioned matrix could be derived.

In a triangular matrix of coefficient with zeros either above or below the main diagonal, any industry is supplied by all sectors with a higher ordering, but sells its products to those with lower ones and to final demand. For example, Industry 1 is supplied by all sectors in the system but sells its products to itself (and perhaps final demand) only. Industry 2 is supplied by all other sectors except Industry 1, and sells its products to Industry 1 and 2, and so forth. The great attraction of such a system is the computational convenience, especially the facility with which an inverse can be calculated. Such systems, alas, are relatively rarely encountered.

$$\begin{bmatrix} x_{11} & 0 & 0 & 0 & \ldots & 0 \\ x_{21} & x_{22} & 0 & 0 & \ldots & 0 \\ x_{31} & x_{32} & x_{33} & 0 & \ldots & 0 \\ \cdot & \cdot & \cdot & \cdot & \ldots & \cdot \\ x_{n1} & x_{n2} & x_{n3} & x_{n4} & \ldots & x_{nn} \end{bmatrix}$$

Of greater practical importance are systems in which industries can be classified into two groups r and s with insignificant trade between them. The table of technical coefficients takes then the form of a partitioned matrix:

$$\mathbf{A} = \begin{bmatrix} A_{rr} & | & A_{rs} \\ -- & -|- & -- \\ A_{sr} & | & A_{ss} \end{bmatrix}$$

In the rare case of no trade whatsoever between groups, or $A_{rs} = A_{sr} = 0$, the system takes the following form:

$$\begin{bmatrix} X_r \\ -- \\ X_s \end{bmatrix} = \begin{bmatrix} A_{rr} & | & 0 \\ -- & + & -- \\ 0 & | & A_{ss} \end{bmatrix} \begin{bmatrix} X_r \\ -- \\ X_s \end{bmatrix} + \begin{bmatrix} Y_r \\ -- \\ Y_x \end{bmatrix} ;$$

The matrix multiplier consists here of inverses of the two submatrices: $(I - A_{rr})^{-1}$ and $(I - A_{ss})^{-1}$.

In the more usual case of some residual trade one of the two assumptions can be made, resulting in either case in a considerable saving of research effort: (1) the amount of goods r available for industries s depends upon the level of output of r industries, itself a function of final and intermediate demand for r products, or (2) amounts of goods r sold to industries s depend upon demand, but averaged over all s-type industries, rather than by individual sectors.

In the first case any flow x_{rs} is supply determined, being a function of X_r rather than X_s. This happens when intergroup flows are comprised mainly of by-products, the level of output of which is technologically determined. This takes the following form:

$$
\begin{bmatrix} X_r \\ X_s \end{bmatrix} = \left[\begin{array}{c|c} A_{rr} + A_{rs} & 0 \\ \hline 0 & A_{ss} + A_{sr} \end{array} \right] \begin{bmatrix} X_r \\ X_s \end{bmatrix} + \begin{bmatrix} Y_r \\ Y_s \end{bmatrix} ;
$$

Hence,

$$
X_r = (I - A_{rr} - A_{rs})^{-1} Y_r ;
$$
$$
X_s = (I - A_{ss} - A_{sr})^{-1} Y_s ;
$$

In the second case A_{rs} is replaced by a row vector a'_{rs} of average coefficients and similarly for A_{sr}. The system takes the following forms:

$$
\begin{bmatrix} X_r \\ X_s \end{bmatrix} = \left[\begin{array}{c|c} A_{rr} & a'_{rs} \\ \hline a'_{sr} & A_{ss} \end{array} \right] \begin{bmatrix} X_r \\ X_s \end{bmatrix} + \begin{bmatrix} Y_r \\ Y_s \end{bmatrix} ;
$$

$$
X_r = A_{rr} X_r + a'_{rs} X_s + Y_r ;
$$
$$
X_r = (I - A_{rr})^{-1} (a'_{rs} X_s + Y_r);
$$
$$
X_s = (I - A_{ss})^{-1} (a'_{rs} X_r + Y_s);
$$

Substituting

$$
X_r = (I - A_{rr})^{-1} [a'_{rs}(I - A_{ss})^{-1}(a'_{sr} X_r + Y_s) + Y_r] ;
$$

$$
X_r = [I - (I - A_{rr})^{-1} a'_{rs}(I - A_{ss})^{-1} a'_{sr}]^{-1} (I - A_{rr})^{-1} [a'_{rs}(I - A_{ss})^{-1} Y_s + Y_r] ;
$$

$$
X_r = [I - A_{rr} - a'_{rs}(I - A_{ss})^{-1} a'_{sr}]^{-1} [a'_{rs}(I - A_{ss})^{-1} Y_s + Y_r] ;
$$

and similarly for X_s.

This assumption is occasionally encountered in regional interindustry studies.[7] Two other simplifying assumptions leading to what is known as "rows only" and "from-to" matrices help overcome the notorious dearth of data and research resources accompanying attempts to analyze regional industrial structure. Both lack the elegance of the model just described.

The intersectoral flows model, dubbed "rows only" was developed by Tiebout and his associates at the University of California at Los Angeles.[8] The distinguishing feature of the "rows only" model is that at the data-collecting stage a sample of firms were asked to break down their 1960 sales by final demand sectors and local industry groups. No information on inputs was requested. The more typical procedure in implementing a regional input-output model is to seek from a sample of firms data on both inputs and sales. After the sample data have been aggregated and "blown up" to cover all transactions by using control totals from published sources, the problem is faced of reconciling differences between the input and output data. This involves a considerable amount of work and exercise of informed judgment. The sample survey itself is obviously also considerably more expensive. These difficulties are avoided in the "rows only" model which uses solely sales data. Since these are arranged in matrix form, the model implicitly assumes that the columns represent inputs, but the inaccuracies likely to result from lack of cross-checks may be substantial.

Another feature of the "rows only" model was that its entries were expressed in terms of employment rather than in dollars. This is, however, more typical of the "form-to" model.[9] The latter matrix is limited to flows between sectors expressed in terms of value-added or employment. There are thus no rows at the bottom covering primary inputs or imports. The model abstracts trade relationship from technical relationship and may thus provide a welcome complement to either income and product, or input-output accounts.

A simplified procedure for developing a regional input-ouput model has been demonstrated by Bonner and Fahle.[10] It represents a compromise between an input-output and an economic base study. Complete information on sales and purchases is obtained from firms in the major or "basic" sectors only, with the minor or nonbasic sectors treated in an aggregate form. The distribution of sales of, and to, minor sectors and the flows between each of them and the households remain unknown.

Routing and Pricing

The method of pricing and the treatment of tertiary sectors in an input-output system are two closely related issues which confront the analyst with a major difficulty. Both revolve around routing or rather the deviations between the paths followed by the goods in reality and those portrayed in the table. Part of the problem is due to the fact that should actual transactions be described in the table, the very interindustry links to be analysed would be missing. The following hypothetical example, in which X_1 and X_2 are producing sectors and X_3 is a tertiary or service sector, illustrates the loss of connection between producing sectors when actual flows only are described:

Case 1

	X_1	X_2	X_3	Y	Σ
X_1	0	0	110	0	110
X_2	0	0	50	0	50
X_3	10	30	0	160	200
V	100	20	40	0	160
Σ	110	50	200	160	520

In the above table, goods are recorded at selling or producers' prices. The table duly records transactions between the first two or the producing sectors, with sector three representing the intermediaries—the trade and transport services—but it fails to indicate the technical links between the producing industries. In the above case, with accounts limited to two manufacturing sectors only, the flows between Industry 1 and Industry 2 can be reconstructed, but for many industries this would be no longer possible, defeating the very purpose of interindustry analysis.

The following two methods of constructing input-output tables remedy some of the deficiencies of direct recording of actual flows. Both are indirect but while case 2 records flows at producers' costs with the values of services charged separately, in case 3 the distribution costs are absorbed by producers and the full prices charged to customers indicated in the appropriate cells. The overhead charges of the tertiary sector recorded in the third row amount to 20 percent of the selling prices, or 25 percent of producers' costs. Notice that the row totals

Case 2

	X_1	X_2	X_3	Y	Σ
X_1	0	24	0	86	110
X_2	8	0	0	42	50
X_3	2	6	0	32	40
V	100	20	40	0	160
Σ	110	50	40	160	360

Case 3

	X_1	X_2	X_3	Y	Σ
X_1	0	30	0	107.5	137.5
X_2	10	0	0	52.5	62.5
X_3	27.5	12.5	0		40
V	100	20	40	0	160
Σ	137.5	62.5	40	160	400

are identical in all three cases, except for the tertiary (service) sector which in case 2 and 3 records only its own value-added. The method presented in case 2 is usually preferred because the costs of services are likely to vary between classes of buyers, a feature not directly observable when the method illustrated in case 3 is followed. Moreover, the price homogeneity in each row is preserved by charging the value-added generated in tertiary activities directly to the user of the product.

In income and product accounts as well as in financial flows analysis, market prices are used as far as possible, but in interindustry accounts, indirect taxes may gravely distort the picture, particularly if different tax rates are imposed on various categories of final and intermediate buyers. Two methods of indirect taxation are possible although the systems encountered in reality are usually a combination of both: (1) a uniform output or excise tax which differentiates only between commodities, or (2) a tax rate which differs according to buyers, with businesses usually exempt from sales taxes.

In the first case, valuation for purposes of interindustry analysis can be based on either market prices or factor costs, as the only difference would be a change in scale. In the second case, valuation at market prices would group in each row entries based on different prices, yielding a table useless for most analytical purposes. For this reason, indirect taxes are usually removed from the structural matrix.

The impact of indirect taxes can be illustrated with the help of a hypothetical example. Let us assume that all indirect taxes are charged in the following way:

Industry 1 = 30%

Industry 2 = 20%

Industry 3 = 0%

In terms of the previous input-output table this would mean that Industry 1 would pay 30 percent from $110 or $33. In addition, however, Industry 1 buys $8 worth of inputs from Industry 2 which are taxed at the rate of 20 percent at source, or $1.60. Moreover, by an extension of this reasoning some of the inputs used by Industry 2 are also already taxed, which gives rise to an interactive process. The total indirect taxes can obviously be ascertained with the help of the inverse matrix. In the present case each dollar of commodities billed to final consumers by the various industries is divided as follows between factor costs and indirect taxes:

Industry	Price	Factor Costs	Indirect Taxes
1	1.000	0.674	0.326
2	1.000	0.643	0.357
3	1.000	1.000	0

In order to transform an interindustry flow table presented in terms of producers' prices to one cast in terms of factor costs, the latter has to be postmultiplied by a vector of factor cost contents per unit of output. In symbols the above amounts to $A^* = AF$; where:

A^* = table of interindustry flows in terms of factor costs;

A = table of interindustry flows in terms of producers' prices less services (Case 2);

F = vector of factor cost contents per unit output of various sectors.

In terms of the previous example this yields:

Case 4

	X_1	X_2	X_3	Y	Σ
X_1	0	16	0	58	74
X_2	5	0	0	27	32
X_3	2	6	0	32	40
V	67	10	40	0	117
Σ	74	32	40	117	263

The type of price relations used is of critical importance in determining several important features and analytic applications of a system of interindustry accounts. The logic of input-output analysis guarantees that the prices from a consistent system, with the unit cost of any good composed of its material costs or inputs from other sectors, and its direct primary costs such as wages, taxes, profits, depreciation, and imports. Since in principle each sector uses inputs from all other sectors (some at zero level), the price of its products is determined as shown on the following page.

$$p_1 = a_{11}p_1 + a_{21}p_2 + \ldots + a_{n1}p_n + v_1;$$

$$p_1 = a_{12}p_1 + a_{22}p_2 + \ldots + a_{n2}p_n + v_2;$$

$$\vdots$$

$$p_n = a_{1n}p_1 + a_{2n}p_2 + \ldots + a_{nn}p_n + v_n;$$

where

p_i = price of good i

a_{ij} = input coefficient

v_i = sum of primary costs per unit of i.

The system consists of n equations with $2n$ unknowns — the n prices of goods and the n primary costs. Accordingly, if all primary costs were known the system could be solved for prices of the n goods. Conversely, the prices of the n goods could be used to determine primary costs. The general solution of the price system in terms of primary costs takes the form

$$p_1 = a^{11}v_1 + a^{21}v_2 + \ldots a^{n1}v_n;$$

$$p_2 = a^{12}v_1 + a^{22}v_2 + \ldots a^{n2}v_n;$$

$$\vdots$$

$$p_n = a^{1n}v_1 + a^{2n}v_2 + \ldots a^{nn}v_n;$$

where any a^{ij} is an element of the inverse.

The price and quantity solutions are independent of one another in the sense that changes in the relative price of the output of any sector are assumed not to affect its disposition, and price is assumed to be unaffected by changes in the level of output. If the technical coefficients a_{ij} are not interpreted as physical constants but as value ratios dependent upon price changes, the two solutions are no longer independent, and the system loses its simplicity, essential for many empirical applications.

Unit primary costs can be split into several items, each of which, except taxes, may be written as the product of their price and quantity.

$$v_i = p_\varrho \ell_i + p_k k_i + p_m m_i + t_i;$$

where

ℓ_i = quantity of labor used per unit output of i;

k_i = quantity of capital used per unit output of i;

m_i = quantity of imports used per unit output of i;

p_ϱ = price of labor;

p_k = price of capital;

p_m = price of imports;

t_i = taxes per unit of output.

If the component factors are substituted for v_i, the resulting system has many more unknowns than equations. Consequently, for an empirically useful system permitting analysis of price-cost relations, the number of primary costs is often reduced to two—labor and nonlabor—yielding

$$v_i = p_\varrho \ell_i + \pi_i;$$

where π_i = all nonlabor cost elements.

Both p_ϱ and π_i must be given in order to obtain a general solution, but since ℓ_i is often a given coefficient, this is tantamount to a single unknown factor input. The distinction between labor and nonlabor costs is useful because of the size of labor costs and the possibility of its measurement in physical units. An empirically useful system then takes the following form:

$$p_1 = a_{11}p_1 + a_{21}p_2 + \ldots + a_{n1}p_n + \ell_1 p_\varrho + \pi_1;$$
$$p_2 = a_{12}p_1 + a_{22}p_2 + \ldots + a_{n2}p_n + \ell_2 p_\varrho + \pi_2;$$
$$\vdots$$
$$p_n = a_{1n}p_1 + a_{2n}p_2 + \ldots + a_{nn}p_n + \ell_n p_\varrho + \pi_n;$$

the elements a_{ij}, ℓ_i and π_i are all constants, so that the system is comprised of n equations in $(n+1)$ unknowns (n p_i's and p_ϱ). In order to obtain a solution, it is necessary to specify one price. The price of labor is often selected as numeraire with the effects of changes in wages accounted for by specifying appropriate values for p_ϱ. Similarly, the effects of changes in taxes, depreciation, imports, and other elements or primary costs are determined by specifying changes in π_i. In summary then,

$$p_j = \sum_j a^{ji} v_i = \sum_j a^{ji} (\ell_i p_\varrho + \pi_i) = \sum_j a^{ji} \ell_i p_\varrho + \sum_j a^{ji} \pi_i;$$

and choosing $p_\varrho = 1$ as numeraire

$$p_j = \sum_j a^{ji}\ell_i + \sum_j a^{ji}\pi_i;$$

The input-output model, which provides a simple way of analyzing the relationship between prices of goods and factors in an economy, may be used in order to assess the differences between prices of groups of goods in advanced and stagnating regions and of the repercussions of differences between the relative prices of labor and capital. It is frequently applied for estimating the consequences of a change in any one price upon the other parts of the price system, although it cannot be used in order to study the effects of a change in price upon the quantities of goods consumed or produced. In centrally planned economies, input-output has been widely used in order to determine the system of prices to be decreed by the government, while in market economies the model has been applied in order to evaluate the effects of such events as changes in the prices of coal, general imports, wage increases greater than productivity, legislation for equal pay for men and women, and changes in rates of taxation.

The limitations in the use of the model for studying price systems stem from the following major causes:

1. Even a very large input-output table lists only aggregates of often heterogeneous commodities. Hence, input-output provides a framework for computing consistent indexes of prices, rather than individual commodity prices.

2. Many prices such as tobacco, alcohol, and housing rents include elements of special taxes or subsidies and deviate from total factor costs.

3. An efficient price system is not based on considerations of costs of production alone. Some account is taken of usefulness of the product, expressed as demand. In fact, even in centrally planned economies, some retail prices, notably of agricultural products, are strongly influenced by market supply and demand and deviate from input-output computations.

Returning to problems related to the construction of regional input-output tables from original data, an efficient method of handling interindustry accounts is to delay the aggregation of commodities and activities into sectors. The result is a rectangular array with columns corresponding to sectors and rows to commodities. One of the early studies of this type has been carried out in the Province of Quebec.[11] The original flow table covered sixty sectors and 250 commodities and services. The table of coefficients was calculated in marginal or incremental terms. The model defined a one-to-one correspondence between commodities and activities while at the same time introducing explicitly the distinction between technical and commercial relations. These two features, incidentally, were present in both Stone's and Moses' model,[12] but the Quebec study sent further by taking into account nonproportional outputs, capacity limits, and changes in input structure resulting from changes in the structure of demand, thus resembling a linear programming approach.

The original data table of the system can be represented by a partitioned matrix AB. Part A is a 150 x 60 matrix of inputs at factor costs with the markups added in the last row, while part B collects indirect taxes, imports and factor payments, or value-added.

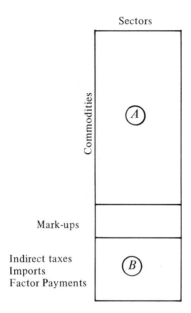

In order to derive an intersectoral flow matrix, AB has to be premultiplied by a weight matrix G, the entries of which conform to

$$\sum_{i=1}^{60} g_{ij} = 1;$$

or all columns add to unity. The result is an intersectoral 60 x 60 matrix C.

The weight matrix distributes the production of each commodity among sectors. In order to have the tables in terms of producers' prices, the markups have to be removed both from the intersectoral flow matrix and from the weight matrix. Hence, the markups column in the weight matrix G has only one entry equal to unity. Its role is straightforward: it transfers the charges for services to a sector "services" in the resulting matrix via the dummy sector "markups."

$$C = G(AB)$$

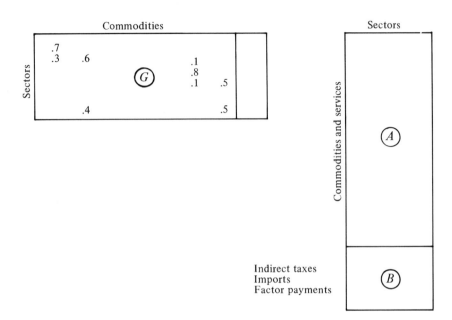

The model can be further refined by removing indirect taxes and imports from the B submatrix, since they refer to commodities rather than to sectors. They properly form part of the G matrix, although for purposes of exposition a separate Q submatrix may be set up.

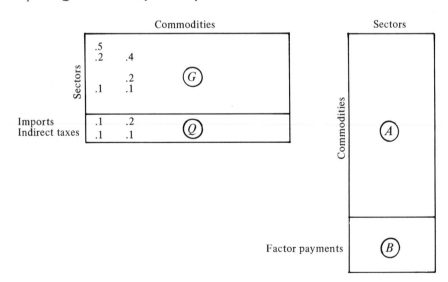

Now

$$\sum_{i=1}^{n} (g_{ij} + q_{ij}) = 1;$$

Rectangular matrices confer great flexibility upon the system. In addition to the obvious convenience at the data-collecting stage, they are eminently suitable for handling capacity constraints. If one assumes that demand is always satisfied, bottlenecks can appear only in terms of sectors but not in terms of commodities. Hence, as soon as a capacity limit is reached demand should be shifted to another sector or, as is most often the case, to imports. Step functions and diagonal matrices have to be introduced for this purpose, but first the system has to be reformulated, by decomposing the Leontief inverse into

$$(I - C)^{-1} = I + C^1 + C^2 + C^3 + \ldots + C^n;$$

Hence, $\qquad x = y + Cy + C^2y + C^3y + \ldots + C^ny;$

and $\qquad v = By + BCy = BC^2y + BC^3y + \ldots + BC^ny;$

or more generally, $x_n = Cx_{n-1};$

and $\qquad v_k = Bx_k;$

It is in the course of the iterative process that the switch can be programmed as soon as capacity is reached. The vectors of intermediate outputs (t_k) can be calculated in terms of commodities, since

$$t_k = Ax_{k-1}$$

and $\qquad x_k = Gt_k;$

while total output levels and factor payments are equal respectively to

$$x = \sum_{n=0}^{\infty} x_n;$$

$$v = \sum_{n=0}^{\infty} v_n = B\sum_{n=0}^{\infty} x_n;$$

Thus the system confers great flexibility and allows at each stage for mapping from the vector space of commodities to the vector of sectors.

Stability of Coefficients

The use of the technical interindustry coefficients for forecasting future events or contingencies is always one of the major immediate or ultimate objectives in constructing input-output tables. Yet any analytic or forecasting applications of the coefficients requires that they be relatively stable over time.

Because of the great importance of this issue, a considerable amount of research has been devoted to it over the past two decades. The numerous attempts at quantifying the variability of the coefficients address themselves to some or all of the following related questions: (1) how to measure and evaluate the intertemporal discrepancies, (2) how to identify the sources of instability, and (3) how to improve the methodology of calculating the coefficients.

The first problem confronting any research is the statistical one of making the tables compiled at different times comparable to one another in the face of changes in industrial classification used. While the difficulties involved are as a rule very considerable, the conceptual aspect of defining criteria for measuring and evaluating the seriousness of the discrepancies rightly deserves even more attention. It is obviously easy to compute—once the tables have been made comparable—the absolute and relative differences between pairs of coefficients, as well as the mean difference, the interquantile or decile ranges, and other measures describing the distribution of discrepancies. Since the various coefficients refer to sectors and flows of widely differing importance to the economy, the results could be made more meaningful by weighting them explicitly by the size of flows before computing the aggregate measures referring to the whole array. Once the latter have been calculated, their evaluation could be left to intuition or some statistical tests of significance could be applied, but this begs the question of the value of the model for economic analyses.

More promising appears to be a rigorous examination of the effects of errors in technical coefficients on the projected levels of operation of various sectors. The importance of errors is here a function of the purpose of the study. For example, the 1953 research program sponsored by the U.S. government[13] established allowable errors in various coefficients, ranging from 3 to 100 percent, which would not preclude the usefulness of the tables for testing the effects of economic war mobilization. Next, all coefficients, one after another, were increased by 100 percent and the effects of such changes upon the other coefficients recorded. It is of some interest that out of 10,000 nonzero coefficients of the 190 x 190 1947 table, only 320 were identified as sensitive to errors. Actually, all industries were affected by changes in at least one a_{ij}; but 134 industries were affected by drastic changes in less than 5 coefficients and 176 industries in less than 10. This approach can be extended to a study of changes in coefficients over a number of years.

Tests applied to individual industries do not reveal the cumulative effects of errors. For overall tests, backward projections are customarily used or, alternatively, projections from a base in the past to the present. Again, statistical difficulties are often encountered in obtaining data on final demand and total output in the industrial breakdown used in the input-output tables. In order to interpret the results of overall tests, these are compared with "naive" projections treated as null hypothesis. Forecasts of each industry's level of output in the target year, calculated as the same proportion of the total final demand as in the base year, are often used as "naive" projections. Alternatively, it is assumed that the share of each industry's output in the target year GNP will be the same as in the base year. Total target-year final demand and GNP are obviously known.

The approach increasingly used in order to assess the quality of input-output tables is based on information theory.[14] Since all entries in a table of input-output coefficients are positive fractions and all columns add up to one, the coefficients can be mathematically regarded as probabilities. The transpose of the table does not differ thus in its form and basic properties from a matrix of transition probabilities. Since entries in an input-output coefficients matrix may be viewed as probabilities, it may be fruitful to consider two tables dealing with the same region, but prepared in the years (t) and $(t+1)$ respectively as two consecutive forecasts of a set of future events. The "forecast" made in the year $(t+1)$ would be generally better, or more reliable, but its information content would depend upon the accuracy of the prior message, or the table for year (t). The better, or less divergent from the target-date table, the values in the (t) year table are, the smaller is the information content of the latter $(t+1)$ year table. These ideas can be succinctly expressed in the following formula:

$$I(A' : A^{t+1}) - I(A' : A^t) = \sum_i \sum_j a'_{ij} \log_2 \frac{a^{t+1}_{ij}}{a^t_{ij}} ;$$

where

$I(A' : A^{t+1}) =$ information content of target year table A' given the table for year $(t+1)$, or equivalently the information value of the prior table A^{t+1}.

$I(A' : A^t)$ =   information value of table A^t.

The term $I(A' : A^{t+1}) - I(A' : A^t)$ measures the increase in our knowledge due to table A^{t+1} given our prior knowledge of A^t. The term $I(A' : A^{t+1}) - I(A' - A^t)$ may be also interpreted as reduction of information content of A^{t+1} caused by the earlier message A^t. The lesser the divergence between the two, the smaller is the information content of the latter and the lower value will the above expression assume. For practical reasons, and in keeping with the objective of measuring changes over time in input-output coefficients, the coefficients for the year $(t + 1)$ could be used as weights instead of those of the hypothetical target year T. The expression measuring the divergence would then become

$$I(A^{t+1}: A^t) = \sum_i \sum_j \left| a_{ij}^{t+1} \log_2 \frac{a_{ij}^{t+1}}{a_{ij}^t} \right| ;$$

An application of this method to the fifteen largest sectors of the ten Dutch 35 x 35 national input-output tables for the years 1948-57 yielded some interesting results. It turned out that the inaccuracy increased almost monotonically and very rapidly with the passage of time, from around 170×10^{-5} bits on the average for the "best" of the fifteen sectors over a time span of one year, to around 20.490×10^{-5} for the "worst" sector over eight years. Further analysis revealed that the stability of coefficients pertaining to primary inputs (wages, imports, and profits) was far greater than of those pertaining to interindustry flows. Yet, because of the highly aggregated level at which the inquiry was conducted, with all inputs of any of the fifteen largest sectors grouped in eight flows, no further insights into the causes of variability were gained.

Generally, some of the variability is undoubtedly due to a host of random factors such as differences in data sources and statistical methods for estimating the technical relationships. A good deal would ordinarily also depend upon the level of aggregation. Changes in production processes due to introduction of new products, substitution of new materials for old, new technologies or substitution of inputs because of changes in their relative prices occur slowly and in orderly fashion. They affect primarily the marginal or incremental coefficients and more gradually the total existing capacity. Because these changes and changes in production mix are less severe the larger and more heterogeneous the sector affected, one would expect the more aggregated tables to show lesser variability. The studies of Sevaldson[15] and Vaccara[16] bear this out, while Isard and Langford[17] have found new confirmation that the differences in input structure among firms belonging to the same sector are greater than variability in coefficients over time. Engineering-type coefficients may be especially misleading in this respect.

The treatment of by-products, secondary and joint products, and of competitive imports can have considerable influence on the stability over time of input-output coefficients. The usually adopted approach, whereby all products other than primary are transferred to the sectors whose main line of activity they form, builds into the table a set of base-year relationships which may no longer correspond to later year realities and in fact may vary quite randomly over time.

The main source of concern is, however, often the change in physical requirements associated with changing technology. The trends over time in input-output coefficients revealed by the work of Sevaldson[18] point strongly to this as a major source of variability. The presence of trends may also be related to a basic divergence between the actual and the strictly proportional relationship assumed between changes in inputs and outputs.

Finally, the often-adopted practice of adjusting for changes in the relative price levels by using price deflators may sometimes aggravate the divergences. The price deflators to be used would have to be specifically developed for each cell to account for changes in the product mix. Quite often the deflated coefficients show greater variability than those expressed in current dollars.[19]

Several approaches have been attempted and explored in order to insure greater stability of input-output coefficients. One interesting approach consists of replacing the intersectoral technological coefficients by commodity coefficients.[20] It is reasonable to assume that commodity technology coefficients are more stable than industrial structures. The latter require not only the assumption of an unchanging technology but also stability of the industrial mix of all sectors. Unfortunately, the transition to sectoral coefficients cannot be avoided, not only because of the obvious necessity of grouping the thousands of articles produced by a modern economy, but also because primary inputs are much more likely to be tied to industry outputs. Delaying the aggregation of commodities into sectors until the latter stages of analysis opens up, nonetheless, interesting possibilities of evaluating separately and in more detail the contributions of secondary and by-products.

Other approaches treat fixed and variable costs separately, thus approximating more closely the situation prevailing in many enterprises. Similar objectives are served by removing capital coefficients from the matrix, dealing separately with them and introducing explicitly into the model changes in technology occurring whenever capacity constraints become binding. Linear programming models usually have to be introduced for handling these problems. Some of these have been briefly alluded to in the preceding section.

An object of major criticism of the input-output model has been the underlying assumption of a linear homogeneous production function. For a dynamic analysis of stability of coefficients the function does not allow taking into account technological changes due to learning, increasing sophistication of the products or simply emerging economies of scale. Some attempts[21] have been made at replacing in interindustry studies the Leontief production function by an exponential formulation of the Cobb-Douglas type, defining the flow from industry i to j as

$$x_{ij} = A X_j^\alpha ;$$

where A, α = parameters with

$$\alpha > 0; \text{ and } 0 < A < \infty ;$$

$\alpha = 1$ would obviously correspond to the Leontief case. The model assumes that changes over time in the input requirement would be a function of the level of output of the purchasing sector, or

$$\frac{dx_{ij}}{dX_j} = x'_{ij} = A\alpha X_j^{\alpha-1} = c_{ij}X_j^{\alpha-1} ;$$

where

$c_{ij} = A\alpha$; and is different from the simple input-output coefficients. x'_{ij} is always positive and is an increasing function of X_j for $\alpha > 1$, decreasing for $\alpha < 1$, and constant for $\alpha = 1$. The two parameters A and α can be estimated from time series data in log form:

$$\log x_{ij} = \log A + \alpha \log X_j ;$$

The studies carried out in Turin show more stable relationships, due to time trends in the variables, and highly significant regression and correlation coefficients.

National and Regional Tables

One of the major limitations in the use of input-output analysis in regional studies is the considerable cost and effort involved in the construction of interindustry flow tables. The regional economist, therefore, is often inclined to use either national coefficients or coefficients originally derived for other regions as a short-cut method for avoiding the substantial amount of field work. The drawbacks of using surrogate coefficients are rather obvious, and this crude method is rarely used effectively.

There have been numerous attempts over the past years at assessing the feasibility of using national coefficients for regional studies. One of the most rigorous examinations was by Shen.[22] He derived an estimate of input-output coefficients for New England from the 1947 U.S. table. The national manufacturing sectors were grouped into a 20 x 20 matrix covering the two-digit SIC manufacturing groups. Value-added by New England manufacturing industries provided the weights for the grouping process. In the absence of a regional input-output study based on direct field surveys, he could not assess the ensuing errors.

The sources of divergence between national and regional input-output coefficients have been abundantly discussed in the literature. The most important ones appear to be related to differences in industrial mix and in the relative importance and structure of foreign trade. Foreign trade is an especially sensitive issue at the regional level because of the notorious lack of reliable data on interregional flows. In addition, the surrogate tables of coefficients are often several years old, which further impairs their value. On the other hand, it is not intuitively obvious whether differences in technology and in the relative prices of inputs between regions within a country as economically integrated as the United States are important.

More recently the problem has been systematically explored in another study.[23] The major objectives of the research were to:

1. Develop and test a model for adjusting national input-output coefficients so as to eliminate all or part of the differences due to (a) changes in the relative level of prices over time, (b) degree of fabrication, (c) composition of demand, (d) industry mix, and (e) structure of imports.

2. Determine which sectors could be handled by short-cut methods without destroying the analytic and forecasting value of the input-output table and which sectors would have to be covered by a field study.

3. Analyze the probable errors introduced by the use of the model and compare these with savings in cost and time.

A case study approach was used in attempting to construct the state of Washington input-output table for 1963 with the help of national input-output coefficients and such information as is readily available from regional income accounts.[24] The results were compared with the Washington State table based on direct data.

The first task was to estimate regional input-output coefficients using as the only source of information regional income and product accounts disaggregated by sectors. This amounts to the knowledge of the bill of goods and of the row and column totals and is by itself insufficient for reconstructing the intersectoral flows. The problem has too many degrees of freedom. In order to reach a solution, an additional source of information is required, the most readily available and frequently used being the national table of technical input-output coefficients. The national coefficients had to be adjusted in order to yield the regional row and column totals when multiplied by total regional output, by making the following assumptions:

1. Price differences operate uniformly along rows; whenever there is a difference in the average prices of the products of a sector, it is charged in the same proportion to all users.

2. Whenever there is substitution of one product for another due to differences in demand or industry mix, it affects all users to the same extent.

3. Wherever there is a change in the degree of fabrication, it uniformly affects all productive processes.

The corollary of the last two assumptions is that differences in selling patterns and/or differences in technology operate uniformly along rows and columns, respectively.

In order to explain the model,[25] the following definitions are introduced:

A = national (1958) input-output coefficients matrix;

B = regional (Washington State 1963) input-output coefficients matrix;

x = regional vector of gross outputs by sector;

t = regional vector of intermediate outputs (row totals);

z = regional vector of intermediate inputs (column totals);

G = grouping matrix;

G_w = weight matrix, where $g_{w.ij} = 0, i, w_{ij}$;

$$0 \leqslant g_{v.ij} \leqslant 1 \text{ and } \sum_{i=1}^{n} g_{w.ij} = 1;$$

p = vector of price ratios $\dfrac{1963}{1958}$;

i = identity vector.

Capital letters refer to matrices.

Lower case letters refer to vectors.

Capped letters refer to diagonal matrices obtained from vectors.

Superscripts: '   = transpose;

              r = regional;

            -1 = inverse or, in case of a diagonal matrix, another diagonal matrix whose nonzero elements are reciprocals of the original matrix.

Subscripts: $1, 2, 3, \ldots, n$ refer to successive estimates.

The equation numbers and steps in the computer program are synonymous.

First the national matrix was adjusted for differences in relative price levels between 1958 and 1963 and both were reduced to the same dimensions.

$$A_1 = \hat{p} A \hat{p}^{-1}; \tag{5-18}$$

$$A_2 = G A G_w'; \tag{5-19}$$

$$B_1 = G^r B G_w^{r.'}; \tag{5-20}$$

Next, it is obviously true that

$$t_2 = A_2 x; \tag{5-21}$$

where t_2 is an estimate of the known t.

Ordinarily $t_2 \neq t$; however,

$$\hat{t}\,\hat{t}_2^{-1}\,\hat{t}_2 = \hat{t}\,\hat{t}_2^{-1}\,A_2\hat{x}; \tag{5-22}$$

Hence,

$$\hat{t} = \hat{t}\,\hat{t}_2^{-1}\,A_2\hat{x}; \tag{5-23}$$

$$A_3 = \hat{t}\,\hat{t}_2^{-1}\,A_2; \tag{5-24}$$

is an improved estimate of B adjusted for row totals, but not for column totals. Now,

$$z_3 = x'A_3'; \tag{5-25}$$

$$\hat{z}\,\hat{z}_3^{-1}\,\hat{z}_3 = \hat{z}\,\hat{z}_3^{-1}\,\hat{x}A_3'; \tag{5-26}$$

$$z = \hat{x}\,(A_3\,\hat{z}\,\hat{z}_3^{-1})'; \tag{5-27}$$

and

$$A_4 = A_3\,\hat{z}\,\hat{z}_3^{-1}; \tag{5-28}$$

is a new improved estimate of B now adjusted for column totals but no longer for row totals. One can use, however, A_4 in equation (5-21) and obtain A_5 in equation (5-24) which then can be used in equation (5-25) and so on. In the corresponding computer program this forms a loop.

The only remaining problem is to find out whether the process converges, at what speed, and whether the limit toward which it converges is the B matrix of true regional coefficients.

The above model was used for testing six different cases in order to isolate the effects of (1) degree of aggregation (size of the matrix of coefficients), (2) differences in the relative level of prices between 1958 and 1963, and (3) differences in the relative size and structure of Washington State and U.S. imports. More specifically, the following cases were studied.

Case I: Both the U.S. and the 54 x 54 Washington State input-output coefficients matrices were aggregated to size 43 x 43 by the use of appropriate grouping and weighting matrices in steps (5-19) and (5-20) of the program. The relative importance of the various sectors in the national and Washington State economy provided the respective weights.

No adjustments were made for differences and changes in the relative price levels; that is, step (5-18) of the program was omitted.

Case II: Repeated case I except that both the U.S. and Washington State matrices were aggregated to size 36 x 36.

Case III: Both matrices were aggregated to size 43 x 43. The U.S. matrix was adjusted for changes in the relative price levels between 1958-63. This was accomplished in step (5-24).

Case IV: Repeated case III except that both the U.S. and Washington State matrices were aggregated to size 36 x 36.

Case V: Both matrices were aggregated to size 36 x 36. The Washington State matrix was adjusted by including domestic imports in the appropriate sectors. The input-output coefficients obtained by applying the model to the U.S. input-output matrix were compared with Washington State coefficients which included inputs per dollar of output imported from the rest of the United States as well as those obtained from other industries in the state.

Case VI: Repeated case V except the U.S. matrix was adjusted for changes in the relative price levels between 1958-63.

In order to assess the validity of the results, the absolute deviations between the Washington State coefficients estimated from national coefficients with the help of the model and the "true" coefficients were calculated. These deviations were transformed into percentages and the mean, standard deviation, and distribution by deciles of errors were derived. More formally, the program covered the following steps:

$$D_1 = B_1 - A_4;$$ (5-29)

$$d^*_{1.ij} = \left[\frac{d_{1.ij}}{b_{1.ij}} \right] ; \text{ where } b_{ij} \neq 0;$$ (5-30)

$$\text{Mean of } D^*_1 = \frac{\sum_i \sum_j d^*_{1.ij}}{m} ;$$ (5-31)

$$\text{Standard deviation of } D^*_1 = \sqrt{ \frac{\sum_i \sum_j d^{*2}_{1.ij}}{m} - \left[\frac{\sum_i \sum_j d^*_{1.ij}}{m} \right]^2 }$$ (5-32)

where

D_1 = matrix of absolute deviations between the calculated and real coefficients;

D^*_1 = matrix of deviations between the calculated and real coefficients expressed as percentages of the real coefficients;

$d_{1.ij}$ = elements of the D_1 matrix;

b_{ij} = elements of the B matrix;

$d^*_{1.ij}$ = elements of the D^*_1 matrix;

m = number of entries in the D^*_1 matrix.

These calculations were repeated after each iteration of the model. Together with the distribution of percentage deviations by deciles, they enable a crude assessment of the relative value of the various approaches and hypotheses tested. The major drawback appears to be, however, the way in which the deviations have been implicitly weighted. Notice that a deviation from a small "true" coefficient affects the end result far more than an equal deviation from a large coefficient. Weighting the deviations by the absolute size of the flows is of no analytic interest since these flows would refer to one particular region only and would not necessarily help to test the basic assumptions of the method used. Obviously, size of flows and of sectors varies greatly from one region to another.

In order to at least partly overcome this shortcoming, the information-theory approach was also used for measuring the accuracy of input-output coefficients. The estimated Washington State input-output table (A_n) was treated as a forecast of the "true" table (B), the information content which was defined as

$$I(B: A_n) = \sum_i \sum_j \left| b_{ij} \log_2 \frac{b_{ij}}{a_{n.ij}} \right|;$$

where each estimate is weighted by the "true" coefficient, b_{ij}.

The case study involved the use of the following sources of data:

1. United States Input-Output Coefficients Table, 1958, which is a 77 x 77 matrix.[26] This table was enlarged to an 89 x 89 table by including additional information provided by the Office of Business Economics.[27] More specifically, three sectors were expanded: (a) food and kindred products, to nine separate sectors; (b) primary nonferrous metals manufacturing, to three sectors; (c) electric, gas, water, and sanitary services, also to three sectors.

2. The Washington State Input-Output Tables for 1963, which included a cross-flows table and a 54 x 54 table of coefficients.

3. Washington State Input-Output Technical Coefficients Table for 1963, calculated in the following way. First, the Washington State gross-flows table was reduced to size 46 x 46. Next, the gross flows and the distribution of Washington State imports from the rest of the United States by receiving sectors were added together. Finally, the flow table was converted into a technical coefficients table.

4. Wholesale price indexes for 89 sectors showing average changes from 1958 to 1963.[28]

5. Sales, receipts, value-added, and value of shipments data for the United

States and Washington State, which were used to calculate the weights needed for aggregating coefficients, as elements of the weighting matrices.[29]

Six different cases were considered and are summarized in Table 5-1. The results were obtained after ten iterations of the process. The striking fact is that the process converges extremely rapidly. As a matter of fact, the differences in the results obtained after ten iterations and those obtained after the first iteration were never nearer than in fourth or fifth decimal place. In most cases, there were no differences whatsoever.

The results almost invariably give rise to different interpretations, depending on whether one considers the mean percentage errors or the "I" values. The mean percentage errors, however, were implicitly weighted inversely to the size of the coefficients. Hence, the analysis was based mainly on the "I" values.

The first six cases summarized in the table above show very wide deviations between the estimates and the real matrix. Whichever way one looks at them, they seem to far exceed any tolerance limits. The adjustment for domestic imports has clearly increased the errors and diminished the value of the estimates. This rather surprising result seems to have something to do with the differences in routing used in the U.S. and Washington tables.

On purely theoretical grounds one would expect the following to be the main sources of deviations: (1) differences in routing practices, (2) fundamental differences in natural conditions, and (3) specialization of the regional economy in some particular sectors.

Differences in the routing practices would be particularly significant in the tertiary sectors. The errors in the seven tertiary sectors (communications, electric companies, gas companies, water services, wholesale and retail trade, finance and insurance, real estate, business services, and personal services) were particularly large. The grouping of the seven tertiary sectors into two considerably improved the results.[30] Of the six cases examined, case II, in which both matrices had been aggregated to order 36 x 36 through grouping of the tertiary sectors and without adjustments for prices or domestic imports, yielded the best results.

Primary activities, which on theoretical grounds were expected to yield poor results, were represented by four sectors: agricultural crops, livestock products, forestry and fishing, and mining. The errors in these sectors were over two standard deviations larger than the mean errors of the whole array.

It can be safely assumed that these high errors can be largely explained by the wide range of activities grouped together. Agricultural crops in Washington State, for example, would include different activities from the U.S. average. This will be even more true of mining, livestock products, or forestry and fishing. Many types of mining included in the U.S. sector do not exist in Washington State.

The last group of sectors in which large deviations were expected to occur were those in which the regional economy is highly specialized. Measuring the

Table 5-1
Deviations between Estimated and "True" Regional Input-Output Coefficients

Case	I	II	III	IV	V	VI	VII[a]
Matrix Size	43 x 43	36 x 36	43 x 43	36 x 36	36 x 36	36 x 36	28 x 28
Price Adjustments	No	No	Yes	Yes	No	Yes	No
Domestic Imports Adjustments	No	No	No	No	Yes	Yes	No
Mean Percentage Error of Coefficients	58.65	71.73	59.03	69.92	80.81	79.20	38.93
Standard Deviation of Percentage Error	2.211	3.716	2.202	3.378	6.314	6.177	2.160
I Values[b]	9.085	6.279	9.266	6.408	54.169	54.262	0.779

[a]Repeats II after removing "problem" sectors (1, 2, 3, 4, 8, 14, 16, 24).

[b]
$$I(B_1 : A_{10}) = \sum_i \sum_j \left| b_{ij} \log_2 \frac{b_{ij}}{a_{n.ij}} \right|$$

degree of specialization by location quotients[31] it is found that six out of the thirty-six sectors had location quotients of 2.0 or more:

3)	Forestry and fishing	3.1
8)	Canning and preserving	2.5
14)	Lumber and wood products	5.1
16)	Paper products	2.0
24)	Nonferrous metals manufacturing	2.4
31)	Aerospace industry	7.7

Of the six sectors, forestry and fishing, a primary industry, has been explained above, while aerospace industry is a case apart.

It seems that sectors in which the regional economy is highly specialized have a different technology from the national average, and their input-output coefficients cannot be estimated by short-cut methods. This is not true, however, for the aerospace industry. In this case, the coefficients estimated on the basis of the U.S. table were quite close to actual. This is undoubtedly due to the fact that aerospace industry in Washington State forms an important part of the national total and therefore influences the structure of national coefficients. In fact, on the basis of employment it would appear that 11 percent of the U.S. aerospace industry is concentrated in this state.

By removing eight sectors (four primary industries and four industries in which Washington State is specialized) from the 36 x 36 table, a considerable decrease in the "I" value was achieved. Notice the "I" value becomes 0.799 after removing the eight sectors, certainly an acceptable level of error by any standard.

It appears, thus, that while national input-output tables cannot be used for purposes of regional studies without considerable adjustments, acceptable results can be achieved by the methods tried on the Washington State table.

In order to obtain acceptable results it seems important (1) to exclude the tertiary sectors through aggregation; and (2) to use field surveys in order to obtain input-output coefficients for (a) primary industries, and (b) industries in which the regional economy is specialized. Successive iterations after the first one, price adjustments, and adjustments for domestic imports do not seem to add anything to the quality of results.

Chapter 5 Appendix
Basic Notions of Information Theory

The use of logs to base 2 is well established in information theory, both because of its additive properties and because of the obvious convenience in measuring the information content of messages referring to two mutually exclusive and equiprobable events. More generally, the information content of any message which announces the occurrence of an event is defined as a function of the probability or likelihood of the event taking place. The function should be decreasing, since the less likely the event E, the greater is the information content of the message announcing its occurrence. Thus

$$I = \log \frac{1}{p};$$

where

$I =$ information content of the message,
$p =$ prior probability of the event described in the message.

The function takes arbitrarily large values for $p = 0$ and decreases to zero for $p = 1$. The information content of a message informing of an event certain to occur is zero.

In case of two independent events E_1 and E_2 with probabilities p_1 and p_2, the probability of their joint occurrence is $p_1 p_2$ and the information content of the message that both occurred is

$$I = \log \frac{1}{p_1 p_2} = \log \frac{1}{p_1} + \log \frac{1}{p_2};$$

so that the value of the "double" message is equal to the sum of two separate messages informing the two events. The use of logs to base 2 is particularly convenient in cases of statements concerning two alternative events, each of which has a 50 percent likelihood of happening. The information content of the message that one of them took place, or of one "bit," is

$$I = \log_2 \frac{1}{0.5} = 1;$$

In cases of n mutually exclusive events with certainty that one will be realized, the information content of the message that one of them occurred is $\log_2 \left(\frac{1}{p_i} \right)$. This message is received with probability p_i, and hence the expected information content of the message is

$$I = \sum_{i=1}^{n} p_i \log \frac{1}{p_i} = -\sum_{i=1}^{n} p_i \log p_i;$$

The function attains maximum values when all p_i's are equal or when dealing with equiprobable events. The expected information content is equal to

$$p \log \frac{1}{p} + p \log \frac{1}{p} + \ldots = (p + p \ldots) \log \frac{1}{p} = \log \frac{1}{p};$$

or the value of a single message, since $\Sigma p = 1$. The expression has zero value when one $p_i = 1$ and all others are equal to zero.

6

Interregional Flows

Construction of Interregional Flow Tables

Economists have long recognized that levels of output, income, and employment in regions which trade with one another are interdependent. Two techniques have been used for studying the existence and strength of the various feedback effects involved: (1) statistical estimation of prices, incomes, and demand propensities, and (2) input-output analysis. The Leontief interindustry model offers the possibility of integrating location theory with a general analysis of production, but it has the serious drawback that it lacks any elements of choice. Moreover, it can explain spatial phenomena only on the assumption of a certain stability in the geographical distribution of production, since it is limited to analyzing changes in capacity.

The simplest framework covering interregional flows can be developed as an extension of income and product accounts. As a first step, an accounts model for a closed system of n regions has to be cast in matrix form by presenting all flows of goods and services, both intra- and interregional, as entries in appropriate cells. By an easy extension, the same method can be applied to open or incomplete systems, treating the rest of the world as another region. For three regions ($n = 3$) the framework is illustrated in Table 6-1. The first subscript indicates the region of origin, the second the region of destination of the various flows. The symbols have the following meanings:

x_{ij} = flows of intermediate products between producing and processing sectors;

C_{ij} = consumption by households and nonprofit organizations;

V_{ij} = capital investments;

G_{ij} = exhaustive government spending, both current and investments;

Y_{ij} = income accruing to factors of production;

F_{ij} = direct and indirect government transfer payments;

U_{ij} = unilateral transfers between households;

D_{ij} = capital consumption;

S_{ij} = savings;

B_{ij} = interregional loans;

133

W_{ij} = indirect taxes less subsidies;

T_{ij} = direct taxes.

Table 6-1
Regional Ordering of Flows

	Region 1				Region 2				Region 3			
Region 1	x_{11}	C_{11}	V_{11}	G_{11}	x_{12}	0	0	0	x_{13}	0	0	0
	Y_{11}	0	0	F_{11}	Y_{12}	U_{12}	0	F_{12}	Y_{13}	U_{13}	0	F_{13}
	D_{11}	S_{11}	0	0	0	0	B_{12}	0	0	0	B_{13}	0
	W_{11}	T_{11}	0	0	W_{12}	T_{12}	0	0	W_{13}	T_{13}	0	0
Region 2	x_{21}	0	0	0	x_{22}	C_{22}	V_{22}	G_{22}	x_{23}	0	0	0
	Y_{21}	U_{21}	0	F_{21}	Y_{22}	0	0	F_{22}	Y_{23}	U_{23}	0	F_{23}
	0	0	B_{21}	0	D_{22}	S_{22}	0	0	0	0	B_{23}	0
	W_{21}	T_{21}	0	0	W_{22}	T_{22}	0	0	W_{23}	T_{23}	0	0
Region 3	x_{31}	0	0	0	x_{32}	0	0	0	x_{33}	C_{33}	V_{33}	G_{33}
	Y_{31}	U_{31}	0	F_{31}	Y_{32}	U_{32}	0	F_{32}	Y_{33}	0	0	F_{33}
	0	0	B_{31}	0	0	0	B_{32}	0	D_{33}	S_{33}	0	0
	W_{31}	T_{31}	0	0	W_{32}	T_{32}	0	0	W_{33}	T_{33}	0	0

The first row summarizes the distribution of products of industries located in region 1, the second row the sources of income of households of region 1, the third sources of financing of local investments, and the fourth sources of government income. Similarly, the first column indicates the inputs both primary and intermediate of industries of region 1, the second column the distribution of expenditures of households of region 1, the third the distribution of savings between investments and interregional loans, and the fourth the major categories of government spending. The blocks on the main diagonal each cover all flows internal to a region while interregional transactions appear in blocks located off the main diagonal. By rearranging the entries, separate interregional accounts can be set up for production, households, savings and investments, and governments. Table 6-2 illustrates such an arrangement with each entry corresponding to a certain class of transactions either intra- or interregional.

If the analysis is conducted at a more disaggregated level, each entry is replaced by a submatrix. In this case the first block represents a complete interregional input-output system of interindustry transactions. Each industry is

Table 6-2
Sectoral Ordering of Flows

	Production			Households			Savings and Investments			Governments		
Production	x_{11}	x_{12}	x_{13}	C_{11}	0	0	V_{11}	0	0	G_{11}	0	0
	x_{21}	x_{22}	x_{23}	0	C_{22}	0	0	V_{22}	0	0	G_{22}	0
	x_{31}	x_{32}	x_{33}	0	0	C_{33}	0	0	V_{33}	0	0	G_{33}
Households	Y_{11}	Y_{12}	Y_{13}	0	U_{12}	U_{13}	0	0	0	F_{11}	F_{12}	F_{13}
	Y_{21}	Y_{22}	Y_{23}	U_{21}	0	U_{23}	0	0	0	F_{21}	F_{22}	F_{23}
	Y_{31}	Y_{32}	Y_{33}	U_{31}	U_{32}	0	0	0	0	F_{31}	F_{32}	F_{33}
Savings and Investments	D_{11}	0	0	S_{11}	0	0	0	B_{12}	B_{13}	0	0	0
	0	D_{22}	0	0	S_{22}	0	B_{21}	0	B_{23}	0	0	0
	0	0	D_{33}	0	0	S_{33}	B_{31}	B_{32}	0	0	0	0
Governments	W_{11}	W_{12}	W_{13}	T_{11}	T_{12}	T_{13}	0	0	0	0	0	0
	W_{21}	W_{22}	W_{23}	T_{21}	T_{22}	T_{23}	0	0	0	0	0	0
	W_{31}	W_{32}	W_{33}	T_{31}	T_{32}	R_{33}	0	0	0	0	0	0

divided into as many sectors as there are regions. This most exacting (as far as data are concerned) system was first proposed by Isard.[1]

The data requirements for implementing it are enormous. It has in fact been utilized only once and even then only on a very small scale.[2] The model is conceptually very attractive since it captures the feedback effects of increased activity in region A on region B, and of B's induced increase on A, in a more precise way than other interregional input-output models. Unfortunately, interregional flow data (X_{ij}) for geographical regions forming subnational units within a country are not immediately available, and cannot be easily reconstructed by sector of origin and destination even with the help of field surveys, while interregional flows of payments to factors of production (Y_{ij}), unilateral transfers (U_{ij}), and loans (B_{ij}) may be hard to get even for regions corresponding to nations.

A possible alternative is to treat the rest of the world, composed in our example of regions 2 and 3, as just one column vector in the bill of goods and one row vector among the primary inputs. This approach has been used quite frequently[3] although at some analytic cost. According to Miller,[4] who has performed some interesting empirical tests, the increase in accuracy resulting from the use of interregional (as opposed to a series of separate regional) input-output models is not significant compared to the higher costs of the more detailed model.

The transition from Isard's full interregional input-output model to a regional one with single row and column summarizing all flows across the region's boundaries, can be formally presented as a process involving two intermediate steps. First, the accounts system outline in Table 6-1 might be bordered by rows and columns containing interregional transactions, while retaining in unchanged form the intraregional ones. Table 6-3 presents the interregional transactions in a simplified form. Notice that, in order to balance the sixteen accounts the terms

$$-\sum_{j}\sum_{k} Y_{jk}; \quad -\sum_{j}\sum_{k} F_{jk}; \quad -\sum_{j}\sum_{k} W_{jk}; \quad \text{for } (j \neq k),$$

representing the negative totals if incomes accruing to factors of production, direct and indirect government transfer payments, and indirect taxes less subsidies have been added. Second, the various entries or submatrices can be again rearranged in order to obtain Table 6-4 organized by type of transaction.[5]

Tables 6-3 and 6-4 are clearly less demanding in terms of data and can be further simplified by netting all interregional flows. Schematically the following relations can be identified in the preceding tables:

Table 6-1	*Table 6-2*
(1) $x + C + V + G = x + Y + D + W$;	(1) $x + C + V + G = x + Y + D + W$;
(2) $Y + F + U \quad = C + S + T + U$;	(2) $Y + U + F \quad = C + U + C + T$;
(3) $D + S + B \quad = V + B$;	(3) $D + S + B \quad = V + B$;
(4) $W + T \quad = G + F$;	(4) $W + T \quad = G + F$;

Table 6-3	*Table 6-4*
(1) $x + Y + W - Y - W = x$	(1) $x + C + V + G = x + Y + D + W$
(2) $U = Y + U + F - Y - F$	(2) $Y + U + F = C + U + S + T$
(3) $B = B$	(3) $V + B = D + S + B$
(4) $F + T - F = W + T - W$	(4) $W + T = G + F$

The reduction in data requirements achieved by transforming Tables 6-1 and 6-2 into Tables 6-3 and 6-4 is illustrated by a comparison between the number of flows, and the number of independent relations for a region.

Tables	*Flows*	*Independent relations*
6-1 and 6-2	24 n	$4n - 1$
6-3 and 6-4	17 n	$4n - 1$

Whenever the number of independent relations is inferior to the number of flows, some of these can be estimated indirectly, as residuals, thus reducing data

Table 6-3
Intranational Ordering of Flows

	Region 1				Region 2				Region 3							
Region 1	x_{11}	C_{11}	V_{11}	G_{11}	0	0	0	0	0	0	0	0	$(x_{12}+x_{13})$	0	0	0
	Y_{11}	0	0	F_{11}	0	0	0	0	0	0	0	0	$(Y_{12}+Y_{13})$	$(U_{12}+U_{13})$	0	0
	D_{11}	S_{11}	0	0	0	0	0	0	0	0	0	0	0	0	$(B_{12}+B_{13})$	0
	W_{11}	T_{11}	0	0	0	0	0	0	0	0	0	0	$(W_{12}+W_{13})$	0	0	0
Region 2	0	0	0	0	x_{22}	C_{22}	V_{22}	G_{22}	0	0	0	0	$(x_{21}+x_{23})$	0	0	0
	0	0	0	0	Y_{22}	0	0	F_{22}	0	0	0	0	$(Y_{21}+Y_{23})$	$(U_{21}+U_{23})$	0	0
	0	0	0	0	D_{22}	S_{22}	0	0	0	0	0	0	0	0	$(B_{21}+B_{23})$	0
	0	0	0	0	W_{22}	T_{22}	0	0	0	0	0	0	$(W_{21}+W_{23})$	0	0	0
Region 3	0	0	0	0	0	0	0	0	x_{33}	C_{33}	V_{33}	G_{33}	$(x_{31}+x_{32})$	0	0	0
	0	0	0	0	0	0	0	0	Y_{33}	0	0	F_{33}	$(Y_{31}+Y_{32})$	$(U_{31}+U_{32})$	0	0
	0	0	0	0	0	0	0	0	D_{33}	S_{33}	0	0	0	0	$(B_{31}+B_{32})$	0
	0	0	0	0	0	0	0	0	W_{33}	T_{33}	0	0	$(W_{31}+W_{32})$	0	0	0
	$(x_{21}+x_{31})$	0	0	0	$(x_{12}+x_{32})$	0	0	0	$(x_{13}+x_{23})$	0	0	0	0	0	0	0
	$(Y_{21}+Y_{31})$	$(U_{21}+U_{31})$	0	$(F_{21}+F_{31})$	$(Y_{12}+Y_{32})$	$(U_{12}+U_{32})$	0	$(F_{12}+F_{32})$	$(Y_{13}+Y_{23})$	$(U_{13}+U_{23})$	0	$(F_{13}+F_{23})$	$-\sum_j\sum_k Y_{jk}$	0	0	0
	0	0	$(B_{21}+B_{31})$	0	0	0	$(B_{12}+B_{32})$	0	0	0	$(B_{13}+B_{23})$	0	0	0	0	0
	$(W_{21}+W_{31})$	$(T_{21}+T_{31})$	0	0	$(W_{12}+W_{32})$	$(T_{12}+T_{32})$	0	0	$(W_{13}+W_{23})$	$(T_{13}+T_{23})$	0	0	$-\sum_j\sum_k W_{jk}$	0	0	0

Table 6-4
Intrasectoral Ordering of Flows

	Production				Households				Savings and Investments				Governments			
Production	x_{11}	0	0	$(x_{12}+x_{13})$	C_{11}	0	0	0	V_{11}	0	0	0	G_{11}	0	0	0
	0	x_{22}	0	$(x_{21}+x_{23})$	0	C_{22}	0	0	0	V_{22}	0	0	0	G_{22}	0	0
	0	0	x_{33}	$(x_{31}+x_{32})$	0	0	C_{33}	0	0	0	V_{33}	0	0	0	G_{33}	0
	$(x_{21}+x_{31})$	$(x_{12}+x_{32})$	$(x_{13}+x_{23})$	0	0	0	0	0	0	0	0	0	0	0	0	0
Households	Y_{11}	0	0	$(Y_{12}+Y_{13})$	0	0	0	$(U_{12}+U_{13})$	0	0	0	0	F_{11}	0	0	$(F_{12}+F_{13})$
	0	Y_{22}	0	$(Y_{21}+Y_{23})$	0	0	0	$(U_{21}+U_{23})$	0	0	0	0	0	F_{22}	0	$(F_{21}+F_{23})$
	0	0	Y_{33}	$(Y_{31}+Y_{32})$	0	0	0	$(U_{31}+U_{32})$	0	0	0	0	0	0	F_{33}	$(F_{31}+F_{32})$
	$(Y_{21}+Y_{31})$	$(Y_{12}+Y_{32})$	$(Y_{13}+Y_{23})$	$-\Sigma\Sigma Y_{jk}$	$(U_{21}+U_{31})$	$(U_{12}+U_{32})$	$(U_{13}+U_{23})$	0	0	0	0	0	$(F_{21}+F_{31})$	$(F_{12}+F_{32})$	$(F_{13}+F_{23})$	0
Savings and Investments	D_{11}	0	0	0	S_{11}	0	0	0	0	0	0	$(B_{12}+B_{13})$	0	0	0	0
	0	D_{22}	0	0	0	S_{22}	0	0	0	0	0	$(B_{21}+B_{23})$	0	0	0	0
	0	0	D_{33}	0	0	0	S_{33}	0	0	0	0	$(B_{31}+B_{32})$	0	0	0	0
	0	0	0	0	0	0	0	0	$(B_{21}+B_{31})$	$(B_{12}+B_{32})$	$(B_{13}+B_{23})$	0	0	0	0	0
Governments	W_{11}	0	0	$(W_{12}+W_{13})$	T_{11}	0	0	$(T_{12}+T_{13})$	0	0	0	0	0	0	0	0
	0	W_{22}	0	$(W_{21}+W_{23})$	0	T_{22}	0	$(T_{21}+T_{23})$	0	0	0	0	0	0	0	0
	0	0	W_{33}	$(W_{31}+W_{32})$	0	0	T_{33}	$(T_{31}+T_{32})$	0	0	0	0	0	0	0	0
	$(W_{21}+W_{31})$	$(W_{12}+W_{32})$	$(W_{13}+W_{23})$	0	$(T_{21}+T_{31})$	$(T_{12}+T_{32})$	$(T_{13}+T_{23})$	0	0	0	0	0	0	0	0	0

requirements, or alternatively can be used in order to check the quality of data and eliminate possible inconsistencies.

Trading Patterns

The models of interregional flows of goods and services so far discussed have rarely been statistically implemented because of the inordinate demands which they make with respect of data. But dearth of data and heavy demands put on research resources are not the only reasons for the relative neglect of this form of analysis. Of even greater importance is the added concern regarding the stability of input-output coefficients raised by the introduction into an interindustry framework of the spatial element.

The model developed independently by Chenery[6] and Moses[7] considerably decreases data requirements and at the same time provides some interesting additional insights into the nature of spatial development processes. The relations between pairs of industries are decomposed into two parts, dealing with technical requirements, and trading patterns respectively. The model is best explained by using a hypothetical example.

Assume three regions with the economy of each comprised of three sectors only. The basic relations in the three economies can be described by a set of nine balance equations.

$$X_1^1 - x_{11}^{11} - x_{12}^{11} - x_{13}^{11} - x_{11}^{12} - x_{12}^{12} - x_{13}^{12} - x_{11}^{13} - x_{12}^{13} - x_{13}^{13} = Y_1^{11} + Y_1^{12} + Y_1^{13};$$

$$X_2^1 - x_{21}^{11} - x_{22}^{11} - x_{23}^{11} - x_{21}^{12} - x_{22}^{12} - x_{23}^{12} - x_{21}^{13} - x_{22}^{13} - x_{23}^{13} = Y_1^{11} + Y_2^{12} + Y_2^{23};$$

.

.

.

$$X_3^3 - x_{31}^{31} - x_{32}^{31} - x_{33}^{31} - x_{31}^{32} - x_{32}^{32} - x_{33}^{32} - x_{31}^{33} - x_{32}^{33} - x_{33}^{33} = Y_3^{31} + Y_3^{32} + Y_3^{33};$$

where subscripts 1, 2, 3, refer to sectors and superscripts 1, 2, 3 refer to regions.

X_i^k = total output of sector i in region k.

x_{ij}^{kl} = flow of goods and services from sector i in region k to sector j in region l.

Y_i^{kl} = total demand in region l for products of sector i produced in region k.

Total shipments of Region 1 on account of final demand in all regions are defined by

$$F_1^1 = Y_1^{11} + Y_1^{12} + Y_1^{13};$$

The above system of nine balance equations contains 117 unknowns and cannot be solved for a given or postulated level of final demand without further assumptions. In order to generate solutions two sets of structural constants are introduced. The first set defines the technology of each sector in each region by postulating absorption strictly proportional to output. Thus, for example,

$$a_{31}^2 = \frac{x_{31}^2}{X_1^2};$$

defines the input of services required per unit output of agriculture in Region 2 as a constant. This is a standard assumption forming part of any input-output model.

The second set of coefficients is developed by analyzing the trading patterns between regions. The ratio of purchases of any commodity by a region from another region is assumed to form a constant proportion of its total purchases of that commodity from all suppliers. These trading constants are the characteristic features of the model. Thus, for example,

$$t_1^{13} = \frac{\rho_1^{13}}{P_1^3};$$

where

t_1^{13} = proportion of total purchases of Region 3 of agricultural products (1), supplied by Region 1.

ρ_1^{13} = amount of agricultural products which Region 3 buys from Region 1 in order to satisfy both intersectoral and final demand.

P_1^3 = total purchases of agricultural products in Region 3 from all other regions including itself in order to satisfy both intersectoral and final demand.

Obviously

$$P_1^3 = \rho_1^{13} + \rho_1^{23} + \rho_1^{33};$$

Combining the production constant (a_{ij}^k) and the trading constant (t_i^{kl}) one can derive a new coefficient

$$c_{ij}^{kl} = a_{ij}^l(t_i^{kl})$$

= the amount of commodity i produced in region k required per unit output of commodity j in region l.

Provided both coefficients (a_{ij}^l) and (t_i^{kl}) are unchanging over time the following system of nine equations can be solved for any set of Y's.

$$X_1^1 - c_{11}^{11}X_1^1 - c_{12}^{11}X_2^1 - c_{13}^{11}X_3^1 - c_{11}^{12}X_1^2 - c_{12}^{12}X_2^2 - c_{11}^{13}X_1^3 - c_{12}^{13}X_2^3 - c_{13}^{13}X_3^3$$

$$= t_1^{11}Y_1^1 + t_1^{12}Y_1^2 + t_1^{13}Y_1^3 ;$$

$$X_1^1 - \sum_{j=1}^{3} c_{1j}^{11}X_j^1 - \sum_{j=1}^{3} c_{1j}^{12}X_j^2 - \sum_{j=1}^{3} c_{1j}^{13}X_j^3 = \sum_{h=1}^{3} t_1^{1h}Y_1^h ;$$

$$X_2^1 - c_{21}^{11}X_1^1 - c_{22}^{11}X_2^1 - c_{23}^{11}X_3^1 - \ldots = t_2^{11}Y_2^1 + t_2^{12}Y_2^2 + t_2^{13}Y_2^3 ;$$

.

.

.

$$X_3^3 - c_{31}^{11}X_1^1 - c_{32}^{11}X_2^1 - c_{33}^{11}X_3^1 - \ldots = t_3^{11}Y_3^1 + t_3^{12}Y_3^2 + t_3^{13}Y_3^3 ;$$

The assumptions insuring stability of trading coefficients are essentially two. The first requires uniformity of trading relationships for all sectors in a region, which means that an average import pattern for all locally operating firms and plants can be derived and considered unchanging. The assumption is crucial as otherwise import and export data would be required not only by region but also by sector of origin and destination. Since these data do not exist and may be unobtainable even with the help of field surveys, such a model could not be statistically implemented. The assumption is strong, but is implied in any discussion of marginal propensity to import.

The second assumption refers to stability of trading relationships over time. This means that, for example, Pennsylvania and Alabama coal must be used in New Jersey in fixed and unchanging proportions. Since trading patterns reflect regional cost-price relationships rather than technological requirements, what is implied is constancy of production costs throughout the system, constancy of transportation costs between any two points, unlimited production and transportation capacity, and an infinitely elastic labor supply curve. Other implied assumptions involve treatment of regions as points in space with no intraregional transportation costs, perfect competition (hardly possible in an economy with a spatial dimension), no freight absorption, and lack of disturbances due to business cycles.

The model requires somewhat less stringent assumptions when applied to two regions only. This has been convincingly shown by Chenery and Clark.[8] Composed of n sectors, their model has $2n$ equations and $6n$ variables, namely a set of n variables each for Y_i^1, Y_i^2, X_i^{11}, X_i^{12}, X_i^{21}, X_i^{22}, $(i = 1, \ldots, n)$. With fixed trading coefficients the output level of each commodity in any of the two regions is defined as

$$X_i^1 = \left[\sum_j t_i^{11} a_{ij}^1 X_j^1 + \sum_j t_i^{12} a_{ij}^2 X_j^2 \right] + \left[t_i^{11} Y_i^1 + t_i^{12} Y_i^2 \right];$$

which states merely that production is equal to the quantities used for further processing in both regions, plus shipments to both regions on account of final demand. In this model autonomous demand (Y_i) is limited to investments and government expenditures, since consumption by households is assumed to be a function of locally generated income and hence has been placed in the structural matrix.

The model has been applied to the study of the Italian economy divided into the industrialized North and the agricultural, in many ways backward, South. It has been implemented with the help of the national input-output coefficients aggregated into twenty three sectors. Coefficients for the households sector were calculated on the basis of budget studies and were different for each of the two regions. The derivation of regional supply coefficients has been greatly facilitated by the economically dissimilar character of the two regions which were united less than 100 years ago. The twenty three sectors were divided into three categories:

1. National sectors, for which supply and demand were balanced only at the national level. Hence, the sources of supply were assumed to be identical for both regions. This group was comprised of ten sectors.

2. Mixed sectors, comprised of four industries, representing 85 percent of southern output. It has been assumed that the South does not import the products of these sectors from the North, relying exclusively on local production and imports from abroad. The North was assumed to use its own production, the available balance of southern output, and to import the rest from abroad.

3. Local sectors, comprised of the remaining nine industries. For those, production and consumption were assumed to be balanced locally for both regions with only small, percentagewise equal for both regions, imports from abroad.

The problem investigated with the help of the model was the amount of activity generated by an investment in the South of 150 billion lire, spent as follows:

Value added generated locally	63 billion
Purchases from other sectors in the South	33 billion
Imports from the North	52 billion
Imports from abroad	2 billion
Total	150 billion

The increased demand gave rise to multiplier effects and the total increase in production was 955 billion lire plus 31 billion lire of direct and indirect imports from abroad, yielding total increase in the volume of disposable goods and services of the order of 985 billion lire. In terms of value added, the North reaped 160 billions of lire and the South 194 billions. The latter figure includes, however, 63 billions directly attributable to the initial increase in final demand. Hence, the indirect repercussions of the investment in the South of 150 billions lire show the following effects:

	In Terms of Value Added	In Terms of Total Output
South	131	335
North	160	472

The remarkable fact emerging from the study is that the developed part of the country reaps greater benefits in terms of output and value added than the underdeveloped South which the original outlays were designed to boost.

Of methodological interest is the finding that when a regional instead of an interregional model is used (i.e., disregarding the feedback effects of increase northern demand for southern products) the increase of households income in the South is 165 instead of 194 billions of lire. The difference amounts to 18 percent, illustrating the strength of foreign trade repercussions within a single country. In the latter case, the investment multiplier is limited to 1.7 instead of 2.0. This then is the analytic gain from using the more sophisticated multiregional model.

Effects of Distance

A more general and conceptually elegant tool was forged earlier by Leontief in the form of the balanced interregional model.[9] Its basic premise is that while some commodities are produced and consumed in adjacent locations, others have to be transported over considerable distances. Consequently, the balances for some goods may be struck regionally, while for others the balance between output and consumption is only established for the nation as a whole. The former might be called regional, and the latter national commodities. The system is thus reminiscent of the central place theory, although in an important way it goes considerably further, since it does not ignore the reality of heavy industrial concentrations or the presence of localized raw materials and resources.

An assumption basic to the method is that the locational pattern of each national industry is known and unchanging, and that the expansion and contraction of each industry takes place in all regions in the same proportion. The spatially fixed distribution of the nationally balanced industries determines, moreover, the demand for a substantial part of the regionally balanced goods, since their products serve as inputs to the nationally balanced ones. The model does not attempt, however, to reconstruct the paths followed by individual commodities, because the balance is struck with the rest of the economy which is treated as one national pool. It can only be conjectured that imports, to the extent possible, come from nearer regions.

For purposes of developing the model, all commodities have to be classified into national and regional. The classification of commodities is largely determined by the regional breakdown applied, since the smaller the regions, the fewer commodities will be regionally balanced. Practically, moreover, there are bound to be many borderline cases of commodities almost balanced within a region.

In order to illustrate the exposition, let us assume that the economy turns out m commodities, of which h are regionally balanced, or

$$
\begin{matrix}
1 \\
2 \\
\cdot \\
\cdot \\
\cdot \\
h \\
h+1 \\
h+2 \\
\cdot \\
\cdot \\
\cdot \\
m
\end{matrix}
\qquad
\begin{array}{l}
\text{Balanced in} \\
\text{region } L
\end{array}
\qquad
\begin{array}{l}
\text{Balanced in} \\
\text{Nation } N
\end{array}
$$

Consequently, the vectors of total outputs and final demands can be partitioned as follows:

$$
X = \begin{bmatrix} X_L \\ X_N \end{bmatrix} ; \qquad Y = \begin{bmatrix} Y_L \\ Y_N \end{bmatrix} ;
$$

where

$$
X_L = \begin{bmatrix} X_1 \\ X_2 \\ \vdots \\ X_h \end{bmatrix} ; \qquad X_N = \begin{bmatrix} X_{h+1} \\ X_{h+2} \\ \vdots \\ X_m \end{bmatrix} ;
$$

$$Y_L = \begin{bmatrix} Y_1 \\ Y_2 \\ \vdots \\ Y_h \end{bmatrix} \; ; \quad Y_N = \begin{bmatrix} Y_{h+1} \\ Y_{h+2} \\ \vdots \\ Y_m \end{bmatrix} \; ;$$

The nation, however, contains many regions, hence for each region j the total output can be described by

$$_jX = \begin{bmatrix} _jX_L \\ _jX_N \end{bmatrix} \; ;$$

where

$$_jX_L = \begin{bmatrix} _jX_1 \\ _jX_2 \\ \vdots \\ _jX_h \end{bmatrix} = \begin{array}{l} \text{production} \\ \text{of regionally} \\ \text{balanced goods} \\ \text{in region } j \end{array} \qquad _jX_N = \begin{bmatrix} _jX_{h+1} \\ _jX_{h+2} \\ \vdots \\ _jX_m \end{bmatrix} = \begin{array}{l} \text{production} \\ \text{of nationally} \\ \text{balanced goods} \\ \text{in region } j \end{array}$$

Similarly for total final demand

$$_jY = \begin{bmatrix} _jY_L \\ _jY_N \end{bmatrix} \; ;$$

where

$$_jY_L = \begin{bmatrix} _jY_1 \\ _jY_2 \\ \vdots \\ _jY_h \end{bmatrix} = \begin{array}{l} \text{final demand} \\ \text{of regionally} \\ \text{balanced goods} \\ \text{in region } j \end{array} \qquad _jY_N = \begin{bmatrix} _jY_{h+1} \\ _jY_{h+2} \\ \vdots \\ _jY_m \end{bmatrix} = \begin{array}{l} \text{final demand} \\ \text{of nationally} \\ \text{balanced goods} \\ \text{in region } j \end{array}$$

The table of technical coefficients $a_{ik} = \dfrac{x_{ik}}{X_k}$ can also be partitioned as follows:

$$
a = \left[\begin{array}{cccc|cccc}
a_{11} & a_{12} & \cdots & a_{1h} & a_{1,h+1} & a_{1,h+2} & \cdots & a_{1,m} \\
a_{21} & a_{22} & \cdots & a_{2h} & a_{2,h+1} & a_{2,h+2} & \cdots & a_{2,m} \\
\vdots & & & & & & & \\
a_{h1} & a_{h2} & \cdots & a_{hh} & a_{h,h+1} & a_{h,h+2} & \cdots & a_{h,m} \\
\hline
a_{h+1,1} & a_{h+1,2} & \cdots & a_{h+1,h} & a_{h+1,h+1} & a_{h+1,h+2} & \cdots & a_{h+1,m} \\
a_{h+2,1} & a_{h+2,2} & \cdots & a_{h+2,h} & a_{h+2,h+1} & a_{h+2,h+2} & \cdots & a_{h+2,m} \\
\vdots & & & & & & & \\
a_{m1} & a_{m2} & \cdots & a_{mh} & a_{m,h+1} & a_{m,h+2} & \cdots & a_{m,m}
\end{array}\right]
$$

or in the compact matrix notation

$$
a = \left[\begin{array}{c|c}
a_{LL} & a_{LN} \\
\hline
a_{NL} & a_{NN}
\end{array}\right] ;
$$

a_{LL} = submatrix of input-output coefficients indicating the required levels of production of regionally balanced goods per unit output of regionally balanced goods.

a_{LN} = submatrix of input-output coefficients indicating the required levels of production of regionally balanced goods per unit output of nationally balanced goods.

a_{NL} = submatrix of input-output coefficients indicating the required levels of production of nationally balanced goods per unit output of regionally balanced goods.

a_{NN} = submatrix of input-output coefficients indicating the required levels of production of nationally balanced goods per unit output of nationally balanced goods.

The Leontief inverse of the matrix takes the form of:

$$
(I - a)^{-1} = A
$$

$$\begin{bmatrix} A_{11} & A_{12} & \cdots & A_{1h} & | & A_{1,h+1} & A_{1,h+2} & \cdots & A_{1,m} \\ A_{21} & A_{22} & \cdots & A_{2h} & | & A_{2,h+1} & A_{2,h+2} & \cdots & A_{2,m} \\ \vdots & & & & | & & & & \\ A_{h1} & A_{h2} & \cdots & A_{hh} & | & A_{h,h+1} & A_{h,h+2} & \cdots & A_{h,m} \\ \hline A_{h+1,1} & A_{h+1,2} & \cdots & A_{h+1,h} & | & A_{h+1,h+1} & A_{h+1,h+2} & \cdots & A_{h+1,m} \\ \vdots & & & & | & & & & \\ \vdots & & & & | & & & & \\ A_{m,1} & A_{m,2} & \cdots & A_{m,h} & | & A_{m,h+1} & A_{m,h+2} & \cdots & A_{m,m} \end{bmatrix} =$$

The output of any commodity in the system can be defined as

$$X_i = \sum_{k=1}^{m} A_{ik} Y_k \quad (i = 1, \ldots, h, \ldots, m);$$

The inverses of the submatrices are defined as

$$(I - a_{LL})^{-1} = A_{LL}; \qquad (I - a_{LN})^{-1} = A_{LN};$$
$$(I - a_{LL})^{-1} = A_{NL}; \qquad (I - a_{NN})^{-1} = A_{NN};$$

The A matrix can also be partitioned into $A = (L^A, N^A)$; where

$$_L A = \begin{bmatrix} A_{LL} \\ A_{NL} \end{bmatrix}; \qquad _N A = \begin{bmatrix} A_{LN} \\ A_{NN} \end{bmatrix}.$$

The output of regionally balanced goods in any region j is defined by the balance equation

$$\begin{bmatrix} I - a_{LL}, & -a_{LN} \end{bmatrix} \begin{bmatrix} {}_j X_L \\ {}_j X_N \end{bmatrix} = {}_j Y_L;$$

$$(I - a_{LL})_j X_L - a_{LN\,j} X_N = {}_j Y_L;$$

which simply states that consumption of regionally balanced goods in region j or $({}_j Y_L)$ equals total output of such goods, less what is needed as intermediate inputs into the production of regionally balanced goods ($a_{LL}\ _jX_L$), and less what is needed as intermediate inputs into the production of nationally balanced goods produced in region j ($a_{LN}\ _jX_N$). The solution of the balance equation is

$$(I - a_{LL})_jX_L = \ _jY_L + a_{LN\ j}X_N\ ;$$

$$_jX_L = A_{LL\ j}Y_L + A_{LL}\ a_{LN\ j}X_N\ .$$

Since the spatial distribution of production of nationally balanced goods is assumed to be known and unchanging over time, the share in the output of all nationally balanced goods of any region j represented by a vector or by a diagonal matrix, is also unchanging.

$$_jR = \begin{bmatrix} _j r_{h+1} & 0 & \cdots & 0 \\ 0 & _j r_{h+2} & \cdots & 0 \\ \vdots & & & \\ 0 & 0 & \cdots & _j r_m \end{bmatrix} ;$$

where

$_j r_{h+i}$ represents the share of region j in the national production of good $h + i$, or

$$_j r_{h+i} = \frac{_jX_{h+i}}{X_{h+i}}\ ;$$

The level of output of national goods in any region j is therefore

$$_jX_N = \ _jR\ X_N\ ;$$

But X_N is known, since national output is a function of national demand Y or

$$X_N = \ _NA\ Y\ ;$$

and therefore the output of nationally balanced goods in any region j is

$$_jX_N = \ _jR\ _NA\ Y\ ;$$

Substituting it into the balance equation for the regionally balanced goods yields

$$_jX_L = A_{LL\ j}Y_L + A_{LL}\ a_{LN\ j}R_N\ A\ Y\ ;$$

However total production in any region j is the sum of outputs of both regionally and nationally balanced commodities or

$$_jX = {_jX_L} + {_jX_N};$$

Substituting

$$_jX = A_{LL}\,{_jY_L} + A_{LL}\,a_{LN}\,{_jR_N}\,A\,Y + {_jR_N}\,A\,Y;\ \text{or,}$$

$$_jX = A_{LL}\,{_jY_L} + (I + A_{LL}\,a_{LN})\,{_jR_N}\,A\,Y;$$

which gives total output of all types of commodities in region j as a function of two sets of variables only: (1) demand for nationally balanced commodities (Y), and (2) regional demand for regionally balanced commodities ($_jY_L$).

The analysis can be further pursued by disaggregating the regions into subregional units. It is not necessary to subdivide all regions, as some may be composed of subregions and others not. It is also not necessary to assume identical input-output structure in the regions and subregions of which the system is comprised. The new symbols introduced are summarized below.

As before the economy turns out m commodities.

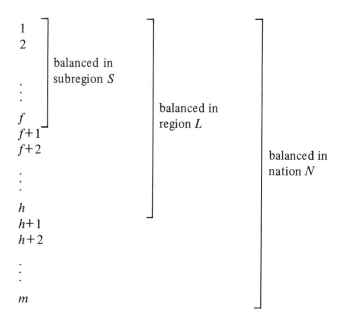

Output and final demand is referred to by the following symbols:

		Commodities		
		Balanced in subregion S	Balanced in region L	Balanced in Nation N
	S_i	$_iX_S,\ _iY_S$	$_iX_L,\ _iY_L$	$_iX_N,\ _iY_N$
Produced or demanded in	L_j	$_jX_S,\ _jY_S$	$_jX_L,\ _jY_L$	$_jX_N,\ _jY_N$
	N	$X_S,\ Y_S$	$X_L,\ Y_L$	$X_N,\ Y_N$

The share in output of nationally balanced goods of any subregion is represented by a diagonal matrix

$$_iR_N = \begin{bmatrix} _ir_{h+1} & 0 & \cdots & 0 \\ 0 & _ir_{h+2} & \cdots & 0 \\ \vdots & & & \\ 0 & 0 & \cdots & _ir_m \end{bmatrix} \ ;$$

and defined by $_iX_N = {}_iR_N\,X_N$;

Similarly, for the output of regionally balanced goods in subregion i, one can write

$$_iR_L = \begin{bmatrix} _ir_{f+1} & 0 & \cdots & 0 \\ 0 & _ir_{f+2} & \cdots & 0 \\ \vdots & & & \\ 0 & 0 & \cdots & _ir_h \end{bmatrix} \ ;$$

and $_iX_L = {}_iR_L\,_jX_L$;

Written out in full outputs in subregion i, in region j, and in the nation, are

Output of subregionally balanced goods

$$_iX_S = \begin{bmatrix} _iX_1 \\ _iX_2 \\ \vdots \\ _iX_f \end{bmatrix} \ ;$$

Output of regionally balanced goods

$$_iX_L = \begin{bmatrix} _iX_{f+1} \\ _iX_{f+2} \\ \vdots \\ _iX_h \end{bmatrix} \ ;$$

Output of nationally balanced goods

$$_iX_N = \begin{bmatrix} _iX_{h+1} \\ _iX_{h+2} \\ \vdots \\ _iX_m \end{bmatrix} \ ;$$

$$_jX_S = \begin{bmatrix} _jX_1 \\ _jX_2 \\ \vdots \\ _jX_f \end{bmatrix} \quad ; \qquad _jX_L = \begin{bmatrix} _jX_{f+1} \\ _jX_{f+2} \\ \vdots \\ _jX_h \end{bmatrix} \quad ; \qquad _iX_N = \begin{bmatrix} _jX_{h+1} \\ _jX_{h+2} \\ \vdots \\ _jX_m \end{bmatrix} \quad ;$$

$$X_S = \begin{bmatrix} X_1 \\ X_2 \\ \vdots \\ X_f \end{bmatrix} \quad ; \qquad X_L = \begin{bmatrix} X_{f+1} \\ X_{f+2} \\ \vdots \\ X_h \end{bmatrix} \quad ; \qquad X_N = \begin{bmatrix} X_{h+1} \\ X_{h+2} \\ \vdots \\ X_m \end{bmatrix} \quad ;$$

A similar set of vectors describes the final demand at the subregional, regional, and national levels.

The table of technical coefficients is now also partitioned as follows:

$$a = \left[\begin{array}{ccc|ccc|ccc} a_{11} & \cdots & a_{1f} & a_{1,f+1} & \cdots & a_{1,h} & a_{1,h+1} & \cdots & a_{1,m} \\ \vdots & & & & & & & & \\ a_{f1} & \cdots & a_{ff} & a_{f,f+1} & \cdots & a_{f,h} & a_{f,h+1} & \cdots & a_{f,m} \\ \hline a_{f+1,1} & \cdots & a_{f+1,f} & a_{f+1,f+1} & \cdots & a_{f+1,h} & a_{f+1,h+1} & \cdots & a_{f+1,m} \\ \vdots & & & & & & & & \\ a_{h,1} & \cdots & a_{h,f} & a_{h,f+1} & \cdots & a_{h,h} & a_{h,h+1} & \cdots & a_{h,m} \\ \hline a_{h+1,1} & \cdots & a_{h+1,f} & a_{h+1,f+1} & \cdots & a_{h+1,h} & a_{h+1,h+1} & \cdots & a_{h+1,m} \\ \vdots & & & & & & & & \\ a_{m,1} & \cdots & a_{m,f} & a_{m,f+1} & \cdots & a_{m,h} & a_{m,h+1} & \cdots & a_{m,m} \end{array} \right] \quad ;$$

In the compact matrix notation it can be represented by

$$a = \begin{bmatrix} a_{SS} & a_{SL} & a_{SN} \\ a_{LS} & a_{LL} & a_{LN} \\ a_{NS} & a_{NL} & a_{NN} \end{bmatrix} ;$$

Similarly, $(I - a)^{-1} = A$, can be partitioned into

$$A = \begin{bmatrix} S^A, & L^A, & N^A \end{bmatrix} ;$$

The total output in any subregion i is composed of the sum of production of goods balanced at the subregional, regional, and national levels. The production of subregionally balanced commodities is described by the following equation.

$$\begin{bmatrix} I - a_{SS}, & -a_{SL} & -a_{SN} \end{bmatrix} \begin{bmatrix} _iX_S \\ _iX_L \\ _iX_N \end{bmatrix} = {}_iY_S ;$$

$$(I - a_{SS}) \, _iX_S - a_{SL} \, _iX_L - a_{SN} \, _iX_N = {}_iY_S ;$$

yielding

$$_iX_S = A_{SS} \, _iY_S + A_{SS} \, a_{SL} \, _iX_L + A_{SS} \, a_{SN} \, _iX_N ;$$

The production of regionally balanced goods in subregion i is defined as a share of output in region j. The latter was described in the two stage model as

$$_jX_L = A_{LL} \, _jY_L + A_{LL} \, a_{LN} \, _jR_N \, A \, Y .$$

Hence,

$$_iX_L = {}_iR_L \begin{bmatrix} A_{LL} \, Y_L + A_{LL} \, a_{LN} \, _jR \, _N A \, Y \end{bmatrix} ;$$

$$_iX_L = {}_iR_L \, A_{LL} \begin{bmatrix} _jY_L + a_{LN} \, _jR \, _N A \, Y \end{bmatrix} ;$$

Here production of regionally balanced commodities in subregion i is defined as a function of two sets of variables pertaining to final demand for regional $(_jY_L)$ and national goods $(_jY_N)$.

The output of nationally balanced goods in subregion i is given as a share of national production:

$$_iX_N = {_iR_N}\, X_N\,; \text{ or substituting}$$

$$_iX_N = {_iR_N}\, {_NA}\ Y\,;$$

Now, total production in subregion i is obviously the sum of outputs of subregionally, regionally and nationally balanced commodities.

$$_iX = {_iX_S} + {_iX_L} + {_iX_N}\,;$$

$$_iX = \left[A_{SS}\, {_iY_S} + A_{SS}\, a_{SL}\, {_iX_L} + A_{SS}\, a_{SN}\, {_iX_N} \right]$$

$$+ \left[{_iR_L}\, A_{LL}\, ({_jY_L} + a_{LN}\, {_jR_N}\, A\ Y) \right] + \left[{_iR_N}\, {_NA}\ Y \right]\,;$$

$$_iX = A_{SS}\, {_iY_S} + (I + A_{SS}\, a_{SL})\, {_iR_L}\, A_{LL}\, {_jY_L}$$

$$+ \left[(I + A_{SS}\, a_{SL})\, {_iR_L}\, A_{LL}\, a_{LN}\, {_jR} + (I + A_{SS}\, a_{SN})\, {_iR_N} \right]\, {_NA}\ Y\,;$$

Again, the level of production in subregion i is a function of three sets of variables, namely vectors of demand for subregionally $({_iY_S})$, regionally $({_jY_L})$, and nationally (Y) balanced goods.

The households sector may be treated either as a datum, outside of the system or placed inside the structural matrix. In the latter case very large multipliers would result, but the problem is not directly related to the use of the balanced model.

The balanced model has been criticized as being not so much interregional as intranational since the trading patterns of each region and subregion are described in terms of relations with a pool composed of all other territorial units of the same rank. The actual pattern of spatial economic interdependence within a nation is obviously more complex. The relation between any two regions can be either direct or indirect if the links are through industries located in a third region, with triangular or multilateral trading patterns emerging in the latter case.

A more sophisticated model encompassing the often involved interregional flows has been developed by Leontief and Strout as the gravity input-output model.[a,10] It was designed to make effective use of the limited amount of data with which economists have to work even in advanced countries and to attack one of the major difficulties of interregional models, stemming from the fact that identical commodities produced and consumed in different regions do not

---

[a]From *Studies in the Structure of the American Economy* by Wassily Leontief. Copyright 1953 by Oxford University Press, Inc. Reprinted by permission.

necessarily give rise to predictable interregional flows without other variables such as distance being explicitly considered. In order to describe their model, a few definitions are introduced:

$X_{i.og}$ = total available quantity of commodity i (production + imports − exports) in region g;

$X_{i.go}$ = total output of commodity i in region g;

$Y_{i.g}$ = final demand for commodity i in region g;

$X_{i.gh}$ = flow (total shipments) of commodity i from region g to region h.

Obviously,

$$X_{i.go} = \sum_{h=1}^{m} X_{i.gh} \ (h = 1, 2, \ldots, m),$$

since total output equals total shipments to all other regions including itself. Similarly,

$$X_{i.og} = \sum_{h=1}^{m} X_{i.hg} \ (h = 1, 2, \ldots, m),$$

since total available quantity equals the sum of received shipments from all other regions including itself. Exports can be included in the above equation with a negative sign.

The aggregate supply of commodity i in the nation can be expressed by summing the above equations over all supplying and receiving regions:

$$X_{i.oo} = \sum_{g=1}^{m} X_{i.go} = \sum_{h=1}^{m} X_{i.oh} = \sum_{g=1}^{m} \sum_{h=1}^{m} \frac{X_{i.gh}}{2};$$

The balance equations can be supplemented by a set of structural equations:

$$X_{i.og} = \sum_{j=1}^{m} (a_{ij.g} X_{j.go}) + Y_{i.g};$$

If the mn elements of final demand are given, the system still contains mn equations in $(2mn - 1)$ unknowns comprised of mn regional outputs and mn regional inputs. A further set of structural equations is added explaining the magnitude of interregional flows of commodities.

$$X_{i.gh} = \frac{X_{i.go} \, X_{i.oh}}{X_{i.oo}} Q_{i.gh}; \ (g \neq h) \quad \begin{cases} i = 1, \ldots, m; \\ g = 1, \ldots, m; \\ h = 1, \ldots, m; \end{cases} \quad \text{where}$$

$Q_{i.gh}$ is an empirical constant which would vary with the distance between region g and h.

Each flow is assumed to be directly proportional to output of commodity i in region g, and to total demand in region h. At the same time the flow is assumed to be inversely proportional to total production in the system. Notice that the multiplicative, nonlinear form follows the gravity model formulation, with the assumptions characteristic of the latter model implied. In order that the above model might describe observed reality, a perfect world must be postulated in which regions are points, goods are homogeneous, and decisions are rational. In such a world there would be no cross-shipments except those due to seasonal factors, not revealed by data referring to long time intervals spanning several seasons.

The equation describing total output and total available quantity can now be reformulated by substituting $X_{i.gh}$.

$$X_{i.go} = \sum_{h=1}^{m} X_{i.hg} = \sum_{h=1}^{m} \frac{X_{i.go} \, X_{i.oh}}{X_{i.oo}} Q_{i.gh}$$

$$= \frac{X_{i.go} \sum_{h=1}^{n} (X_{i.oh} \, Q_{i.gh})}{X_{i.oo}} + X_{i.gg};$$

$$X_{i.og} = \sum_{h=1}^{m} X_{i.hg} = \frac{X_{i.og} \sum_{h=1}^{m} (X_{i.ho} \, Q_{i.hg})}{X_{i.oo}} + X_{i.gg};$$

The terms $X_{i.gg}$ which represent the internally absorbed part of output of i have to be added because obviously $Q_{i.gg} = 0$.

Proceeding toward a numerical solution of a system which now contains $3mn$ equations and $3mn$ unknowns, one can reduce the number of equations and unknowns by eliminating the terms $X_{i.gg}$ among the last two equations.

$$X_{i.go} - \frac{X_{i.go} \sum_{h=1}^{m} (X_{i.oh} \, Q_{i.gh})}{X_{i.oo}} = X_{i.og} - \frac{X_{i.og} \sum_{h=1}^{m} (X_{i.ho} \, Q_{i.hg})}{X_{i.oo}};$$

$$X_{i.go} X_{i.oo} - X_{i.go} \sum_{h=1}^{m} (X_{i.oh} \, Q_{i.gh}) = X_{i.og} X_{i.oo} - X_{i.og} \sum_{h=1}^{m} (X_{i.ho} \, Q_{i.hg});$$

Since $\Sigma X_{i.og} = \Sigma X_{i.go} = X_{i.oo}$, we have

$$X_{i.go} \sum_{h=1}^{m} (X_{i.oh} - X_{i.oh} Q_{i.gh}) = X_{i.og} \sum_{h=1}^{m} (X_{i.ho} - X_{i.ho} Q_{i.hg});$$

and defining

$$L_{i.gh} = 1 - Q_{i.gh}; \text{ where } L_{i.gg} = 0;$$

yields

$$X_{i.go} \sum_{h=1}^{m} (X_{i.oh} L_{i.gh}) = X_{i.og} \sum_{h=1}^{m} (X_{i.ho} L_{i.hg});$$

For the m commodities and n regions this results in a set of mn equations and $2mn$ variables, namely all $X_{i.og}$ and $X_{i.go}$. However in each set of equations one (or n equations in all) describes the interdependence between all regional outputs and inputs of one particular commodity and is redundant. Hence, omitting from each set of equations for which $g = m$, only $(mn - n)$ independent equations remain.

On the other hand, the n identities, one for each commodity

$$\Sigma X_{i.og} = \Sigma X_{i.go};$$

impose constraints on the system and should be counted.

The remaining equations can be added to yield an identity

$$\sum_{g=1}^{m} \sum_{h=1}^{m} (X_{i.go} X_{i.oh} L_{i.gh}) = \sum_{g=1}^{m} \sum_{h=1}^{m} (X_{i.og} X_{i.ho} L_{i.hg});$$

Thus, with final demand (Y_{ig}) levels given, for the n commodities in m regions a general solution giving the output level of each industry in each region is obtainable. The solution contains, nonetheless, nonlinear equations, which for computational convenience have to be approximated by linear ones in which each variable is split into two parts: a base-year component and an additive deviation.

Industrial Complexes and Growth Poles

The empirical question most often facing the regional scientist springs from the policy objective to "rehabilitate" the regional economy and start a growth process. In a small open economy a major breakthrough can result only from the introduction of new productive activities. Among the various types of spatial groupings acting as growth poles, an important category is formed by industrial complexes. Both location and development theory support the view that the attractiveness of a region and the pull that it exercises upon industries looking for suitable locations are a function of the existence of a prior industrial agglomeration. Accordingly, a group of industries complementary to one another, characteristic of an industrial complex, forms the most propitious background for initiating self-supporting growth processes. Under modern conditions, the strength and variety of forward and backward interindustry links generates economies of scale and agglomeration that are the basis of regional growth and development.

The problem can also be viewed in a slightly different way. The importance of a new industry to a depressed region resides not only in the volume of new employment and income that it generates but very often primarily in its indirect impact, the strength of which can be effectively measured with the help of input-output analysis. A common feature of depressed regions is the general weakness of multiplier effects generated in their economies, due mainly to the size of leakages present. The absence of substantial indirect effects ordinarily accompanying new investments constitutes one of the greatest obstacles to efforts aimed at invigorating the economies of depressed regions and makes the process at best a slow and expensive one.

Yet the introduction of new industries progressively reduces leakages and reinforces the indirect impact of new activities until a point is reached when, in a group of related industries linked by flows of goods and services, the multiplier effects become significantly stronger, signalling a qualitative as well as a quantitative change. It is assumed that such a breakthrough can hardly be recognized by examining one industry after another in isolation, since an analysis on a sector by sector basis will fail to reveal effects characteristic of, and advantages accruing to, groups of industries only.

In order to assess the ability of the regional economy to generate multiplier effects, a technique has been developed for indentifying, from among all the sectors of which a regional economy is comprised, those forming an industrial cluster with strong internal and relatively weak external flows.[11] The technique can be used to test the hypothesis that in some regions such subsystems might account for a substantial part of total multiplier effects capable of being generated. The implications of the existence of identifiable clusters of interlinked industries for investment policy are obvious, since by fostering the establishment of new complementary plants, the emergence of a full industrial complex may be advanced. Investments rejected when examined in isolation in favor of alternatives offering greater imeediate payoffs might prove more efficient because of long-run considerations brought to the fore by the comprehensive approach suggested.

The second hypothesis which can be tested is that in an urban agglomeration the various ancillary links with suppliers of technical, commercial, or financial services take precedence over links based on flows of raw materials, basic production ingredients, or outputs. If the hypothesis were vindicated, it would mean that in a metropolitan agglomeration industrial complexes based on technical affinity among plants are relatively rare and that economies of urbanization are more important than those due to localization.[12]

An *industrial complex* is usually defined as a set of activities with total output above a certain minimum size, occurring at a given location, and belonging to a subsystem subject to important production, marketing, or other interrelations. The extent of relative "closeness" of a local economy, or conversely its dependence upon exports and imports, can be simply measured with the help of the following index:

$$S = \sum_i \sum_j x_{ij} / \sum_i X_i;$$

where

S = index of relative "closeness" of the regional economy;

x_{ij} = flow of goods and services in dollars from industry i to industry j, both located in the study region;

X_i = total output of industry i.

Alternatively, one could use value added rather than flows, although the results are slightly different.

$$U = \sum_j V_j / \sum_i X_i;$$

where

V_j = value added (primary inputs) in industry j.

Other indexes could measure the dependence of the regional economy upon particular types of imports or take into account differences in price levels. Such synthetic measures fail, however, to account explicitly for the important indirect and induced effects that are at the heart of a growing agglomeration. This failure and their generality make them devoid of analytic and policy applications.

The alternative approach described below starts by identifying industries belonging to a subgroup with closer links among themselves than with the rest of the local economy. Two industries, k and l, may be operationally defined as "forming" an industrial complex if they are connected by strong flows of goods or services. Four coefficients may describe this type of relationship:

$$a_{kl} = \frac{x_{kl}}{X_l}; \quad a_{lk} = \frac{x_{lk}}{X_k}; \quad b_{kl} = \frac{x_{kl}}{X_k}; \quad b_{lk} = \frac{x_{lk}}{X_l}.$$

An "a" coefficient exceeding a certain cutoff point $(a_l \geq a^*)$ indicates a dependent industry, while a large "b" coefficient ($b_k \geqslant b^*$) indicates a complementary industry. An example of a dependent industry may be a plant producing glue out of waste products of a fish-processing plant, while an example of a complementary industry may be a plant producing, say, windshields for a car factory, with the relationship being important in terms of the supplying unit.

Far more significant analytically are indirect links. Two industries, k and l, may be members of an industrial complex in the absence of direct links. For example, an oil refinery and a pharmaceutical plant may both belong to a petro-chemical complex even though they may not trade with one another. The link in this more typical and important case is established thorugh other activities of the complex. More generally, two industries, k and l, may be considered to be members of a complex if their trading pattersn with suppliers or purchasers involve the same group of industries. This type of link is revealed by correlation analysis.

Specifically, four coefficients of correlation describe the similarity between the input-output structures of two industries:

$$r(a_{ik} \cdot a_{il}), \ r(b_{ki} \cdot b_{li}), \ r(a_{ik} \cdot b_{li}), \ r(b_{ki} \cdot a_{il}) .$$

A high $r(a_{ik} \cdot a_{il})$ coefficient iddicates that the two industries, k and l, have similar input structures or draw their supplies from the same producers. A high $r(b_{ki} \cdot b_{li})$ coefficient signifies that the two industries, k and l, supply their products to a similar set of users. A high $r(a_{ik} \cdot b_{li})$ coefficient implies that the supplier of k industry are users of the products of l. Finally, a high $r(b_{ki} \cdot a_{il})$ coefficient points toward a reserve relationship between k and l, namely the users of the products of k are suppliers of l. Provision has to be made to eliminate similarities based on high import and export content of the two industries, undifferentiated by region and sector of origin or destination.

The formal model for studying the interindustry linkages consists of the following major steps:

1. A set of four zero order correlation coefficients of the form

$$r(u_{ik} \cdot u_{il}), \ r(b_{ki} \cdot b_{li}), \ r(a_{ik} \cdot b_{li}), \ r(b_{ki} \cdot a_{il}) ; \ (i = 1, \ldots, n);$$

is derived for all possible pairs of industries included in the interindustry flow table examined.

2. A symmetric intercorrelation matrix $\mathbf{R}$ is set up by selecting the highest of the four coefficients,[13] or

$$r_{lk} = r_{kl} = \max \left[r(a_{ik} \cdot a_{il}), \ r(b_{ki} \cdot b_{li}), \ r(a_{ik} \cdot b_{li}), \ r(b_{ki} \cdot a_{il}) \right] ;$$

It appears that generally an examination of intercorrelation matrices $\mathbf{R}$ set up by selecting the highest of the four zero order correlation coefficients is most fruitful. The entries in the **R** matrix help to identify affinities between pairs of industries based on their links with a subgroup forming a hypothetical complex.

More formally, the first two steps can be summarized as follows:
Given an $n \times n$ matrix of input-output flows expressed in dollars

$$\mathbf{X} = \begin{bmatrix} x_{11} & x_{12} & \cdots & x_{1n} \\ x_{21} & x_{22} & \cdots & x_{2n} \\ \vdots & & & \\ x_{n1} & x_{n2} & \cdots & x_{nn} \end{bmatrix}$$

an $n \times 4n$ matrix of zero order correlation coefficients is derived

$$\mathbf{r} = \begin{bmatrix} r(a_{ik} \cdot a_{il}) & | & r(b_{ki} \cdot b_{li}) & | & r(a_{ik} \cdot b_{li}) & | & r(b_{ki} \cdot a_{il}) \end{bmatrix} ;$$

Each entry in the first submatrix is a measure of the degree of affinity between any two industries k and l on the basis of similarity in their buying patterns. Each entry in the second submatrix is a measure of the degree of affinity between any two industries k and l on the basis of similarity in their selling patterns. The entries in the third and fourth submatrices measure the degree of affinity between pairs of industries by correlating the suppliers of the one with customers of the other. Each complete row of the matrix is interpretable as a description of an industry in terms of $4n$ characteristics, each of which measures its affinity to other industries in terms of various relations to the remaining sectors in the system.

Next an $n \times n$ covariance matrix is formed

$$K = E[(r - \bar{r})(r - \bar{r})^T] ;$$

Notice that the matrix of deviations was postmultiplied by its transpose, since the purpose of this step was to compare pairwise industries on the basis of their characteristics, with the final objective of reducing the number of industries while maximizing total variance.

The covariance matrix is transformed into an $n \times n$ correlation matrix

$$R = D \frac{1}{\sigma_i} K D \frac{1}{\sigma_i} ;$$

where

D = diagonal matrix of standard deviations of the variates (r's).

3. In order to identify, from the set of all industries, the subgroup belonging to a complex, an iterative process is applied. For this purpose all industries having either a null column or a null row vector [or all k industries for which either $r_{ik}, r_{ki} = 0$; ($i = 1, \ldots, n$)] are removed from the **R** matrix, and the whole process repeated until no more null vectors are left.

4. The relative strength of the links binding the remaining industries together is assessed with the help of eigenvalues of the **R** matrix, computed as:

$$(Ra - Ia\lambda) = \underline{0};$$
$$(R - I\lambda)a = \underline{0};$$
$$|R - I\lambda| = \underline{0};$$

where

a = eigenvector, or characteristic vector;
λ = eigenvalue, or characteristic root.

The ratios of the characteristic roots to the trace of the **R** matrix define an index of association:

$$C_n = \frac{\lambda_n}{\text{tr } \mathbf{R}} \times 100;$$

This provides an aggregate measure of the strength of the ties connecting the industries remaining in the **R** matrix—a large C_1 indicating the existence of an industrial complex, and a fairly large C_1 and C_2 pointing toward the existence of two identifiable complexes.

The eigenvalues, λ_i, are interpretable as variances along a particular dimension, and determine the degree of affinity of industries forming a subsystem because the elements of the eigenvectors were standardized by setting

$$a_i' a_i = 1;$$

5. Finally, in order to eliminate similarities based on high import and export contents, all industries are removed from the matrix for which both

$$\frac{m_i}{x_i} \geqslant \alpha^*; \quad \text{and} \quad \frac{e_i}{x_i} \geqslant \beta^*;$$

where

m_i = total imports of industry i;

e_i = total exports of industry i ;

α^*, β^* = constants determined by an iterative process and finally set, in one empirical study, at $\alpha^* = \beta^* = 0.30$.

The removed industries are those with relatively weak links with the regional economy. Any similarities in trading patterns of such industries revealed by correlation analysis are thus deemed to be spurious, based solely on ancillary inputs and outputs.

While without extensive applications no definite conclusions can be drawn, it appears that multivariate analysis may be a useful tool for analyzing linkages existing in regional economies. The sample of input-output tables so far examined is far too small for any regularities to emerge. Nonetheless, the pervasiveness of links based on spatial proximity rather than technical affinity in the first subsystems falls in line with theoretical considerations and deserves careful attention.[14]

7 Toward a Fused Framework

The Uses of Regional Social Accounts

Social accounts are rightly considered to be the most widely useful and versatile tool of regional analysis. In assessing proposals for altering the framework of social accounts, it is necessary to analyse the various uses to which they are currently being put. A comprehensive classification or even listing of the main applications of regional social accounts would have to distinguish the following main groups of institutions interested in this form of analysis of data:

1. Local governments with jurisdictions corresponding to or approximating the study area. Also into this category would fall emanations of local governments formed for the purpose of developing regional plans or coordinating activities transcending the boundaries of individual members.
2. Supraregional government organizations such as federal agencies, state governments, international bodies, or combinations of the three.
3. Scientific institutions such as universities, institutes, or nonprofit organizations.
4. Private groups such as business or labor organizations, households, and so forth.

The applications of accounts by the various users are numerous and heterogeneous.[1] The following list, covering the main uses, is by no means exhaustive:

1. A check on coverage or consistency of statistics or, more generally, a framework for developing a comprehensive system of regional data.
2. A source of data or instrument for developing indicators periodically measuring regional progress or performance.
3. A basis for deriving *ad hoc* indicators of the contribution of a public body to an aggregate, especially for measuring the impact of federal policies upon a regional economy.
4. A framework for projections and forecasts of future trends either economic or, less frequently, social.
5. A basis for analyzing and studying causal and functional relationships either by direct comparisons (interregional, over time, or structural), or as part of more elaborate models.

163

6. An aid in formulating policies by providing a means of assessing their impact upon phenomena only indirectly influenced by the measure considered.

7. A data basis for regional planning. In this category the very different requirements due to changing time horizons (short, intermediate, and long-range planning) and to differences in coverage (partial and comprehensive planning) should be mentioned.

It is rather doubtful that a single system of accounts could be developed satisfying the myriad needs and uses to which they are presently being put. Of the five main types of social accounts, the income and products accounts are most useful in providing a current check on the performance of the regional economy. The analysis is most often based on major aggregates—gross regional product, net regional product, and regional income. Closely related to it is regional production analysis and the measurement of coefficients of a production function. The latter is, however, often concerned with long-run trends as well, and not infrequently is carried out in a more disaggregated form than would be feasible on the basis of income and product accounts alone.

Analysis of income distribution and consumption patterns, on the other hand, as a running check of the fulfillment of various social and political goals in order to provide for an in-depth analysis of consumer behavior, does not exceed the possibilities of this form of social accounting. Closely related is demand analysis, both as part of a study of market structure, and as a method of forecasting the most likely directions of development in the composition of regional production. Closely related to consumption, in terms of accounting, is analysis of savings and of their sectoral and spatial distribution. The economic significance of savings in regional studies is not so much related to the balance between savings and investments as to their sectoral distribution and impact upon future productive capacity.

Moneyflow or flow-of-funds accounts have not been sufficiently explored at the regional level, regarding their potential and usefulness. Yet moneyflows are obviously relevant as far as sensitivity of the regional economy to cyclical variations is concerned, and their study is capable of making an important contribution to capital market analysis. The results of recent research reveal that within a spatially unbalanced national economy there is very often a drain of savings and financial resources from the poorer to the more developed parts of the nation.[2] The lack of interest in regional moneyflows accounts is due partly to the very great difficulties encountered in their construction and partly to the remote likelihood of using monetary policy measures with regional objectives in mind.

The third type of social accounting, balance-of-payments accounts, has often been suggested as an indirect method of implementing export base studies. Aside from this rather limited objective, balance-of-payments accounts are useful in measuring the dependence of the regional economy upon national and international capital markets. When fully implemented, they are an important source of information concerning interregional transfers, both public and private, as well as interregional investments and returns on capital invested abroad.

The importance of wealth accounts as a form of social accounting at the regional level is potentially enormous. Properly developed, they are capable of revealing the major wealth aggregates and the composition and structure of each wealth aggregate, according to a variety of criteria. Extended over time and space, they may yield important insights into the ability of a region to generate growth and attract capital and labor resources from outside. The various aggregates derived from wealth accounts such as assets by type, by sector, by ownership, by use, by asset size, or by age composition, are important elements of regional econometric models. Of lesser importance for regional studies are financial assets, as the implications of differences in their composition by type and maturity class have never been worked out theoretically or practically. Standard ratios, such as capital stock to output relationship or capital productivity, are quite revealing for projected capital requirements and are frequently invoked. The importance of capital density analysis, of trends in capital deepening, is of obvious importance in assessing the effects of government policies. The difficult area of natural resources and of human capital has been discussed at some length in chapter 4. Progress in this respect is likely to bring about a significant improvement in our ability to analyze the working of a regional economy.

The interindustry flow accounts are of obvious importance in regional studies. They help to assess the size of existing multipliers, especially of those generated by changes in demand and in levels of government expenditures. They are used for such diverse purposes as assessing the interregional repercussions of investments in depressed regions or impacts of changes in defense spending upon regional economies. More generally, the disaggregated input-output accounts are indispensable in the study of repercussions attending upon changes in national policies. They might also be used to study price changes and the consequences for the regional price structure of changes in prices of some staples. The relevance of interindustry accounts for production analysis, for determining industrial dependency of the regional economy, and for market analysis is obvious. Another application is the identification of emerging industrial complexes, the promotion of which might be one of the main objectives of government policy.

Multiple Classifications and Converters

In order to examine the regional structure, it is necessary to consider the various phenomena from several points of view. Some regional studies and models may stress the sectoral structure of the regional economy or its institutional composition. For other problems, a classification of flows by type of commodities produced or by specific government programs may be more meaningful. For still other purposes, a classification in terms of employment either by industry or by type of skills may be relevant. It is not at all certain that a single system, satisfying all the diverse needs connected with regional analysis, can be developed.

Technically, the preliminary task of transforming sets of data to make them conform to different classification criteria can be handled by a set of interlocking rectangular matrices.[3] The off-diagonal blocks in the resulting partitioned matrix are referred to as converters. The system may be presented schematically.

The first classification is in terms of sectors or industries. All submatrices in the first row and column include a classification of flows by sector. The first entry on the main diagonal, T_{11}, is a square matrix with both rows and columns referring to sectors. The various entries show the incomings and outgoings of goods and services of different branches of production.

The second classification is in terms of commodities. All submatrices in the

$$
\begin{array}{cccccc}
 & \text{sectors} & \text{commodities} & \text{institutions} & \text{government programs} & \text{rest of the world} & \text{employment} \\
\end{array}
$$

T_{11}	T_{12}	T_{13}	T_{14}	T_{15}	0	sectors
T_{21}	T_{22}	T_{23}	T_{24}	T_{25}	0	commodities
T_{31}	T_{32}	T_{33}	0	T_{35}	T_{36}	institutions
0	0	T_{43}	0	0	0	government programs
T_{51}	T_{52}	T_{53}	T_{54}	0	0	rest of the world
T_{61}	T_{62}	T_{63}	T_{64}	T_{65}	0	employment

second row and second column include a classification of flows in terms of commodities. The commodities required as inputs in the production of each commodity are shown in the square submatrix T_{22} on the main diagonal. This square array with both rows and columns showing identical classification is an input-output flow matrix in terms of commodities. It is sometimes held that the coefficients derived with help of this matrix show greater stability than those based on the more usual intersectoral flows. The submatrix T_{12} in the first row is a rectangular array with rows corresponding to sectors and columns to commodities. Its rows thus show the composition of output of each sector in terms of commodities, while its columns show the sectoral origin of inputs into each group of commodities. The symmetrically located rectangular matrix T_{21} indicates, in each column, the commodity composition of inputs into each industry. Its rows, which correspond to commodity groups, summarize the destination of flows by receiving industrial sectors. Together the two submatrices T_{12} and T_{21} are very useful in analyzing the commodities-sectors relationships. The method is widely used in Canada both at the national and provincial levels. It gives rise to some interesting models dealing with capacity constraints.

The third classification is in terms of institutional groupings such as households (possibly disaggregated by type of household), unincorporated business, corporations, governments (by level and possibly by type of agency), and nonprofit organizations. The flows between aggregates defined in these terms are recorded in the square submatrix T_{33}, located on the main diagonal. The intersection with the flows classified in terms of industrial sectors is shown in the rectangular submatrix T_{31}. Its rows indicate, for each institutional sector, primary inputs contributed to each industry; each column indicates primary inputs of each industry disaggregated by institutional sectors in which they originate. The symmetrically located submatrix T_{13} indicates the destination of sectoral outputs by institutional groupings. It corresponds roughly to the bill of goods of a simple input-output table organized by industrial sectors.

The intersection between the system of flows grouped according to type of commodity and those grouped according to institutional sector is summarized in the two rectangular submatrices T_{23} and T_{32}. The rows of the former show the composition of consumers of each commodity—and thus indirectly its position in the economic system—while the columns indicate the total of commodities and services consumed by each institutional grouping of economic units. The rows of submatrix T_{32} show the contribution of primary inputs supplied by each institutional sector to the production of each commodity. Its columns indicate the sources of primary inputs used in producing each commodity within the system.

The fourth classification deals with the role of government and classifies flows according to government programs of which they form a part. For many purposes, classification by programs such as education, fire protection, military spending, or public housing, is more meaningful than by the government agencies responsible for their operation, despite the fact that very heterogeneous flows are thus locked together. The relationship between this classification and the one formerly discussed dealing with institutional groupings is demonstrated in the rectangular array T_{43}. This submatrix shows in each row the amounts earmarked for financing government programs. The sources are grouped according to institutional sectors covering mainly the government agencies responsible for portions of a particular program. The rows of the submatrix indicate various government programs, and the columns indicate the institutional sectors with emphasis on government agencies.

The flows of goods and services consumed by each government program are summarized in submatrices T_{14} and T_{24}. The former concentrates on the relationships between industrial sectors and government programs. Each of its rows indicates the contribution of an industrial sector to the various government programs, while each column of the submatrix indicates the sources of the commodities and services consumed by each government program according to the industrial sector producing them. The matrix T_{24} is similar to it, except that its rows refer to commodities. Thus each row indicates the destination in quantitative terms of a particular commodity to the extent that it is consumed by various government programs, while each column indicates the commodities content of a particular program.

The fifth classification deals with the rest of the world. For purposes of regional social accounting, the rest of the world might be disaggregated into the rest of the nation and foreign countries. More elaborate classifications might also be useful under special circumstances. Thus the rest of the nation might be divided into the rest of the state or the rest of the region of which the particular jurisdiction forms a part and the rest of the nation. Similarly, foreign countries might be divided into certain groupings. Less frequently, transactions with the rest of the world might be subdivided into some functional subcategories.

The submatrices T_{51} and T_{15} deal with imports and exports respectively, cross-classified by the regions supplying or receiving them, and by the local industrial sector concerned. Similarly, submatrices T_{53} and T_{35} show imports and exports grouped according to the institutional sectors concerned. Submatrix T_{54} indicates imports according to the government program consuming them.

The sixth classification is concerned with employment by type of skills required. These converters, important for many purposes, are contained in the submatrices T_{61}, T_{62}, T_{63}, T_{64}, T_{65}, and T_{36}. The flows are in terms of men-years, by type of skills.

Submatrix T_{61} indicates the inputs of labor into the various industrial sectors. Each row refers to one particular type of skill and indicates its use in men-years by various industrial sectors. Submatrix T_{62} indicates the labor requirements in men-years of various commodities produced in the system, by type of skills. The rows indicate the distribution of the flows of labor by type of skills into various commodities, and the columns indicate the men-years of labor, by type of skill, required for the production of a particular commodity. Submatrix T_{63} indicates the requirements of labor in men-years, by type of skills, according to various institutional groupings, while submatrix T_{64} indicates the labor requirements of various government programs. Submatrix T_{65} indicates the labor content of exports to the rest of the world. Its rows refer to labor possessed of various skills, while its columns indicate various portions of the rest of the world. Submatrix T_{36} refers to educational and training activities and indicates the output of skills by various institutional sectors. Its entries are negative. Each row indicates the output of a particular institutional sector divided according to various skills. Each column refers to a particular skill and indicates the institutional origin of people possessing that skill in a particular year.

A Generalized System of Accounts

The system of multiple classifications and converters, extensive and difficult to implement as it undoubtedly is, fails to encompass several phenomena which are often of crucial importance to the regional planner. The flows so far considered were the "real" ones, that is, those limited to goods, services, and contributions of factors of production. To them could be added financial flows which, although often omitted at the less sophisticated level of inquiry, nonetheless provide some important insights into the decision-making processes, at the regional as well as at the national level. But even the "real" flows are often not sufficiently disaggregated to provide a basis for in-depth analysis. A classification of flows in terms of current production and consumption, on the one hand, and of capital account, on the other, is often of significant interest. The problem of separating flows relating to capital accumulation is conceptually straightforward, but its implementation is beset by many practical difficulties.

Far more involved, both practically and conceptually, are problems relating to integration of stock and flow accounts. Not only do regional stock accounts exist only at one point in time, but their relation to other phenomena is by no means as clear-cut as one might expect. It has already been mentioned that many significant components of wealth accounts are not easily quantifiable in money terms, while some are difficult to quantify in any units. Moreover, the relation of social accounts to the ecosystem within which the regional economy operates has hardly been explored or systematized even at the abstract theoretical level. Many functional relations of great importance at the local level are involved and almost all of them seem to be nonlinear in character.

Recently, there have been several attempts to develop generalized systems of national social accounts, but the important differences in scope and objectives of regional studies require an approach specifically designed for dealing with problems within a more limited frame of reference.[4] A crude synthesis of the several types of accounts is presented in Figure 7-1.

The upper part of diagram represents the accumulations of various types of assets in the form of regional wealth accounts at the beginning of the accounting period. The components of regional wealth are cross-classified according to a number of criteria. The first distinction is between appropriable and non-appropriable assets. The former are further divided into real assets, comprised of both tangible and intangible assets, and financial assets. The classification by sectors corresponds to control over wealth, while the classification by institutions corresponds to ownership. The nonappropriable assets are comprised of assets often classified as free goods such as water or clean air. This classification forms part of the more general classification by commodities. Furthermore, the nonappropriable assets comprise also human resources which form a category apart.

The next part of the table deals with various aspects of the working of the regional economy: production, consumption, and capital accumulation. Production processes taking place in a market economy can be described in three different ways by recording: (1) the contributions of factors of production which correspond to the distribution of claims to the goods and services produced, (2) the distribution or the uses made of the products, or (3) the summation of the value-added in the various processes. The threefold aggregate classification forms the regional income and products account which, however, are ordinarily limited to only two of the three classifications possible.

In disaggregated form, the production processes are customarily presented in the form of input-output tables. The most commonly used input-output tables are square, employing sectors or industries as the criteria of classification. In terms of the symbols introduced in the preceding sections, they correspond to submatrix T_{11}.

An extension of the input-output accounts model to comprise commodities, institutions, programs and employment, has already been discussed in detail. The submatrices corresponding to the second classification criteria and describing complementary aspects of the working of the regional economy are listed in part 2 of Figure 7-1.

Activities broadly related to consumption may be roughly divided into the consumption of private goods on the one hand, and of public goods and services on the other. The first, in aggregate form, are represented by entries in the personal income and expenditures accounts forming part of the regional income and product accounts. The latter correspond roughly in the aggregate form to the government accounts. In both accounts the "sources" sides indicate the sector in which the claims to goods and services produced by the regional economy originate, while the "uses" sides indicate the type of goods and services purchased with their help. In a disaggregated form, consumption and the claims

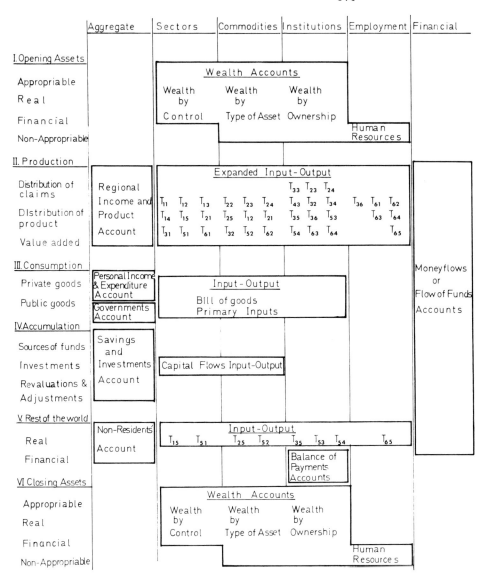

Figure 7-1. Hypothetical System of Regional Accounts.

arising out of the use of factors of production are presented in an input-output accounts model in the set of columns corresponding to the bill of goods, and in the set of rows corresponding to the primary inputs. Both can be classified or cross-classified in terms of sectors, commodities, or institutions. A discussion of the problems encountered in attempting to reconcile totals of flows classified according to different criteria was presented in the preceding section and in Chapter 5. These problems are schematically indicated in part 3 of Figure 7-1.

The accounts dealing with activities related to accumulation must display the sources of funds, especially of savings, and the way in which those funds are invested. In aggregate form, the accumulation processes are presented in the savings and investments account of the income and product accounts. In addition, the savings and investment account encompasses revaluations and various adjustments, although these items are of lesser analytical importance. In a disaggregated form, investments form the capital flows or dynamic input-output table. In principle, the capital flows input-output model may be constructed so as to emphasize the sectoral structure of investments or their commodities content. The accounts dealing with capital flows are indicated in part 4 of Figure 7-1.

The dealings with the rest of the world often assume for the regional economy an importance greater than that for the nation as a whole. They can be presented either in "real" terms or in terms of financial flows. In aggregate form, the "real" flows across regional boundaries are summarized in the nonresidents' account of the regional income and product accounts. The left- and right-hand side of this account show respectively the amounts earned from nonresidents and the amounts due to nonresidents for goods and services received.

In a disaggregated form, the rest of the world is represented by several columns and rows of an input-output flows matrix. Again, the flow matrix may be constructed in terms of sectors or in terms of commodities. Only infrequently are the relations with the rest of the world described in terms of institutions dealing with nonresidents. The theoretical possibility of an extension of the input-output accounts to encompass the institutional or employment aspects of foreign trade were discussed in connection with submatrices T_{35}, T_{53}, T_{54}, and T_{65}.

Financial transactions with the rest of the world are usually summarized in the balance-of-payments account. This type of social accounting is far more significant for the national economy but may also yield interesting analytical insights when dealing with an open region. The accounts related to the rest of the world are schematically presented in part 5 of Figure 7-1.

All real flows within the regional economy, that is, flows of goods and services, have their counterparts in financial transactions. The latter are summarized in moneyflows or flow-of-funds accounts which were previously discussed. The flow of funds accounts cover production, consumption, accumulation, and rest-of-the-world accounts, but are not limited to transactions appearing in the income and product or interindustry accounts. So far they have been disaggregated almost exclusively in terms of the institutional characteristics of these flows.

The last part of the system deals with closing assets. The wealth accounts established at the end of the accounting period would be theoretically equivalent to those describing the opening assets. The numerical differences between corresponding entries in the two accounts could be used to derive incremental changes during the reporting period. The closing wealth accounts are indicated in part 6 of Figure 7-1.

Some Tentative Conclusions

The review of the existing systems of regional social accounts, and of their various uses and potential extensions, highlights several features of this approach to regional planning and analysis. They appear to be an eminently useful tool of inquiry at an early stage of regional research. They complement the existing collections of regional data whether in the form of data banks or *ad hoc* efforts related to a planning operation. They integrate the often scattered pieces of numerical information into a comprehensive system yielding some preliminary insights into the operation of the regional economy.

However, the study also underlines the important shortcomings of the main social and accounting systems used at the regional level. They are all derived directly or indirectly from the corresponding national economic accounting practices. But in view of the vast differences in objectives, scope, and instruments available for implementing economic policies, it is necessary to develop regional accounts systems that differ in important respects from the national ones. Such systems, nonetheless, are likely to emerge only gradually, through a relatively slow process of change and addition. Because of the peculiarities of regional planning, any regional social accounting system would have to stress more strongly stock phenomena, with some emphasis on the difficult problem of goods lacking some or even all of the attributes of a commodity. Far more weight has also to be given to the phenomena related to the production and consumption of public goods and services, even though little progress has so far been made in developing methods of quantifying and expressing them in money terms. Once accomplished, this alone would permit their full integration into the analytical framework upon which social accounting and regional economic analysis are based.

Because of the specific needs and demands placed on regional social accounts, the question of indicators to be derived from numerical data arises. The usual major aggregates, which form part of national income and product accounts either directly or indirectly, do not appear to be the most significant or even the most relevant tools of inquiry into a regional economy. The methods that could be used to develop indicators of the performance of a regional economy and of its attractiveness in terms of potential flows of goods, investments, and migrants, are far from clear. Even less progress has been achieved so far in constructing indicators of the welfare of the inhabitants of a region and its geographic subdivisions. The latter indicators are likely to be far more important for regional studies with emphasis on welfare and equity than for studies dealing with the nation as a whole.

With so much yet to be accomplished in developing both theoretical and applied aspects of regional social accounts, the difficulties arising from an inadequate data basis are understandably receiving a lot of attention. It would appear, however, that the development of a centralized system of regional data banks covering the whole nation is as yet premature. While intensive pilot studies are certainly called for, the major investments required in making such a system operational should be delayed until more progress has been made in constructing the conceptual and practical framework for regional social accounting.

Notes

1. According to Bert G. Hickman, ed., *Quantitative Planning of Policy*, The Brookings Institution, 1965, p. 10, "the closest link between quantitative economic analysis and actual policy decisions is clearly to be found in the Netherlands. There the short-term macroeconomic model is used not only to make forecasts on the assumption of unchanged policies but also to predict the policy outcomes associated with proposed action programs or to predict the instrumental combinations needed to achieve specified targets. . . . The quantitative estimates of the Central Planning Bureau do indeed importantly affect the actual decisions . . . ."

2. Chile, Equador, France, Germany, Hungary, Italy, Japan, Netherlands, Norway, Puerto Rico, U.S.A., Yugoslavia.

3. Regional development is obviously also affected by decisions of such diverse nongovernment bodies as boards of large corporations, nonprofit organizations, or private citizens.

4. Peter Hall, *Von Thünen's Isolated State*, Pergamon Press, 1966; and Alfred Weber, *Theory of the Location of Industries*, University of Chicago Press, 1929. Both von Thünen and Weber treated space as largely continuous and they were followed by several others including, more recently, Louis Lefeber, *Allocation in Space*, North Holland Publishing Co., 1958.

5. T. C. Koopmans, "Measurement without Theory," *Review of Economic Statistics*, 29 (1947): 161 ff.

6. There are, of course, several alternative ways of classifying regional studies. For a possible approach see Stanislaw Czamanski, "Industrial Location and Urban Growth," *The Town Planning Review*, Liverpool, 36, no. 3 (October 1965): 165-80; and Czamanski, "Regional Policy Planning."

7. For an examination and evaluation of several types of simple multipliers, see Walter Isard, and Stanislaw Czamanski: "Techniques for Estimating Local and Regional Multiplier Effects of Changes in the Level of Major Governmental Programs," *Papers, Peace Research Society (International)* 3 (1965): 19-45.

8. There is currently, however, considerable interest in regional applications of such related concepts as integer programming, quadratic programming, and game theory.

9. E. Malinvaud, "Notes sur l'étude des procedures de planification," *Canadian Journal of Economics* 1, no. 1 (February 1968): 28.

10. Social accounts as developed at the national level are, in fact, economic accounts. Hardly any variables other than economic ones were ever included in those accounts. The word "social" in the name means that they refer to society

as a whole to distinguish them from business accounts. For attempts to generalize from economic relationships and the price mechanism to all types of social interaction see, for example, George C. Homans, *Social Behavior: Its Elementary Forms,* Harcourt, Brace & World, 1961.

11. See, for example, Walter Isard, et al., *Methods of Regional Analysis: An Introduction to Regional Science,* The M.I.T. Press and John Wiley, 1960, 8-121; Charles L. Leven, "Theory and Method of Income and Product Accounts for Metropolitan Areas, Including the Elgin-Dundee Area as a Case Study," Iowa State University, 1958 (mimeo.); and Stanislaw Czamanski, *Regional Income and Product Accounts of North-Eastern Nova Scotia,* Institute of Public Affairs, Dalhousie University, 1966.

12. For details, see Stanislaw Czamanski, "Regional Science and Regional Planning," *Plan: Journal of the Town Planning Institute of Canada,* 9, no. 2 (1968): 63.

13. The most extensive studies completed to date are P. J. Bourque, et al., *The Washington Interindustry Study for 1963,* Reprint No. 10, Center for Urban and Regional Studies, University of Washington, Seattle, Washington, 1966; Walter Isard, T. W. Langford, Jr., and E. Romanoff, *Philadelphia Region Input-Output Study,* 4 vols., Regional Science Research Institute, 1966; W. L. Hansen, and Charles M. Tiebout: "An Intersectoral Flows Analysis of the California Economy," *Review of Economics and Statistics,* 45 (November 1963): 409-418; Werner Z. Hirsch, "Interindustry Relations of a Metropolitan Area," *Review of Economics and Statistics,* 45 (November 1959): 360-69; and Frederich T. Moore, and James W. Peterson: "Regional Analysis: An Interindustry Model of Utah," *Review of Economics and Statistics,* 37 (November 1955): 368-83. A more complete listing is given in Phillip J. Bourque, and Millicient Cox: *An Inventory of Regional Input-Output Studies in the United States,* Occasional Paper no. 22 University of Washington, Graduate School of Business Administration, 1970.

14. Hollis B. Chenery, and Paul G. Clark: *Interindustry Economics,* John Wiley, 1962, p. 7.

15. Wassily Leontief, et al.: *Studies in the Structure of the American Economy,* Oxford University Press, 1953, Ch. 3.

16. Stanislaw Czamanski, with the assistance of Emil Malizia, "Applicability and Limitations in the Use of National Input-Output Tables for Regional Studies," *Papers and Proceedings of the Regional Science Association* 23 (1969): 65-77.

17. See Rose Knight, ed., *Bibliography on Income and Wealth,* International Association for Research in Income and Wealth, vol. 8, Bowes and Bowes, 1964, and Emil E. Malizia, "Regional Wealth Accounting as a Means of Quantitative Evaluation of Regional Resources," Ph.D. dissertation, Cornell University, 1969.

18. See, for example, Glenn O. Johnson, "An Automated Data System: The

Los Angeles Approach:, in University of California, Department of City and Regional Planning, Center for Planning and Development Research and Institute of Urban and Regional Research, eds., *Proceedings of the Fourth Annual Conference on Urban Planning Information Systems and Programs,* University of California, November 1966, 10-23; and L. S. Jay, "Data Collection Systems for Metropolitan Planning," *Papers and Proceedings of the Regional Science Association,* 16 (1966): 77-92.

19. Harvey S. Perloff and Charles L. Leven: "Towards an Integrated System of Regional Accounts: Stocks, Flows, and the Analysis of the Public Sector," in Werner Z. Hirsch, ed., *Elements of Regional Accounts,* Johns Hopkins Press, 1964, pp. 180-81.

20. More detailed discussion of the accounts and their interrelationships is found in G. Stuvel, *Systems of Social Accounts,* Clarendon Press, 1965; M. Yanovsky, *Social Accounting Systems,* Aldine Publishing Co., 1965; Sam Rosen, *National Income: Its Measurement, Determination, and Relation to Public Policy,* Holt, Rinehart and Winston, 1963; Erik Lundberg, ed., *Income and Wealth, Series 1,* Bowes and Bowes, 1951; and National Bureau of Economic Research, National Accounts Review Committee, *The National Economic Accounts of the United States: Review, Appraisal, and Recommendations— Extract,* Government Printing Office, 1958.

21. Walter Isard provides an excellent introductory discussion in *Methods of Regional Analysis,* pp. 122-81. Also, see Bowsher, N., J. Daane, and R. Einzig: "The Flows of Funds between Regions of the United States," *Papers and Proceedings of the Regional Science Association* 3 (1957): 139-65; and Charles L. Leven, "A Moneyflows Analysis of Metropolitan Saving and Investment," *Papers and Proceedings of the Regional Science Association* 7 (1961): 53-65.

Notes to Chapter 2
Intersectoral Flows of Goods and Services

1. For a general history of income and product accounts, see Paul Studenski, *The Income of Nations,* New York University Press, 1958; and Rosen, *National Income.*

2. Producing unit is any firm, individual or government agency that creates values by combining factors of production. By definition all productive activities are carried out by producing units, mainly business enterprises, although post offices and private doctors provide examples of the fairly numerous exceptions.

3. Notice that dividends and interest received from other corporations have been eliminated.

4. See, for example, Charles L. Leven, "Regional Income and Product Accounts: Construction and Applications," in Werner Hochwald, ed., *Design of*

Regional Accounts, John Hopkins Press, 1961, for a discussion of the direct approach; and Edwin F. Terry: "Regional Income Accounts Estimates" in Werner Z. Hirsch: *Elements of Regional Accounts,* Johns Hopkins Press, 1964; and Isard et al., *Methods of Regional Analysis,* for a review and general appraisal of the disaggregated approach.

5. Some systems treat sectors as aggregates of similar economic units, while others prefer the functional approach, viewing sectors as aggregates of similar transactions. These differences are sometimes reflected in names of sectors such as "producers" and "consumers" as against "enterprises" and "households."

6. By netting is meant the elimination of identical but opposite flows between pairs of transactors so that only the balances are shown. By consolidation is meant the elimination of flows between transactors belonging to the same sector.

7. The methodology of the Nova Scotia income and product accounts has been discussed in Czamanski, *Regional Income and Product Accounts of North Eastern Nova Scotia.*

8. The Canadian system of national income and expenditure accounts is somewhat similar to the one in use in the United States until 1957. It has six sector accounts, as against five in the present United States system. More important, at variance with the United States system, the major aggregates are not derived directly as part of the sectoral accounts.

9. The term "local governments" is used here to include both provincial and municipal governments (as distinct from federal) and certain public bodies as well.

10. Military personnel stationed in the area are considered as residents to the extent that during the 1961 census they declared their place of residence to be Nova Scotia. Other members of the military forces are treated in the accounts in much the same way as tourists. Their pay is thus indirectly considered in the accounts as invisible exports.

11. They are further broken down according to origin into wages and salaries received from business; local governments; nonlocal governments; other households; and nonresidents. This item is treated as income accruing to households rather than as total cost to business and other employers of obtaining the services of labor. Hence, employers' and employees' contributions to social insurance and government pension plans are deducted. Military pay and allowances, although similar in nature, are singled out as a separate entry.

12. Consumption was assumed to be identical to purchases of goods and services by households and nonprofit organizations. The estimates of purchases are broken down into those from business, direct services (the counterpart of this item is to be found in the same account), and expenditure abroad. Personal net saving is the balancing item and thus contains the residual error of estimate involved in all the items enumerated above.

13. The dividing line between these two categories is sometimes tenuous because the differences between certain types of indirect taxes and government services are elusive.

14. By exhaustive government expenditures are meant those which compete for scarce resources with other uses. The nonexhaustive government expenditures are those which simply recirculate or redistribute the claim to the national product. An illustration of an exhaustive government expenditure might be the construction of military aircraft using up raw materials, labor, and so forth, which could find alternative uses in production of consumer goods. On the other hand, veterans' benefits, for example, simply withdraw the money (claim on goods) from one section of the population (taxpayers) and give it to another (veterans).

15. For a detailed discussion of the problems involved, see Czamanski, *Regional Income and Product Accounts of North-Eastern Nova Scotia.*

16. Payments accruing to other factors of production are dealt with in the investment income appropriation account, to which the relevant balance is transferred from the business operating account.

17. Other estimates comprise unilateral transfer payments to residents and payments collected by local governments from nonresidents in respect of various (mainly property) taxes.

18. The reason usually advanced is that the bulk of federal debt has been contracted in order to finance the two World Wars and during the Great Depression. Interest paid in respect of it is thus not considered as payment for the use of borrowed capital (factor of production) but rather as a charge against social product. Whatever the arguments for or against this approach may be, the practice is long established in national social accounting in the United States and many other countries.

19. These undistributed profits are actually accruing to stockholders, whose place of residence is unknown. In regional social accounting the practice has been followed of allocating these amounts to the region in which the corporation has its headquarters irrespective of place of residence of ultimate owners or of where the actual operations take place.

20. For a discussion of problems involved in the construction of aggregates at the national level see, for example: Rosen, *National Income*; Richard Ruggles and Nancy D. Ruggles, *National Income Accounts and Income Analysis,* McGraw-Hill, 1956.; Wallace C. Peterson, *Income, Employment, and Economic Growth,* W.W. Norton, 1962.; and Charles L. Schultze, *National Income Analysis,* Prentice-Hall, 1964, pp. 18-39.

21. The last method is actually more appropriate for calculating gross domestic product or value of goods and services produced within the geographic boundaries of the region.

22 See, for example, Leven, "Theory and Method of Income and Product Accounts for Metropolitan Areas."

23. For more details see Leven: "Regional Income and Product Accounts."

24. Something similar could be observed on the national scale in the United States and other countries during the Great Depression. At that time it was largely, though not exclusively, due to increased government transfer payments in the face of mass unemployment and to generally increased government spending related to efforts to boost the economy.

25. For details concerning this type of multiplier, often described as foreign trade multiplier or interregional trade multiplier, and differences existing between these concepts, see J.S. Chipman, *The Theory of Intersectoral Money Flows and Income Formation,* Johns Hopkins Press, 1950, pp. 13-15; Isard, *Methods of Regional Analysis,* pp. 205-8; Peterson, *Income,* pp. 174-5, 225-6 and 301-3; and Lloyd A. Metzler, "A Multiple Region Theory of Income and Trade," *Econometrica* 18, no. 4 (1950): 329-54.

26. Analytically, far greater importance would attach to merginal multipliers of the form

$$\Delta Y = \frac{1}{1 - \bar{c} + \bar{m}} \Delta(I + G + E);$$

where

$$\bar{c} = \frac{\partial C}{\partial Y} = \text{marginal propensity to consume;}$$

$$\bar{m} = \frac{\partial M}{\partial Y} = \text{marginal propensity to import.}$$

These may be subject to very great fluctuations the magnitude and persistence of which may be only partly related to real causes, the greater part being simply due to the fact that marginal propensities are based on differences between successive estimates of GRP, consumption, and imports as recorded in the income and product accounts. The total estimates contain errors commensurate with the magnitude of the quantities involved and hence are acceptable, but these errors become overwhelming when referred to the much smaller yearly changes.

Notes to Chapter 3
Financial Flows

1. For a thorough discussion of the theory of international trade, see Charles P. Kindleberger, *International Economics,* Richard D. Irwin, 1953, ch. 5, 6, 7.

2. It may dissipate its advantage through, for example, lavish foreign aid, military ventures abroad, or indefensible in the long-run foreign investments.

3. For development of basic trade, comparative cost, and balance-of-payments concepts see Seymour E. Harris, *International and Interregional Economics,* McGraw-Hill, 1957, especially parts I & II.

4. Wojciech Morawski, "Balances of Interregional Commodity Flows in Poland: A Value Approach," *Papers, Regional Science Association* 20 (1968): 30.

5. Economic base theory is treated in detail in Charles M. Tiebout, *The Community Economic Base Study,* Supplementary paper no. 16, Committee for Economic Development, 1962, and Ralph Pfouts, ed., *The Techniques of Urban Economic Analysis,* Chandler-Davis, 1960.

6. Bertil Ohlin, *Interregional and International Trade,* Harvard University Press, 1933.

7. The seminal work in flow-of-funds accounting was Morris A. Copeland, *A Study of Money Flows in the United States,* National Bureau of Economic Research, 1952.

8. One of the few exceptions is the treatment of tax deductions from wages and salaries, which are shown as two distinct flows although wages and salaries are typically paid net of income tax.

9. Raymond Goldsmith, *The Flow of Capital Funds in the Postwar Economy,* National Bureau of Economic Research, 1965, p. 49.

10. Mcir Ileth, *The Flow of Funds in Israel,* Studies in International Economics and Development, Praeger, 1970, p. 36.

11. See Kindleberger, *International Economics,* p. 38, for typical national flow of funds accounting format.

12. See Heth, *Flow of Funds,* pp. 256-262.

13. Ibid., p. 263.

14. Ibid., p. 256.

15. For a more detailed statement on the difficulties in determining flows, see L. Grebler, "California's Dependence on Capital Imports for Mortgage Investment," *California Management Review,* 5 (1963): 47-54.

16. See, for example, J. C. Ingram, "State and Regional Payments Mechanism," *Quarterly Journal of Economics,* 63 (1959): 619-32, and Francis A. Lees, "Interregional Flows of Funds Through State and Local Government Securities (1957-1962)," *Journal of Regional Science,* 9 (April 1969): 79-86.

17. Bowsher, Daane, and Einzig, "Flows of Funds."

18. Leven, "A Moneyflows Analysis."

19. Grebler, "California's Dependence."

20. J. T. Romans, *Capital Exports and Growth among U. S. Regions,* Wesleyan University Press, 1965.

21. Penelope C. Hartland, *Balance of Interregional Payments of New England,* Brown University, 1950. See also, Isard, et al., *Methods of Regional Analysis,* pp. 144-63.

22. Isard discusses and reviews this type of study in his *Methods of Regional Analysis,* pp. 146-49.

23. Hartland, *Balance of Interregional Payments,* p. 1.

24. Ibid., pp. 150-63.

25. Bowsher, Daane, and Einzig, "Flows of Funds."

26. José Raymon Lasuén, "Regional Income Inequalities and the Problems of Growth in Spain," *Papers, Regional Science Association,* 8 (1962): 169-88.

Notes to Chapter 4
Regional Wealth

1. Sir William Petty, "Verbum Sapienti," in Edwin Cannan: *A History of the Theories of Production and Distribution in English Political Economy,* P.S. King & Sons, 1903, presents wealth estimates for 1679 and 1691.

2. Gregory King, "Natural and Political Observations and Conclusions upon the State and Condition of England, 1696," (Herald of Armes, 1696) in *Gregory King: Two Tracts,* ed. George E. Barnett, Johns Hopkins Press, 1936.

3. Simon Kuznets with Elizabeth Jenks, *Capital in the American Economy: Its Formation and Financing,* Princeton University Press, 1961.

4. Raymond W. Goldsmith, "A Perpetual Inventory of National Wealth Since 1896," in Conference on Research in Income and Wealth, *Studies in Income and Wealth,* 14, National Bureau of Economic Research, 1952.

5. Anthony Scott, "Canada's Reproducible Wealth," in International Association for Research in Income and Wealth, *Income and Wealth Series VIII;* and William C. Hood and Anthony Scott, *Output, Labour and Capital in the Canadian Economy,* Study for Royal Commission on Canada's Economic Prospects, Queen's Printer, 1957.

6. Jerome Rothenberg, "Values and Value Theory in Economics," in Sherman R. Krupp, ed., *The Structure of Economic Science,* Prentice-Hall, 1966, p. 222.

7. For a brief discussion, see Raymond W. Goldsmith, "Measuring National Wealth in a System of Social Accounting," Conference on Research in Income and Wealth, *Studies in Income and Wealth,* 12, National Bureau of Economic Research, 1950.

8. The addition of financial assets and liabilities, however, introduces some ambiguity in the definition. It is no longer quite clear whether regional wealth should be confined to elements located within specific geographic boundaries or

should be defined as wealth owned or controlled by economic units domiciled in the region.

9. Anthony Scott, *Natural Resources: The Economics of Conservation,* Canadian Studies in Economics, no. 3, University of Toronto Press, 1955, pp. 8, 86.

10. Edgar F. Palmer, *The Meaning and Measurement of the National Income and of other Social Accounting Aggregates,* University of Nebraska Press, 1966.

11. Goldsmith, "Measuring National Wealth in a System of Social Accounting," pp. 63-64; and Jack Revell, "The National Balance Sheet of the United Kingdom, *Review of Income and Wealth,* series 13 (December 1966), p. 286.

12. See J. C. Bonbright, "May the Same Property Have Different Values for Different Purposes?" *Proceedings of the National Tax Association,* 1927, p. 287.

13. Franco Modigliani, "Comment," Conference on Research in Income and Wealth, *Studies in Income and Wealth,* 12, National Bureau of Economic Research, 1950, p. 144.

14. See Raleigh Barlowe, *Land Resource Economics: The Political Economy of Rural and Urban Resource Use,* Prentice-Hall, 1958, pp. 157-60.

15. Land and imporvements might be treated as a joint product yielding services. See Ernest M. Fisher, *Urban Real Estate Markets: Characteristics and Financing,* Financial Research Program Studies in Urban Mortgage Financing, National Bureau of Economic Research, 1951, p. 5.

16. Karl Scholz, "Inadequacy of Actual Selling Price of Real Estate as Fvidence of Fair Present Value for Purposes of Taxation," *Annals of the American Academy of Political and Social Science,* 158 (March 1930): 157-64.

17. Walter Isard, et al., "On the Linkage of Socio-Economic and Ecological Systems," *Papers, Regional Science Association,* 21 (1968): 79-99.

18. Quality refers not only to the broad distinction between fresh and saline waters but to such characteristics as mineral content, presence of organic substances, temperature, and color.

19. A significant exception is the project of transporting water from northern to southern California.

20. The average annual supply of fresh water or water surplus potentially available for human use corresponds to the difference between precipitation in the catchment area and evapotranspiration and run-off. To the extent that the study region does not correspond to the catchment area, surface and underground inflows have to be accounted for.

21. See, for example, J. S. Nicholson, "The Living Capital of the United Kingdom," *Economic Journal,* 1 (March 1891): 95-107; Alfred de Fouville, "Ce que c'est que la richesse d'un peuple et comment on peut la mesurer," *Bulletin de l'Institut International de Statistique,* 14, no. 2 (1903): 62-74; Francesco Coletti, "Il costo di produzione dell'uomo e il valore economico degli

emigranti," *Giornale degli Economisti,* series 2, 30 (March 1905): 260-291; and J. R. Walsh, "Capital Concept Applied to Man," *Quarterly Journal of Economics,* 49 (1934-35): 255-85.

22. Charles H. Hull, ed., *The Economic Writings of Sir William Petty together with the Observation upon the Bills of Morality More Probably by Captain John Graunt,* Reprints of Economic Classics, I, August M. Kelley, 1963, pp. 259 and 267.

23. Adam Smith, *An Inquiry into the Nature and Causes of the Wealth of Nations,* edited by Edwin Connan with Max Lerner, Modern Library, 1937, pp. 265-66.

24. Irving Fisher, *Investment in Human Capital,* Macmillan Company, 1906, p. 1.

25. Alfred Marshall, *Principles of Economics,* 8th ed. Macmillan Company, 1920.

26. Theodore W. Schultz, "Investment in Human Capital," *American Economic Review,* 51 (March 1961): 2-3.

27. Schultz, "Investment in Human Capital," p. 6-7; and Theodore W. Schultz, "Investment in Man: An Economist's View," *Social Science Review,* 33 (June 1959): 114-16.

28. See, for example, P. J. Wiles, "The Nation's Intellectual Investment," *Bulletin of the Oxford University Institute of Statistics,* 18 (August 1956): 279-90; Eli Ginsberg, ed., *The Nation's Children,* 2 vols., Columbia University Press, 1960; Commission of Human Resources and Advanced Training, *America's Resources of Specialized Talent: A Current Appraisal and a Look Ahead,* Report prepared by Dael Wolfle, Director, Harper and Brothers, 1954; Eli Ginsberg, *Human Resources: The Wealth of a Nation,* Simon and Schuster, 1958; Harry G. Shaffer, "Investment in Human Capital: Comment," *American Economic Review,* 51 (December 1961): 1026-35; and, for good bibliographies on the subject, B. F. Kiker, *The Concept of Human Capital,* Essays in Economics, no. 14, College of Business Administration, University of South Carolina, November 1966; Marian C. Alexander-Frutsche, ed., *Human Resources and Economic Growth: An International Annotated Bibliography on the Role of Education and Training in Economic and Social Development,* Stanford Research Institute, 1963; and Mark Perlmen, ed., *Human Resources in the Urban Economy,* Johns Hopkins Press, 1963.

29. Consumption and investment are distinguished by their results. Pure consumption satisfies needs but has no effect on productivity, while pure investment changes capabilities and future productivity without satisfying needs.

30. Wiles, "Nation's Intellectual Investment"; Theodore W. Schultz, "Capital Formation by Education," *Journal of Political Economy,* 68, no. 6 (1960): 571-74; and Walsh, "Capital Concept," pp. 265-66.

31. See Fritz Machlup, *The Production and Distribution of Knowledge in the United States,* Princeton University Press, for the National Bureau of Economic Research, 1962, pp. 51-55.

32. For example, see Burton A. Weisbrod, "The Valuation of Human Capital," *Journal of Political Economy,* 69, no. 5 (1961): 425-36.

33. Kenneth J. Arrow, "The Economic Implications of Learning by Doing," *Review of Economic Studies,* 29 (June 1962): 155-73.

34. A. W. Phillips, "The Relation between Unemployment and the Rate of Change of Money Wage Rates in the United Kingdom, 1861-1957," *Economica,* 25 (1958): 283-99.

35. W. G. Bowen and R. A. Berry, "Unemployment Conditions and Movements of the Money Wage Level," *Review of Economics and Statistics,* 55 (1963): 162-72.

36. Frederick W. Bell, "An Econometric Forecasting Model for a Region," *Journal of Regional Science,* 7, no. 2 (1967): 109-127.

37. The following three forms were used:

$$(1)\ \frac{W_t - W_{t-1}}{W_{t-1}} = \underset{(2.037)}{-2.621} + \underset{(0.3284)}{0.7324}\left(\frac{U}{N_o}\right)_{t-1};\qquad \begin{array}{l} R^2 = 0.276; \\ d\ = 2.42; \end{array}$$

$$(2)\ \frac{W_t - W_{t-1}}{W_{t-1}} = \underset{(0.587)}{1.595} - \underset{(0.3852)}{0.7204}\left[\left(\frac{U}{N_o}\right)_t - \left(\frac{U}{N_o}\right)_{t-1}\right];$$

$$\begin{array}{l} R^2 = 0.212; \\ d\ = 2.57; \end{array}$$

$$(3)\ \frac{W_t - W_{t-1}}{W_{t-1}} = \underset{(2.371)}{-1.583} = \underset{(0.3946)}{0.5447}\left(\frac{U}{N_o}\right)_{t-1}$$

$$- \underset{(0.4431)}{0.3890}\left[\left(\frac{U}{N_o}\right)_{t-1} - \left(\frac{U}{N_o}\right)_{t-1}\right];\qquad \begin{array}{l} R^2 = 0.320; \\ d\ = 2.49; \end{array}$$

where

W = real wages
U = unemployment
N_o = labor force

d = Durbin-Watson statistic.
Numbers in parentheses refer to standard errors of regression coefficients.

The first equation shows a positive relationship between movement in real wages and unemployment, with a barely significant coefficient at the 5 percent level. Equations (2) and (3) have correct negative signs but the regression coefficients are not significant even at the 5 percent level. In the third equation, unemployment rate has again a positive sign.

38. Frederick W. Bell, "The Elasticity of Substitution, Regional Wage Differentials and Structural Unemployment in Urban Economies," Ph.D. dissertation, 1964.

39. Philip Ross, "Labor Market Behavior and the Relationship Between Unemployment and Wages," *Industrial Relations Research Association: Fourteenth Annual Proceedings,* 1961, pp. 275-88.

40. S. Czamanski, et al, *An Econometric Model of Nova Scotia,* Institute of Public Affairs, Dalhousie University, 1968.

41. Bernard Okun and Richard W. Richardson, "Regional Income Inequality and Internal Population Migrations," in John Friedmann and William Alonso, eds., *Regional Development and Planning,* M.I.T. Press, 1964, p. 306.

42. Talcott Parsons and Neil J. Smelser, *Economy and Society: Integration of Economic and Social Theory,* Free Press, 1965, p. 24.

43. See also Charles L. Leven, John B. Leglar, and Perry Shapiro, *An Analytical Framework for Regional Development Policy,* The M.I.T. Press, 1970.

44. Tibor, Barna, "On Measuring Capital," in F. A. Lutz, chairman, *The Theory of Capital,* D. C. Hague, ed., Macmillan, 1963, pp. 76-77.

45 The perpetual inventory method has been explained in detail in Raymond W. Goldsmith, "Measuring National Wealth in a System of Social Accounting;" idem, "A Perpetual Inventory of National Wealth Since 1896;" idem, *A Study of Saving in the United States,* Princeton University Press, 1955; idem, "The Growth of Reproducible Wealth of the United States: Trends and Structure," *Income and Wealth,* International Association for Research in Income and Wealth, 1961; idem, *The National Wealth of the United States in the Postwar Period,* Princeton University Press, for National Bureau of Economic Research, 1962; idem, with Robert E. Lipsey: *Studies in the National Balance Sheet of the United States,* Princeton University Press for National Bureau of Economic Research, 1963; Philip Redfern, "Net Investment in Fixed Assets in the United Kingdom, 1938-1953," *Journal of the Royal Statistical Soceity,* 118 pt 2 (1955): 141-92; Hood and Scott: *Output, Labour and Capital in the Canadian Economy;* and the work of T. K. Rymes in Statistics Canada, *Fixed Capital Flows and Stocks, Manufacturing, Canada, 1926-1960: Methodology* (Catalogue no. 13-522), 1967.

46. The estimates of Kuznets go back to 1869. Simon Kuznets, "On the Measurement of National Wealth," Conference on Research in Income and Wealth, *Studies in Income and Wealth,* 2, National Bureau of Economic Research, 1938.

47. Statistics Canada, *Fixed Capital Flows and Stocks.*

48. Malizia, "Regional Wealth Accounting."

Notes to Chapter 5
Interindustry Flows

1. For details, see Isard et al., *Methods of Regional Analysis,* pp. 270-73.

2. Charles P. Newman, *The Development of Economic Thought* (discussion of Quesnay's work with illustrations), Prentice-Hall, 1952; L. Walras, *Elements of Pure Economics,* translated by W. Jaffe; Richard D. Irwin, 1954; and Karl Marx, *Capital,* University of Chicago Press, 1906.

3. Isard et al., *Methods of Regional Analysis.* For a clear exposition, see William H. Miernyk, *The Elements of Input-Output Analysis,* Random House, 1965; U.N. Department of Economic and Social Affairs, *Problems of Input-Output Tables and Analysis,* United Nations, series F, no. 14, 1966. A complete recent bibliography is given in U.N. Department of Economic and Social Affairs, *Input-Output Bibliography 1966-1970* (2 vols.), United Nations, series M, no. 55, 1972.

4. P. Sargant Florence, *Investment, Location and Size of Plant,* Cambridge University Press, 1948, introduced the notions of index of specialization and index of exclusiveness. The following example makes it clear.

		Y	XXXXX	X YY
(A)	Z	Y	XXXXX	X YYY	(B)
	Z	Y	XXXXX	X YYY
		ZZZ	XX	X and
(C)		ZZZ	XX	other	(D)
		$ZZZZ$	XX	products

Assume A, B, C, and D are four plants composing the whole economy and X, Y, and Z, three of the products produced. In this case the economy produces, for example, 25 units of X, of which 15 are produced in plant A, 3 in plant B, 6 in plant C, and 1 in plant D. Thus 60 percent of X is produced in plant A. This fact is often summarized in an index of exclusiveness, which indicates the proportion of a product produced in a specific type of plant. Alternatively, switching the point of view from the whole economy to plant A alone, it is possible to conclude that A specializes in X to the extent of 75 percent of its output. Ideally, both indexes should be equal to one, but this is rarely the case; it occurs occasionally in such industries as grain mills, tobacco manufacturing, or production of matches. Both indexes are highly sensitive to the extent of disaggregation applied, and this severely limits their usefulness.

5. In the hypothetical example introduced in the previous footnote, Z is a subsidiary product in A while forming the main product in C.

6. The following discussion of treatment of by-products and most of the examples are based on Richard Stone, *Input-Output and National Accounts*, Organisation for Economic Cooperation and Development, 1961. Used by permission.

7. See Roland Artle, "Planning and Growth—A Simple Model of an Island Economy: Honolulu, Hawaii," *Papers, Regional Science Association*, 15 (1965): 29-44.

8. See Hansen and Tiebout, "California Economy;" and W. Lee Hansen, R. Thayne Robson, and Charles M. Tiebout, *Markets for California Products*, State of California Economic Development Agency, 1961.

9. See Leven, "Regional Income and Product Accounts: Construction and Applications."

10. Ernest R. Bonner and Vernon L. Fahle, *Techniques for Area Planning*, A Manual for the Construction and Application of a Simplified Input-Output Table, Regional Economic Development Institute, Pittsburgh.

11. T. J. Matuszewski, "Some Remarks on an Econometric Model of a Provincial Economy," Paper presented at the Congress of the Canadian Political Science Association, Vancouver, 1965.

12. Stone, *Input-Output and National Accounts*; and Leon Moses, "The Stability of Interregional Trading Patterns and Input-Output Analysis," *American Economic Review* 45 (1955): 803-32.

13. See Chenery and Clark, *Interindustrial Economics*.

14. The information theory approach was largely developed and extensively used by H. Theil. See F. Attneave, *Applications of Information Theory to Psychology*, Holt, Rinehart, 1959; Henri Theil et al., *Applied Economic Forecasting*, Rand McNally & Co., 1966, pp. 256-82; and C. B. Tilanus and H. Theil, *The Information Approach to the Evaluation of Input-Output Forecasts*, Econometric Institute of the Netherlands School of Economics, 1964. For a brief discussion of information theory as it applies to input-output studies, see appendix to this chapter.

15. Per Sevaldson, "The Stability of Input-Output Coefficients," in A. P. Carter and A. Brody, eds., *Applications of Input-Output Analysis*, North Holland, 1970, pp. 207-237.

16. Beatrice N. Vaccara, "Changes Over Time in Input-Output Coefficients for the United States," in A. P. Carter and A. Brody, eds., *Applications of Input-Output Analysis*, North Holland, 1970, pp. 238-260.

17. Walter Isard and Thomas W. Langford, *Regional Input-Output Study: Recollections, Reflections, and Diverse Notes on the Philadelphia Experience*, MIT Press, 1971.

18. Sevaldson, "Stability of Input-Output Coefficients."

19. Technically, the adjustment for changes in the price level is done by premultiplying the table of coefficients by a diagonal matrix whose nonzero elements are the relevant price ratios and postmultiplying it by its inverse.

$$A^* = \hat{p} \, A \, \hat{p}^{-1} \; ;$$

where

A = matrix of original technical coefficients;
A^* = matrix of adjusted technical coefficients;
$\hat{p}$ = diagonal matrix of price ratios, the elements of which are

$$p_i = \frac{p_i^t}{p_i^0} \; ;$$

p_i = average price ratio of the i-th sector;

p_i^0 = average price of outputs of sector i in year 0;

p_i^t = average price of outputs of sector i in year t.

20. T. Gigantes, "The Representation of Technology in Input-Output Systems," in A. P. Carter and A. Brody, eds., *Applications of Input-Output Analysis*, North Holland, 1970, pp. 270-90.

21. Felix Rosenfeld, et al., "Structure et Perspectives Économiques de la Province de Turin," *Metra*, 3, no. 4 (1964).

22. T. Y. Shen, "An Input-Output Table with Regional Weights," *Papers, Regional Science Association* 6 (1960): 113-19.

23. Czamanski and Malizia, "Applicability and Limitaitons in the Use of National Input-Output Tables for Regional Studies." See also the later work of Michael Bacharach, *Biproportional Matrices and Input-Output Change*, Cambridge University Press, 1970.

24. Bourque, et al., *The Washington Interindustry Study for 1963.*

25. The model is an adaptation of a model presented by Richard Stone and Alan Brown and used by them in order to adjust for changes in national input-output tables over time. See Richard Stone, *Mathematics in the Social Sciences and Other Essays*, Chapman & Hall, 1966, pp. 243-44; and Richard

Stone and Alan Brown, "Behavioral and Technical Change in Economic Models," in E.A.G. Robinson, ed., *Problems in Economic Development*, Macmillan & Co., 1965, pp. 433-36.

26. Malizia, "Regional Wealth Accounting."

27. Office of Business Economics, U.S. Department of Commerce, *Survey of Current Business* 46, no. 4 (April 1966): 14-17.

28. Bureau of Labor Statistics, U.S. Department of Labor, *Wholesale Prices and Price Indexes–1963,* Bulletin no. 1513, (June 1966).

Bureau of the Budget, Committee Staff, Subcommittee on Economic Statistics of the Joint Economic Committee and Office of Statistical Standards, "Consumer Price Index for Urban Wage Earners and Clerical Workers," *Economic Indicators,* Supplement, 1964, p. 91.

29. Bureau of Business, U.S. Department of Commerce, *Census of Business: 1963, Selected Services,* vol. 7, Area Statistics, pt 3, table 7, sect. 49, Washington: U.S. Government Printing Office, 1966, p. 5.

Bureau of the Census, U.S. Department of Commerce, *Census of Agriculture: 1959, Final Report, Counties,* vol. 1, state table 17, Washington: U.S. Government Printing Office, 1962, p. 42.

_____ , 1963, *Census of Manufacturers,* vol. 3, Area Statistics, Section 48, table 6, Washington: U.S. Government Printing Office, 1966, pp. 11-12.

_____ , 1963 *Census of Mineral Industries*: Washington, Area Statistics MIC 63(2), Section 46, Washington: U.S. Government Printing Office, 1962, pp. 4-5.

_____ , *Census of Population: 1960, Characteristics of the Population,* vol. 1, Washington, pt 49, table 62, Washington: U.S. Government Printing Office, 1962, pp. 114-115.

Guy G. Gordon, *A Study to Measure Direct and Indirect Impacts of Defense Expenditures on an Economy,* (A Report Submitted to the Arms Control and Disarmament Agency) Graduate School of Business Administration, University of Washington, November 1966.

30. Compare case I to II and III to IV, which are otherwise identical.

31. The location quotients were compiled by taking the ratio

$$L = \frac{E_{ir}}{E_r} \div \frac{E_{i.us}}{E_{us}} \; ;$$

where

L = location quotient;
E_{ir} = employment in industry i in Washington, 1963;
E_r = total employment in Washington State, 1963;
$E_{i.us}$ = employment in industry i in the U.S., 1963;
E_{us} = total employment in the U.S., 1963.

Notes to Chapter 6
Interregional Flows

1. W. Isard, "Interregional and Regional Input-Output Analysis: A Model of a Space Economy," *Review of Economics and Statistics* 33 (1951): 318-28.

2. E. O. Heady and H. W. Carter, "Input-Output Models as Techniques in the Analysis of Interregional Competition," *Journal of Farm Economics* 41 (1960): 978-91.

3. Werner Z. Hirsch, "An Application of Area Input-Output Analysis," *Papers and Proceedings of the Regional Science Association* 5 (1959): 79-92; and Roland Artle, *The Structure of the Stockholm Economy*, Cornell University Press, 1965.

4. R. E. Miller, "Interregional Feedback Effects in Input-Output Models; Some Preliminary Results," *Papers, Regional Science Association* 17 (1966): 105-25; idem, "Interregional Feedbacks in Input-Output Models: Some Experimental Results," *Western Economic Journal* 7 (1969): 41-50. See also David Greytak, "Regional Impact of Interregional Trade in Input-Output Analysis," *Papers, Regional Science Association* 25, (1970): 203-217.

5. For an early concise exposition, see Stone, *Mathematics in the Social Sciences and Other Essays.*

6. Hollis B. Chenery, "Interregional and International Input-Output Analysis," in Tibor Barna, ed., *The Structure Interdependence of the Economy,* John Wiley, 1956, pp. 341-55; and Chenery and Clark, *Interindustry Economics.*

7. Moses, "The Stability of Interregional Trading Patterns and Input Output Analysis".

8. Chenery and Clark, *Interindustry Economics.*

9. Leontief, et al., *Studies.* The formulas on pages 144 to 153 are largely drawn from Leontief's work and use his symbols. Used with permission. Copyright 1953 by Oxford University Press, Inc.

10. For the recent application of extensive interregional analysis, see Karen R. Polenske, *A Multiregional Input-Output Model of the United States,* report no. 21, U.S. Department of Commerce, Economic Development Administration, October 1970.

11. Stan Czamanski, "Some Empirical Evidence of the Strengths of Linkages between Groups of Related Industries in Urban-Regional Complexes," *Papers, Regional Science Association* 27 (1971): 137-50.

12. External economies, as opposed to economies of scale, are customarily classified into economies of agglomeration resulting from spatial concentration of like plants and into economies of urbanization resulting from agglomeration of unlike activities. Together they are referred to as economies of spatial juxtaposition.

13. Two additional approaches might be considered. The weaker involves the use of pooled coefficients of correlation in the construction of the matrix, whose entries become:

$$\rho_{ij} = \frac{(n_1 - 3)z'_1 + (n_2 - 3)z'_2 + (n_3 - 3)z'_3 + (n_4 - 3)z'_4}{\sqrt{(n_1 - 3) + (n_2 - 3) + (n_3 - 3) + (n_4 - 3)}};$$

where

$$z' = \tfrac{1}{2} \log_e \frac{1 + r}{1 - r};$$

A somewhat stronger alternative involved constructing an **R** matrix in which in addition each coefficient is set equal to zero, or $r_{lk} = r_{kl} = 0$; whenever

$$t \geqslant t_{.05};$$

and where

$$t = \frac{r}{s_r}; \quad \text{and } s_r = \frac{1 - r^2}{n - 2};$$

Furthermore, one could also examine four separate matrices of coefficients of correlation, or construct an **R** matrix by selecting the smallest of the four coefficients describing the relations between any pair of industries.

14. M. E. Streit, "Spatial Associations and Economic Linkages between Industries," *Journal of Regional Science*, 9, no. 2, (1969): 177-88; and Walter Isard, Eugene W. Schooler, and Thomas Vietorisz, *Industrial Complex Analysis and Regional Development*, The M.I.T. Press and John Wiley, 1959.

Notes to Chapter 7
A Generalized System of Accounts

1. See Czamanski, "Regional Policy Planning."

2. Lasuén, "Regional Income Inequalities," and Ramon Trias-Fargas and Ernesto Lluch Martin, "Balance of Payments Studies for the Region of Catalonia," *Papers, Regional Science Association* 10 (1962): 143-51.

3. Stone, *Input-Output and National Accounts*, idem, *Mathematics in the Social Sciences and Other Essays*, pp. 118-51.

4. Nancy and Richard Ruggles, *The Design of Economic Accounts*, NBER, distributed by Columbia University Press, 1970; John W. Kendrick, *Economic Accounts and Their Uses*, McGraw Hill Book Co., 1972.

Bibliography

Alexander-Frutschi, Marian C., ed. *Human Resources and Economic Growth: An International Annotated Bibliography on the Role of Education and Training in Economic and Social Development.* Stanford Research Institute, 1963.

Arrow, Kenneth J. "The Economic Implications of Learning by Doing," *Review of Economic Studies* 29 (June 1962): 155-73.

Artle, Roland. "Planning and Growth–A Simple Model of an Island Economy, Honolulu, Hawaii," *Papers, Regional Science Association* 15 (1965): 29-44.

_____. *The Structure of the Stockholm Economy.* Cornell University Press, 1965.

Attneave, F. *Applications of Information Theory to Psychology.* Holt, Rinehart, 1959.

Bacharach, Michael. *Biproportional Matrices and Input-Output Change.* Cambridge University Press, 1970.

Barlowe, Raleigh. *Land Resource Economics: The Political Economy of Rural and Urban Resource Use.* Prentice-Hall, 1958.

Barna, Tibor. "On Measuring Capital," in F. A. Lutz, Chairman: *The Theory of Capital,* D. C. Hague, ed. Macmillan, 1963, pp. 75-94.

Bell, Frederick W. "An Econometric Forecasting Model for a Region," *Journal of Regional Science* 7, 2, (1967): 109-127.

_____. *"The Elasticity of Substitution, Regional Wage Differentials and Structural Unemployment in Urban Economies."* Ph.D. dissertation, 1964.

Bonbright, J. C. "May the Same Property Have Different Values for Different Purposes?" *Proceedings of the National Tax Association,* 1927, pp. 279-95.

Bonner, Ernst R. and Fahle, Vernon L. *Techniques for Area Planning. A Manual for the Construction and Application of a Simplified Input-Output Table.* Regional Economic Development Institute, Pittsburgh, undated.

Bourque, Phillip J. and Cox, Millicent. *An Inventory of Regional Input-Output Studies in the United States.* Occasional Paper no. 22, University of Washington, Graduate School of Business Administration, 1970.

Bourque, Phillip J.; Chambers, E. J.; Chin, J. S.; Derman, F. L.; Dowdle, B.; Gordon, G. G.; Thomas, M.; Tiebout, C. M.; and Weeks, E. E. *The Washington Interindustry Study for 1963.* Reprint no. 10, Center for Urban and Regional Studies, University of Washington, Seattle, Washington, 1966.

Bowen, W. G. and Berry, R. A. "Unemployment Conditions and Movements of the Money Wage Level," *Review of Economics and Statistics* 45 (1963): 163-72.

Bowsher, N., Daane, J., and Einzig, R. "The Flows of Funds between Regions of the United States," *Papers and Proceedings of the Regional Science Association* 3 (1957): 139-59.

Bureau of the Budget, Committee Staff, Subcommittee on Economic Statistics of the Joint Economic Committee and Office of Statistical Standards, "Consumer Price Index for Urban Wage Earners and Clerical Workers," *Economic Indicators,* Supplement, 1964, p. 91.

Bureau of Business, U. S. Department of Commerce. *Census of Business, 1963, Selected Services,* vol. 7, Area Statistics, part 3, table 7, section 49, Washington, U. S. Government Printing Office, 1966, p. 5.

Bureau of the Census, U. S. Department of Commerce, *U. S. Census of Agriculture, 1959, Final Report, Counties,* vol. 1, state table, 17, Washington: U. S. Government Printing Office, 1962. p. 42.

_____ , 1963 *Census of Manufacturers,* vol. 3, Area Statistics, sect. 48, table 6, Washington: U. S. Government Printing Office, 1966.

_____ , 1963 *Census of Mineral Industries,* Washington, Area Statistics M I C 63 (2), sect. 46, Washington: U. S. Government Printing Office, 1962.

_____ , *Census of Population: 1960, Characteristics of the Population,* vol. 1, Washington, part 49, table 62, Washington: U. S. Government Printing Office, 1962.

Bureau of Labor Statistics, U. S. Department of Labor, *Wholesale Prices and Price Indexes—1963,* Bulletin no. 1513, 1966.

Canada. Statistics Canada. *Fixed Capital Flows and Stocks, Manufacturing, Canada, 1926-1960: Methodology.* Catalogue no. 13-522.

Chenery, Hollis B. "Interregional and International Input-Output Analysis" in Tibor Barna, ed. *The Structural Interdependence of the Economy,* John Wiley, 1956.

Chenery, Hollis B. and Clark, Paul G. *Interindustry Economics.* John Wiley, 1959, 1962.

Chipman, J. S. *The Theory of Intersectoral Money Flows and Income Formation.* Johns Hopkins Press, 1950.

Coletti, Francesco. "Il costo di produzione dell'uomo e il valore economico degli emigranti," *Giornale degli Economisti,* series 2, 30 (March 1905): 260-91.

Commission of Human Resources and Advanced Training. *America's Resources of Specialized Talent: A Current Appraisal and a Look Ahead.* Report prepared by Dael Wolfle, Director. Harper and Brothers, 1954.

Copeland, Morris A. *A Study of Money Flows in the United States,* National Bureau of Economic Research, 1952.

Czamanski, Stanislaw. "Industrial Location and Urban Growth," *The Town Planning Review,* Liverpool, 36, 3 (October 1965): 165-80.

_____ . *Regional Income and Product Accounts of North-Eastern Nova Scotia.* Institute of Public Affairs, Dalhousie University, 1966.

_____ . "Regional Policy Planning: Some Possible Implications for Research," *Annals of Regional Science* 4, 2 (December 1970).

_____ . "Regional Science and Regional Planning," *Plan: Journal of the Town Planning Institute of Canada,* 9, 2 (1968).

_____ . "Some Empirical Evidence of the Strengths of Linkages between Groups of Related Industries in Urban-Regional Complexes," *Papers, Regional Science Association* 27 (1971): 137-50.

Czamanski, Stanislaw, with the assistance of Emil E. Malizia. "Applicability and Limitations in the Use of National Input-Output Tables for Regional Studies," *Papers, and Proceedings Regional Science Association,* 23 (1969): 65-77.

Czamanski, S., et al. *An Econometric Model of Nova Scotia.* Institute of Public Affairs, Dalhousie University, 1968.

Fisher, Ernest M. *Urban Real Estate Markets: Characteristics and Financing.* Financial Research Program Studies in Urban Mortgage Financing. National Bureau of Economic Research, 1951.

Fisher, Irving. *Investment in Human Capital.* Macmillan Company, 1906.

Florence, P. Sargant. *Investment, Location and Size of Plant.* Cambridge University Press, 1948.

Fouville, Alfred de. "Ce que c'est que la richesse d'un peuple et comment on peut la mesurer," *Bulletin de l'Institut International de Statistique* 14, 2, (1903): 62-74.

Gigantes, T. "The Representation of Technology in Input-Output Systems," in Carter and Brody, eds. *Applications of Input-Output Analysis,* North Holland Publishing Company, 1970.

Ginsberg, Eli. *Human Resources: The Wealth of a Nation.* Simon and Schuster, 1958.

_____ , ed. *The Nation's Children.* 2 vols. Columbia University Press, 1960.

Goldsmith, Raymond W. *The Flow of Capital Funds in the Postwar Economy.* National Bureau of Economic Research, 1965.

_____ . "The Growth of Reproducible Wealth of the United States: Trends and Structures," *Income and Wealth,* International Association for Research in Income and Wealth, 1961.

_____ . "Measuring National Wealth in a System of Social Accounting," *Studies in Income and Wealth* 12, National Bureau of Economic Research, 1950.

_____ . *The National Wealth of the United States in the Postwar Period.* Princeton University Press for National Bureau of Economic Research, 1962.

_____ . "A Perpetual Inventory of National Wealth," *Studies in Income and Wealth* 14, National Bureau of Economic Research, 1952.

_____ . *A Study of Saving in the United States.* Princeton University Press, 1955.

Goldsmith, Raymond W., with Robert E. Lipsey. *Studies in the National Balance Sheet of the United States.* Princeton University Press for National Bureau of Economic Research, 1963.

Gordon, Guy G. *A Study to Measure Direct and Indirect Impacts of Defense Expenditures on an Economy.* A Report Submitted to the Arms Control and Disarmament Agency. Graduate School of Business Administration, University of Washington, 1966.

Grebler, L. "California's Dependence on Capital Imports for Mortgage Investment," *California Management Review* 5 (1963): 47-54.

Greytak, David, "Regional Impact of Interregional Trade in Input-Output Analysis," *Papers, Regional Science Association* 25 (1970): 203-17.

Hall, Peter, *Von Thünen's Isolated State.* Pergamon Press, 1966.

Hansen, W. Lee and Tiebout, Charles M., "An Intersectoral Flows Analysis of the California Economy," *Review of Economics and Statistics,* 45 (November 1963): 409-18.

Hansen, W. Lee, Robson, R. Thayne, and Tiebout, Charles M., *Markets for California Products,* State of California Economic Development Agency, 1961.

Harris, Seymour E. *International and Interregional Economics,* McGraw-Hill, 1957.

Harland, Penelope C. *Balance of Interregional Payments of New England.* Brown University, 1950.

Heady, E. O. and H. W. Carter. "Input-Output Models as Techniques in the Analysis of Interregional Competition," *Journal of Farm Economics* 41 (1960): 978-91.

Heth, Meir. *The Flow of Funds in Israel.* Special Studies in International Economics and Development. Praeger, 1970.

Hickman, Bert G., ed. *Quantitative Planning of Policy.* Brookings Institution, 1965.

Hirsch, Werner Z. "An Application of Area Input-Output Analysis," *Papers and Proceedings of the Regional Science Association* 5 (1959): 79-92.

———. "Interindustry Relations of a Metropolitan Area," *Review of Economics and Statistics* 41 (November 1959): 360-69.

Homans, George C. *Social Behavior: Its Elementary Forms.* Harcourt, Brace & World, 1961.

Hood, Wm. C. and Scott, Anthony. *Output, Labour and Capital in the Canadian Economy.* Report of the Royal Commission on Canada's Economic Prospects. Queen's Printer, 1957.

Hull, Charles H., ed. *The Economic Writings of Sir William Petty Together with the Observation upon the Bills of Morality More Probably by Captain John Graunt.* Reprints of Economic Classics, I, August M. Kelley, 1963.

Ingram, J. C. "State and Regional Payments Mechanisms," *Quarterly Journal of Economics* 73 (1959): 619-32.

Isard, Walter. "Interregional and Regional Input-Output Analysis: A Model of a Space-Economy," *Review of Economics and Statistics,* 33 (November 1951): 318-28.

Isard, Walter and Czamanski, Stanislaw. "Techniques for Estimating Local and Regional Multiplier Effects of Changes in the Level of Major Governmental Programs," *Papers, Peace Research Society (International),* 3 (1965): 19-45.

Isard, Walter and Langford, Thomas W., Jr. *Regional Input-Output Study: Recollections, Reflections and Diverse Notes on the Philadelphia Experience.* The M.I.T. Press, 1971.

Isard, Walter, Langford, T. W.,Jr., and Romanoff, E. *Philadelphia Region Input-Output Study,* 4 vols., Regional Science Research Institute, 1966.

Isard, Walter, Schooler, Eugene W., and Vietorisz, Thomas. *Industrial Complex Analysis and Regional Development.* The M.I.T. Press and John Wiley, 1959.

Isard, Walter et al. "On the Linkage of Socio-Economic and Ecological Systems," *Papers, Regional Science Association* 21 (1968): 79-99.

_____ . *Methods of Regional Analysis: An Introduction to Regional Science.* The M.I.T. Press and John Wiley, 1960.

Jay, L. S. "Data Collection Systems for Metropolitan Planning," *Papers and Proceedings of the Regional Science Association* 16 (1966): 77-92.

Johnson, Glenn O. "An Automated Data System: The Los Angeles Approach," in University of California, Department of City and Regional Planning, Center for Planning and Development Research and Institute of Urban and Regional Research, eds., *Proceedings of the Fourth Annual Conference on Urban Planning Information Systems and Programs,* University of California, November 1966.

Kendrick, John W., assisted by Carson, Carol S. *Economic Accounts and Their Uses.* McGraw-Hill, 1972.

Kiker, B. F. *The Concept of Human Capital.* Essays in Economics, no. 14. College of Business Administration, University of South Carolina, November 1966.

Kindleberger, Charles P. *International Economics,* Richard D. Irwin, 1953.

King, Gregory, "Natural and Political Observations and Conclusions upon the State and Condition of England, 1696" (Herald of Armes, 1696) in *Gregory King: Two Tracts,* George E. Barnett, ed., Johns Hopkins Press, 1936.

Knight, Rose, ed. *Bibliography on Income and Wealth,* International Association for Research in Income and Wealth, vol. 8, Bowes and Bowes, 1964.

Koopmans, T. C. "Measurement without Theory," *Review of Economics and Statistics* 29 (1947): 161-72.

Kuznets, Simon. "On the Measurement of National Wealth," Conference on

Research in Income and Wealth, *Studies in Income and Wealth* 2. National Bureau of Economic Research, 1938.

Kuznets, Simon, with Jenks, Elizabeth. *Capital in the American Economy: Its Formation and Financing,* Princeton University Press, 1961.

Lasuén, José Raymon. "Regional Income Inequalities and the Problems of Growth in Spain," *Papers, Regional Science Association* 8 (1962): 169-88.

Lees, Francis A. "Interregional Flows of Funds Through State and Local Government Securities (1957-1962)," *Journal of Regional Science* 9 (1969): 79-86.

Lefeber, Louis. *Allocation in Space.* North Holland Publishing, 1958.

Leontief, Wassily W. *Input-Output Economics.* Oxford University Press, 1966.

Leotief, Wassily W., et al. *Studies in the Structure of the American Economy.* Oxford University Press, 1953.

Leven, Charles L. "A Moneyflows Analysis of Metropolitan Saving and Investment," *Papers and Proceedings of the Regional Science Association* 8 (1961): 53-65.

_____ . "Regional Income and Product Accounts: Construction and Applications," in Werner Hochwald, ed., *Design of Regional Accounts.* Johns Hopkins Press, 1961.

_____ . "Theory and Method of Income and Product Accounts for Metropolitan Areas, Including the Elgin-Dundee Area as a Case Study." Ames, Iowa State University, 1958 (mimeo.).

Leven, Charles L., Legler, John B., and Shapiro, Perry. *An Analytical Framework for Regional Development Policy,* The M.I.T. Press, 1970.

Lundberg, Erik, ed. *Income and Wealth, Series I.* Bowes and Bowes, 1951.

Machlup, Fritz. *The Production and Distribution of Knowledge in the United States.* Princeton University Press, for the National Bureau of Economic Research, 1962.

Malinvaud, E. "Notes sur l'étude des procedures de planification," in *Canadian Journal of Economics* 1, no. 1 (February 1968).

Malizia, Emile E. "Regional Wealth Accounting as a Means of Quantitative Evaluation of Regional Resources." Ph.D. dissertation, Cornell University, 1969.

Marshall, Alfred. *Principles of Economics.* 8th ed. Macmillan Company, 1920.

Marx, Karl. *Capital.* University of Chicago Press, 1906.

Matuszewski, T. J. "Some Remarks on an Econometric Model of a Provincial Economy." Paper presented at the Congress of the Canadian Political Science Association, Vancouver, 1965.

Metzler, Lloyd A. "A Multiple Region Theory of Income and Trade," *Econometrica* 18 (1950): 329-54.

Miernyk, William H. *The Elements of Input-Output Analysis,* Random House, 1965.

Miller, R. E. "Interregional Feedback Effects in Input-Output Models: Some Preliminary Results," *Papers, Regional Science Association* 7 (1966): 105-25.

———. "Interregional Feedbacks in Input-Output Models: Some Experimental Results," *Western Economic Journal* 7 (1969).

Modigliani, Franco. "Comment," Conference on Research in Income and Wealth, *Studies in Income and Wealth,* 12. National Bureau of Economic Research, 1950.

Moore, Frederich T. and Peterson, James W. "Regional Analysis: An Interindustry Model of Utah," *Review of Economics and Statistics* 37 (November 1955): 368-83.

Morawski, Wojciech. "Balences of Interregional Commodity Flows in Poland: A Value Approach," *Papers, Regional Science Association* 20 (1968): 29-41.

Moses, Leon N. "The Stability of Interregional Trading Patterns and Input-Output Analysis," *American Economic Review* 45 (1955): 803-32.

National Bureau of Economic Research, National Accounts Review Committee, *The National Economic Accounts of the United States: Review, Appraisal, and Recommendations–Extract.* Government Printing Office, 1958.

Newman, Charles P. *The Development of Economic Thought.* Discussion of Quesnay's work with illustrations. Prentice-Hall, 1952.

Nicholson, J. S. "The Living Capital of the United Kingdom," *Economic Journal* 1 (1891): 95-107.

Office of Business Economics, U. S. Department of Commerce, *Survey of Current Business,* vol. 46, no. 4, 1966.

Ohlin, Bertil. *Interregional and International Trade,* Harvard University Press, 1933.

Okun, Bernard and Richardson, Richard W. "Regional Income Inequality and Internal Population Migrations," in John Friedmann and William Alonso, eds. *Regional Development and Planning.* The M.I.T. Press, 1964.

Palmer, Edgar Z. *The Meaning and Measurement of the National Income and of Other Social Accounting Aggregates.* University of Nebraska Press, 1966.

Parsons, Talcott and Smelser, Neil J. *Economy and Society: Integration of Economic and Social Theory.* Free Press, 1965.

Perlman, Mark, ed. *Human Resources in the Urban Economy.* Johns Hopkins Press, 1963.

Perloff, Harvey S. and Leven, Charles L. "Towards an Integrated System of Regional Accounts: Stocks, Flows, and the Analysis of the Public Sector," in Werner Z. Hirsch, ed., *Elements of Regional Accounts,* Johns Hopkins Press, 1964.

Peterson, Wallace C. *Income, Employment, and Economic Growth*. W. W. Norton, 1962.

Petty, Sir William. "Verbum Sapienti," in Edwin Cannan: *A History of the Theories of Production and Distribution in English Political Economy*. P. S. King & Sons, 1903.

Pfouts, Ralph, ed. *The Techniques of Urban Economic Analysis*. Chandler-Davis, 1960.

Phillips, A. W. "The Relation between Unemployment and the Rate of Change of Money Wage Rates in the United Kingdom, 1861-1957," *Economica* 25 (1958): 283-99.

Polenske, Karen R. *A Multiregional Input-Output Model of the United States*, report no. 21, U. S. Department of Commerce, Economic Development Administration, October 1970.

Redfern, Philip. "Net Investment in Fixed Assets in the United Kingdom, 1938-1953," *Journal of the Royal Statistical Society*, 118, pt. 2 (1955): 141-92.

Revell, Jack. "The National Balance Sheet of the United Kingdom," *Review of Income and Wealth*, series 13, 1966.

Romans, J. T. *Capital Exports and Growth among U. S. Regions*. Wesleyan University Press, 1965.

Rosen, Sam. *National Income, Its Measurement, Determination, and Relation to Public Policy*. Holt, Rinehart and Winston, 1963.

Rosenfeld, Felix, et al. "Structure et Perspectives Economiques de la Province de Turin," *Metra* 3, no. 4 (1964).

Ross, Philip. "Labor Market Behavior and the Relationship between Unemployment and Wages," *Industrial Relations Research Association: 14th Annual Proceedings*, 1961. pp. 275-88.

Rothenberg, Jerome. "Values and Value Theory in Economics," in Sherman R. Krupp, ed. *The Structure of Economic Science*. Prentice-Hall, 1966.

Ruggles, Nancy and Ruggles, Richard. *The Design of Economic Accounts*. National Bureau of Economic Research. Distributed by Columbia University Press, 1970.

———. *National Income Accounts and Income Analysis*. McGraw-Hill, 1956.

Rymes, T. K. in *Statistics Canada: Fixed Capital Flows and Manufacturing, Canada, 1926-1960: Methodology*. (Catalogue no. 13-522), 1967.

Scholz, Karl. "Inadequacy of Actual Selling Price of Real Estate as Evidence of Fair Present Value for Purposes of Taxation," *Annals of the American Academy of Political and Social Science* 148 (1930): 157-64.

Schultz, Theodore W. "Capital Formation by Education," *Journal of Political Economy* 68, no. 6 (1960): 517-74.

_____. "Investment in Human Capital," *American Economic Review,* 51 (1961): 1-17.

_____. "Investment in Man: An Economist's View," *Social Science Review* 33 (1959): 109-17.

Schultze, Charles L. *National Income Analysis.* Prentice-Hall, 1964.

Scott, Anthony. *Natural Resources: The Economics of Conservation.* Canadian Studies in Economics, no. 3, University of Toronto Press, 1955.

_____. "Canada's Reproducible Wealth," International Association for Research in Income and Wealth, *Income and Wealth Series 8. The Measurement of National Wealth.* Raymond W. Goldsmith and Christopher Saunders, eds. Bowes and Bowes, 1959.

Sevaldson, Per. "The Stability of Input-Output Coefficients," in A. P. Carter and A. Brody, eds., *Applications of Input-Output Analysis,* North Holland Publishing Co. 1970.

Shaffer, Harry G. "Investment in Human Capital: Comment," *American Economic Review* 51 (1961): 1026-35.

Shen, T. Y. "An Input-Output Table with Regional Weights," *Papers of the Regional Science Association* 6 (1960): 113-19.

Smith, Adam. *An Inquiry into the Nature and Causes of the Wealth of Nations.* Edited by Edwin Connan with Max Lerner. Modern Library, 1937.

Stone, Richard. *Input-Output and National Accounts.* Organisation for Economic Co-operation and Development, 1961.

_____. *Mathematics in the Social Sciences and Other Essays.* Chapman & Hall, 1966.

Stone, Richard and Brown, Alan. "Behavioral and Technical Change in Economic Models," in E. A. G. Robinson, ed., *Problems in Economic Development.* Macmillan & Co., 1965.

Streit, M. E. "Spatial Associations and Economic Linkages between Industries," *Journal of Regional Science* 9, no. 2 (1969): 177-88.

Studenski, Paul. *The Income of Nations.* New York University Press, 1958.

Stuvel, G. *Systems of Social Accounts.* Clarendon Press, 1965.

Terry, Edwin F. "Regional Income Accounts Estimates" in Werner Z. Hirsch, ed., *Elements of Regional Accounts.* Johns Hopkins Press, 1964.

Theil, Henri, et al. *Applied Economic Forecasting.* Rand McNally & Co., 1966.

Tiebout, Charles M. *The Community Economic Base Study.* Supplementary Paper no. 16. Committee for Economic Development, 1962.

Tilanus, C. B. and Theil, H. *The Information Approach to the Evaluation of Input-Output Forecast.* Econometric Institute of the Netherlands School of Economics, 1964.

Trias-Fargas, Ramon and Martin, Ernesto Lluch, "Balance of Payments Studies for the Region of Catalonia," *Papers, Regional Science Association,* vol. 10, 1962.

U.N. Department of Economic and Social Affairs, *Problems of Input-Output Tables and Analysis,* United Nations, series F, no. 14, 1966.

———, *Input-Output Bibliography 1966-1970* (2 vols.), United Nations, series M, no. 55, 1972.

Vaccara, Beatrice N. "Changes Over Time in Input-Output Coefficients for the Unites States," in A. P. Carter and A. Brody, eds., *Applications of Input-Output Analysis.* North Holland Publishing, 1970.

Walras, L. *Elements of Pure Economics.* Translated by W. Jaffe, Richard D. Irwin, 1954.

Walsh, J. R. "Capital Concept Applied to Man," *Quarterly Journal of Economics.* 49 (1934-35): 255-85.

Weber, Alfred. *Theory of the Location of Industries.* Translated by Carl J. Friedrich. University of Chicago Press, 1929.

Weisbrod, Burton A. "The Valuation of Human Capital," *Journal of Political Economy* 59, no. 5, (1961): 425-36.

Wiles, P. J. "The Nation's Intellectual Investment," *Bulletin of the Oxford University Institute of Statistics* 18 (1956): 279-90.

Yanovsky, M. *Social Accounting System.* Aldine Publishing Co., 1965.

Index

About the Author

Stan Czamanski was born in 1918 in Poland. He studied textile engineering at the Federal Institute of Textile Technology and business administration at the College for Foreign Trade, both in Vienna, economics at the University of Geneva, history of philosophy at the Hebrew University in Jerusalem, and regional science at the University of Pennsylvania in Philadelphia. He earned a Lic. es Sc. Comm. degree from the University of Geneva and a Ph.D. from the University of Pennsylvania.

After teaching for some years at the University of Pennsylvania he joined Cornell University in 1966, where he is Professor of City and Regional Planning and Field Representative, Graduate Field of Regional Science. At various times he held visiting appointments at the University of Pittsburgh, University of Puerto Rico, Harvard University, Technion-Israel Institute of Technology, The Florida State University, and Tel-Aviv University.

In 1966 Professor Czamanski organized a Regional Studies Group at the Institute of Public Affairs, Dalhousie University, Halifax, Nova Scotia, which he has directed since. Among his numerous research and planning activities over the past twenty years his work in Nova Scotia, in Hawaii, and in Baltimore has led to the development of several new and improved techniques of regional analysis.

He is the author of *Regional Science Techniques in Practice* (Lexington Books, D.C. Heath & Co. 1972) and has published in professional journals over forty papers, articles, and research reports ranging over a wide variety of topics. Professor Czamanski is President Elect of the Regional Science Association (International), and General Editor of Regional Science Monograph Series of Lexington Books.